GRE® Exam Advanced
Verbal

Other Kaplan Books Related to Graduate School Admissions:

GRE Exam: Strategies, Practice, and Review

GRE Exam: Premier Live Online

GRE Exam Verbal Workbook

GRE Exam Math Workbook

GRE & GMAT Exams Writing Workbook

GRE Exam Vocabulary in a Box

Get Into Graduate School

GRE® Exam Advanced
Verbal

PUBLISHING

New York

© 2009 Kaplan, Inc.

Published by Kaplan Publishing, a division of Kaplan, Inc.
1 Liberty Plaza, 24th Floor
New York, NY 10006

Printed in the United States of America

10 9 8 7 6 5 4 3

ISBN: 978-1-60714-496-0

Table of Contents

About the Experts

Lucy Green is a student, teacher, and freelance writer in State College, Pennsylvania, where she is earning her Master's degree in creative writing at Penn State University. She has a degree in journalism from the University of North Carolina at Chapel Hill. As a Kaplan instructor, she has been helping students succeed on the GRE, SAT, LSAT, and TOEFL since August 2008.

Andrew Taggart finished his Ph.D. in English literature from the University of Wisconsin in 2009. From 2004–08, he taught LSAT and MCAT courses at Kaplan. He currently resides in Madison, Wisconsin.

Lisa Wolf, a graduate of Harvard-Radcliffe, has been an instructor for Kaplan Test Prep since 1983. She has taught courses ranging from LSAT, GMAT and GRE preparation to General Intensive English and TOEFL preparation. She loves coming up with new and interesting ways to help students be more effective, efficient and successful in their studies.

kaptest.com/publishing

The material in this book is up-to-date at the time of publication. However, the Graduate Management Admission Council may have instituted changes in the test after this book was published. Be sure to carefully read the materials you receive when you register for the test.

If there are any important late-breaking developments—or any changes or corrections to the Kaplan test preparation materials in this book—we will post that information online at **kaptest.com/publishing**. Check to see if there is any information posted there regarding this book.

kaplansurveys.com/books

We'd love to hear your comments and suggestions about this book. We invite you to fill out our online survey form at **kaplansurveys.com/books**. Your feedback is extremely helpful as we continue to develop high-quality resources to meet your needs.

The Perfect Score

Ah, *perfection* . . . We humans are a demanding bunch. We don't bound out of bed in the morning aspiring to mediocrity, but rather striving for *perfection*. The *perfect* mate. The *perfect* job. The *perfect* shoes to go with the *perfect* outfit.

Webster's defines *perfection* as "the quality or state of being complete and correct in every way, conforming to a standard or ideal with no omissions, errors, flaws or extraneous elements." The GRE test makers define perfection as a score of 800. If GRE perfection is what you're after, then you've come to the right place. Kaplan has been training test takers to ace the GRE for decades, and we salute your quest for perfection. The *perfect* GRE score. The *perfect* business school. The *perfect* career. We have the *perfect* book for you.

ABOUT THE GRE

Let's take a look at the current GRE. As someone famous once said, "Know thine enemy." And you need to know firsthand the way this test is put together if you want to take it apart. Before you begin, though, remember that the test makers sometimes change the content, administration, and scheduling of the GRE too quickly for a published guide to keep up with. For the latest, up-to-the-minute news about the GRE, visit Kaplan's website at **kaptest.com**.

The GRE is a test that is designed to assess readiness for graduate school for a wide variety of programs. The ways in which graduate schools use GRE scores vary. Scores are often used as part of the application packet for entrance into a program, but they can also be used to grant fellowships or financial aid.

The GRE is administered on computer and is between two and three-quarters and three and a quarter hours long. The exam consists of three scored sections, with different amounts of time allotted for you to complete each section.

Verbal	
Time	30 minutes
Length	30 multiple-choice questions
Format	Sentence Completion, Analogy, Reading Comprehension, and Antonym
Content	Tests vocabulary, verbal reasoning skills, and the ability to read complex passages with understanding and insight

Quantitative	
Time	45 minutes
Length	28 multiple-choice questions
Format	Quantitative Comparison, Word Problems, and Data Interpretation (graph questions)
Content	Tests basic mathematical skills, ability to understand and apply mathematical concepts, and quantitative reasoning skills

Analytical Writing	
Time	75 minutes
Length	2 essay prompts
Format	Perspective on an Issue and Analyze an Argument
Content	Tests ability to understand and analyze arguments, to understand and draw logical conclusions, and to write clearly and succinctly

The Verbal and Quantitative sections each yield a scaled score within a range of 200 to 800. These scaled scores are like the scores that you received if you took the SAT. You cannot score higher than 800 on either section, no matter how hard you try. Similarly, it's impossible (again, no matter how hard you try) to get a score lower than 200 on either section.

But you don't receive *only* scaled scores. You will also receive a percentile rank, which will place your performance relative to those of a large sample population of other GRE takers. Percentile scores tell graduate schools just what your scaled scores are worth, in a large pool of applicants.

For complete GRE registration information, visit the Educational Testing Service at **gre.org** for the Registration Bulletin.

WHO SHOULD USE THIS BOOK

This book is comprised exclusively of examples of the toughest material you're likely to see on the GRE. No easy stuff, no run-of-the-mill strategies—just killer problems, passages, and questions, complete with Kaplan's proven techniques to help you transcend "above average" and enter the rarefied arena of GRE elite. Even if a perfect score is not your immediate goal, diligent practice with the difficult material in this book can help develop your skills and raise your score. If you're looking for more traditional practice for the GRE, then we recommend working through *Kaplan GRE Exam Premier Live Online* or *GRE Exam Strategies, Practice, and Review* books as a prerequisite for the highly challenging material contained in this volume. You can find the latest edition of these books in stores nationwide, as well as by visiting us at kaplanpublishing.com or through other online retailers.

HOW TO USE THIS BOOK

This book is divided into sections corresponding to the scored question types contained on the GRE. (*Note: The Analytical Writing Assessment is not included in this book because it doesn't contribute to your 200–800 score, and no AWA prompt is written to be any more difficult than any other.*) Each section provides detailed guidelines on how to make the most of the material. Jump right to the section that gives you the most trouble, or work through the sections in the order presented—it's up to you. No matter what you do, try not to overload; remember that this is dense, complicated material and not representative of the range of difficulty you'll see on Test Day. One thing's for sure: if you can ace this stuff, the real thing will be a breeze.

Good luck!

A Special Note for International Students

About 250,000 international students pursue advanced academic degrees at the master's or PhD level at U.S. universities each year. This trend of pursuing higher education in the United States, particularly at the graduate level, is expected to continue. Business, management, engineering, and the physical and life sciences are popular areas of study for international students. If you are an international student planning on applying to a graduate program in the United States, you will want to consider the following:

- If English is not your first language, you will probably need to take the Test of English as a Foreign Language (TOEFL®) or show some other evidence that you're proficient in English prior to gaining admission to a graduate program. Graduate programs will vary on what is an acceptable TOEFL score. For degrees in business, journalism, management, or the humanities, a minimum TOEFL score of 600 (250 on the computer-based TOEFL) or better is expected. For the hard sciences and computer technology, a TOEFL score of 550 (213 on the computer-based TOEFL) is a common minimum requirement.

- You may also need to take the Graduate Record Exam (GRE®) or the Graduate Management Admissions Test (GMAT®) as part of the admission process.

- Since admission to many graduate programs and business schools is quite competitive, you may want to select three or four programs you would like to attend and complete applications for each program.

- Selecting the correct graduate school is very different from selecting an undergraduate school. You should research the qualifications and interests of faculty members teaching and doing research in your chosen field. Also, select a program that meets your current or future employment needs, rather than simply a program with a big name.

- Begin the application process at least a year in advance. Be aware that many programs offer only August or September start dates. Find out application deadlines and plan accordingly.

- Finally, you will need to obtain a 1-20 Certificate of Eligibility in order to obtain an F-1 Student Visa to study in the United States.

Kaplan English Programs*

If you need more help with the complex process of graduate school admissions or assistance preparing for the TOEFL, GRE, or GMAT, you may be interested in Kaplan's programs for international students. Kaplan English Programs were designed to help students and professionals from outside the United States meet their educational and career goals. At locations throughout

*Kaplan is authorized under federal law to enroll nonimmigrant alien students.
Kaplan is accredited by ACCET (Accrediting Council for Continuing Education and Training).

the United States, international students take advantage of Kaplan's programs to help them improve their academic and conversational English skills, raise their scores on the TOEFL, GRE, GMAT, and other standardized exams, and gain admission to top programs.

General Intensive English

Kaplan's General Intensive English classes are designed to help you improve your skills in all areas of English and to increase your fluency in spoken and written English. Classes are available for beginning to advanced students, and the average class size is 12 students.

TOEFL and Academic English

This course provides you with the skills you need to improve your TOEFL score and succeed in an American university or graduate program. It includes advanced reading, writing, listening, grammar, and conversational English. You will also receive training for the TOEFL using Kaplan's exclusive computer-based practice materials.

GRE for International Students

The Graduate Record Exam (GRE) is required for admission to many graduate programs in the United States. Nearly one-half million people take the GRE each year. A high score can help you stand out from other test takers. This course, designed especially for non-native English speakers, includes the skills you need to succeed on each section of the GRE, as well as access to Kaplan's exclusive computer-based practice materials and extra verbal practice.

GMAT for International Students

The Graduate Management Admissions Test (GMAT) is required for admission to many graduate programs in business in the United States. Hundreds of thousands of American students have taken this course to prepare for the GMAT. This course, designed especially for non-native English speakers, includes the skills you need to succeed on each section of the GMAT, as well as access to Kaplan's exclusive computer-based practice materials and extra verbal practice.

Other Kaplan Programs

Since 1938, more than three million students have come to Kaplan to advance their studies, prepare for entry to American universities, and further their careers. In addition to the above programs, Kaplan offers courses to prepare for the SAT®, LSAT®, MCAT®, DAT®, USMLE®, NCLEX®, and other standardized exams at locations throughout the United States.

To get more information or to apply to any of Kaplan's programs, contact us at:

Kaplan English Programs
700 S. Flower, Suite 2900
Los Angeles, CA 90017 USA
Phone (if calling from within the United States): 800-818-9128
Phone (if calling from outside the United States): (213) 452-5800
Fax: (213) 892-1364
Website: www.kaplanenglish.com
Email: world@kaplan.com

THE SHORT VERBAL SECTION

Every GRE test taker wants to improve, and for many people, the process of improving performance simply consists of learning how to do the things they don't yet know how to do and practicing the ones they do know in order to improve their skill, speed, and confidence. But this may not be sufficient for those who already know the basic material and who already have the ability to work reasonably quickly and accurately. Achieving a superior score on the GRE requires another level of analysis.

To improve their performance on the GRE Verbal section, high-scoring test takers need to be very analytical about where they are going wrong, in order to uncover the two danger zones of test preparation: the Blind Spot and the Lucky Guess. The good news is that both of these problem areas will be revealed through the use of one simple practice strategy: Rating Your Confidence. If you resolve to Rate Your Confidence on every GRE Verbal problem you do between now and Test Day, you will move yourself much closer to getting a fabulous score! So let's see how this process works.

RATING YOUR CONFIDENCE

Have you ever noticed that your performance on a quiz or Practice CAT turned out much better—or much worse—than you expected while taking it? If so, this strategy can really help you! After answering a GRE Verbal question, note the question number, your answer, and your confidence level on a scale of 1 to 5, where a rating of 1 represents utter certainty and a 5 indicates complete uncertainty. Here is a breakdown of the ratings:

1. You would bet your life!

2. Pretty sure, but not quite as certain as 1

3. Had to guess between two choices (was able to definitively eliminate three answer choices)

4. Had to guess between three or four choices (was only able to definitively eliminate one or two answer choices)

5. A random guess

Once you have done this, you will be much better able to evaluate your work and to find any Blind Spots or Lucky Guesses.

BLIND SPOTS

A Blind Spot can be defined as any problem that you get wrong after having given your answer a confidence rating of 1 or 2.

These are GRE Verbal problems you don't understand or simply don't know how to do or vocabulary words about whose meaning you are confused. The big problem here is that you **think** you understand these things, so the likelihood of your studying and thus improving your performance in these areas is vanishingly small—at least, it is without a technique such as Rating Your Confidence, which draws your attention to these areas. High confidence and poor performance is a very bad combination, and Rating Your Confidence is the best way to discover these Blind Spots on the road to a high GRE score.

What to do when you discover a Blind Spot? Go over the answer explanations for these problems very carefully. If necessary, create flash cards in order to make sure you learn any confusing vocabulary, review Kaplan Methods for the problem type, and you might even try doing the problems again after a sufficient amount of time has passed to allow you to forget the details.

LUCKY GUESSES

What is a Lucky Guess? It can be defined as any problem that you get right, for which you have given your answer a confidence rating of 3, 4, or 5.

These are GRE Verbal problems that you actually do not understand well or vocabulary words that you actually do not know. The problem here is that you have managed to answer questions about these things correctly, thus concealing your confusion from yourself. Using ordinary study methods, you would never uncover these problem areas, but by Rating Your Confidence, you give yourself a fighting chance of improving your performance on Test Day by identifying areas of confusion beforehand.

What to do when you discover a Lucky Guess? The process is identical to that suggested above for working on Blind Spots: review answer explanations carefully, learn the material and strategies you do not know (vocabulary words, Kaplan Methods, etc.), and try the problems again later.

As you take quizzes and Practice Tests, get into the habit of Rating Your Confidence on each Verbal problem, and you will find that your estimate of your own performance becomes more and more accurate. Of course, the real goal here is that your self-confidence becomes more and more justified!

CHAPTER ONE

Sentence Completions

Short Verbal questions constitute more than three-quarters of all GRE Verbal questions, so students who want to achieve a very high score on the GRE Verbal section must master them. The easiest of these to master is the Sentence Completion question, since it contains a multiplicity of clues that can help the discerning student find the right answer.

Sentence Completions, as the name implies, require you to complete a single sentence by filling in one or two words or short phrases, which you will select from a list of five options. There will be around six of these questions on your test, half containing one blank and half containing two, and your target time for each Sentence Completion is no more than 45 seconds. The directions for this section are as follows:

> **Directions:** Each sample question in this section consists of a sentence with one or two blanks, each blank indicating that something has been omitted. Beneath the sentence are five lettered words or sets of words. Choose the word or set of words for each blank that best fits the meaning of the sentence as a whole.

If you get early questions right, the questions will get more difficult as you move through the section, featuring both harder vocabulary and longer, more complex sentences.

So how can you successfully sleuth out the answers in the Sentence Completion section and achieve a superior score? The most important skill you can cultivate in the Verbal section of the GRE is **predicting an answer.** This skill is crucial to help you avoid the biggest pitfall of the GRE Verbal: allowing yourself to be persuaded to choose a "trap" answer—one that sounds good or sounds plausible, but is not the correct answer. So how do you predict the correct answer and avoid the traps?

As an advanced GRE test taker, your best strategy is to use the available clues. The two clues to look for in Sentence Completions are road signs and keywords. Let's take a closer look at each one of these.

ROAD SIGNS

Road signs are the words or phrases that tell you what to expect in a sentence, and they fall into two categories, Straight Ahead road signs and Detour road signs. The savvy (and high-scoring) test taker will need to recognize both the more obvious examples of these and the more subtle—sometimes even deceptive—versions.

Straight Ahead Road Signs	Detour Road Signs
because	although
since	but
and	yet
as well as	however
similarly	nevertheless
in addition to	despite
likewise	whereas
…	on the other hand
also	conversely
not only…but also	struck by, amazed to find, etc.
; (a semicolon)	

KEYWORDS

Keywords are the words or phrases that allow you to figure out exactly what should go in the blank(s) in a Sentence Completion problem. They are the keys to the meaning of the missing word(s), and a skillful test taker can use them to his or her advantage to predict an answer. (Keywords are as varied as the sentences in Sentence Completion, so it would be impossible to make a list of them.)

Take a look at this sentence, which contains both a road sign you should already be able to recognize and a set of keywords that will allow you to predict an answer.

> Although she earned her reputation for excellence for her impressive murals, the artist felt that her sculpture merited greater _____.
>
> (A) disdain
> (B) acclaim
> (C) refute
> (D) viewing
> (E) popularity

KAPLAN

In this sentence, the word *although* is the road sign, and it indicates a contrast (since it is a Detour road sign) so we know that there will be a change of direction in the sentence. What is this change? The artist was famous for her murals, but she thought that another category of her work was superior. (Notice that even in explaining this, it is necessary to use a Detour road sign: *but*!) And what is the word that fits in the blank? The keywords "reputation for excellence" provide the clue we need; the missing word will echo that phrase. So that is our prediction, and we find a match in answer (B), *acclaim*.

Notice that among the answer choices for this example are some interesting, and possibly tempting, wrong choices. This brings us to the second important GRE test-taking strategy—know thine enemy. More specifically, know and recognize the common trap answers so you do not fall into the test maker's trap and pick them! Not only that, but if you find yourself totally stumped (which could happen to a high-scoring student, considering the high-difficulty words you should expect to see on your test), you can use your knowledge of trap answers to eliminate your way to a correct answer.

ANSWER CHOICES

Trap answer choices in GRE Short Verbal questions include the 180°, the Close Second, the Sound-Alike, and the Clunker; in two-blank Sentence Completions, there is an additional type: the Half-right, Half-wrong.

- The 180° has the exact opposite meaning as the word we seek, and answer (A), *disdain*, is a good example of this type of trap answer choice.

- The Close Second is a word that echoes part of the keyword, or reminds you of it, or seems closely related to the idea expressed, but isn't quite synonymous with it. This is the wrong answer that sounds plausible—one could imagine a well-formed English sentence that contains this word. The problem is that the original sentence lacks clues to lead you to this answer choice, so there is no basis for picking it other than the wistful idea that "it *could* work." In this example, answer (E), *popularity*, typifies the Close Second. *Popularity* describes the state of being widely admired, accepted, or sought after, which (perhaps sadly!) we all know is not exactly the same thing as *excellence*.

- The Sound-Alike is one that sounds like, and therefore reminds the test taker of, a word that could work in the sentence. Answer (C), *refute*, is such a word since it sounds like (and could be mistaken for) *repute*, a word that means good character or reputation and is a close synonym for the keywords "reputation for excellence."

- Finally, the Clunker is an answer choice that just does not sound right. It could be un-idiomatic or just a word that sounds odd with the rest of the sentence. Answer (D), *viewing*, is an example of a Clunker.

There is also one more trap answer you need to learn to recognize, one that is found only in two-blank Sentence Completions. In these problems (which are not necessarily harder than one-blank Sentence Completions—and may even be easier, because they give you more ways to predict right answers and eliminate wrong ones), you need to find two words and they must fit both blanks. The trap wrong answer unique to two-blank Sentence Completions is called the Half-right, Half-wrong answer.

- The Half-right, Half-wrong answer is one where one of the words fits the corresponding blank in the sentence, while the other is one of the wrong answers listed above: a 180°, a Close Second, a Sound-Alike, or a Clunker.

DRILL

Try out what you have just learned about road signs and keywords with these example sentences (which get progressively harder):

1. The winning argument was _____ and persuasive (cogent, flawed).

2. The winning argument was _____ but persuasive (cogent, flawed).

3. Fred was so annoyed with his publicist that he repeatedly _____ him in public (praised, lambasted).

4. Because Mabel had the reputation of being a mediocre cook, most believed her chances of winning the bake-off were _____ (good, slim).

5. The play's script lacked depth and maturity; likewise, the acting was altogether _____ (sublime, amateurish).

6. Because she has often been regarded as an author of entertaining light fiction, critics were struck by the _____ of her latest novel (jocularity, somberness).

7. The majority of the city's police officers have nothing but _____ things to say about their new chief, a novel situation for that chronically disgruntled organization (querulous, laudatory).

8. Paradoxically, Collinsworth's remonstrations against the banality of most detective novels attest to his _____ the genre (devotion to, antipathy toward).

Focusing on road signs and keywords would have helped you to find the correct answers here (1. cogent, 2. flawed, 3. lambasted, 4. slim, 5. amateurish, 6. somberness, 7. laudatory, 8. devotion to).

CONCEPTS TO KEEP IN MIND

There are a few other concepts that can help you in your quest for a superior score on the GRE. Let's look at them one at a time.

Paraphrase Long or Complex Sentences

Many high-difficulty Sentence Completion problems are categorized as such because of their complexity. Here's an example:

> Museum directors understand the need to establish the provenance of every work of art they acquire, from its creation to its most recent owner; such establishment can be hindered, however, by a number of obstacles, including disingenuous dealers who attempt to _____ the truth.
>
> (A) impede
> (B) reveal
> (C) overshadow
> (D) ascertain
> (E) obscure

What a mouthful! A summary of this sentence will be much easier to grasp. For example: "It can be difficult to establish provenance because insincere dealers try to _____ the truth."

If dealers are *disingenuous,* or insincere, what would they try to do with the truth? They would try to hide it. The word *overshadow* has to do with hiding, but it means "to take attention away from something by appearing more important." *Obscure* is the better fit in the context (so the correct answer is (E)). Notice, too, that in simplifying the sentence above, we introduced the Straight Ahead road sign *because.* Restating sentences in simpler terms can help clarify their direction.

Use Word Charge

Although we cannot always predict the word that goes in the blank, often we will be able to tell whether it is a positively charged word or a negatively charged word—and that may be enough to successfully answer a tough one-blank Sentence Completion question. In a two-blank Sentence Completion, we have an additional strategy: We may be able to determine the relationship between the blanks. For instance, we may be able to tell that the blanks have the same charge or the opposite charge. One more point: although predicting an answer is our main strategy in Sentence Completions, it's important for an advanced GRE student to remain flexible, as you will see in the second example below.

> Unfortunately, there are some among us who equate tolerance with immorality; they feel that the _____ of moral values in a permissive society is not only likely, but _____.
>
> (A) decline...possible
> (B) upsurge...predictable
> (C) disappearance...desirable
> (D) improvement...commendable
> (E) deterioration...inevitable

The road signs are *unfortunately* in the first half of the sentence, and *not only* in the second. *Unfortunately* tells us that the answer will consist of words with a negative charge. *Not only* tells us that both blanks will have the same charge. Now, here is the tricky part—and this is what separates the advanced students from the average ones. While *inevitable,* by itself, actually has no positive or negative charge, think about what it refers to and is describing. Its referent in this sentence is the group of words in and after the first blank: *the _____ of moral values.* And we have already decided that the word that goes into that blank must be negatively charged; we might predict that it is something like *loss* or *decline.* When coupled with these keywords, *inevitable* takes on a negative charge. The correct answer here is (E).

> Considering the _____ era in which the novel was written, its tone and theme are remarkably _____.
>
> (A) enlightened...disenchanted
> (B) scholarly...prosaic
> (C) superstitious...medieval
> (D) permissive...puritanical
> (E) undistinguished...commonplace

The road sign here is the subtle clue *remarkably,* which indicates a contrast between the blanks. However, the lack of keywords makes the content of the blanks impossible to predict. Here is a case where we will need to abandon the strategy of predict-and-search, and instead examine the answer choices one by one for pairs of words that contrast with one another. The correct answer here is (D).

Use Word Roots

Using your knowledge of word roots, prefixes, and suffixes can help you get a sense of the meaning of an otherwise obscure word that is needed to understand a sentence, or one found among the answer choices. Your knowledge of other languages can also provide clues to meaning.

The attorney was frustrated because her attempts to _____ the defendant were complicated by the revelations of his malfeasance brought forward by a witness.

(A) uphold

(B) abjure

(C) commend

(D) exculpate

(E) incriminate

Here, the road sign phrases *frustrated* and *were complicated by* indicate a contrast; the keyword *malfeasance* is going to be crucial in figuring out what goes in the blank. Examining *malfeasance* more closely, we see the prefix *mal,* meaning "bad" (which may be familiar to speakers of Romance languages, and which is found in English words such as *malinger, malodorous,* and *malfunction*), a clue to its negative charge. So "revelations of malfeasance" must be quite negative, and the word we seek for the blank must therefore be positive. What might an attorney do to a defendant that is positive? Well, most defendants would like to be proven innocent! Which word on the list of choices could work here? Answer (A), *uphold,* simply means "support," and while it is used to describe support of a principle, law, or rule, it would not really be idiomatic to speak of upholding a person. Let's look for a stronger candidate. Answer (B), *abjure,* means "to renounce, avoid, or shun," so it will not work here. Answer (C), *commend,* which means "praise," is not quite the answer we seek. How about choice (D)? If you don't know the meaning of *exculpate* ("to free from blame"), recognizing the prefix *ex,* meaning "out of," and the root *culp,* meaning "guilt" (found in words such as *culpable* and *culprit*) can help you to identify this as the winner. Answer (E), *incriminate,* has the opposite meaning of the word we seek.

However, you won't always want to rely on these kinds of clues—in fact, this approach can backfire on you. Which brings us to our next point.

Watch Out for Deceptive Vocabulary

Difficult GRE tests are littered with words that do not mean what they may sound like to you and words that may look to you like other words with different meanings.

Its _____ plot made the spy movie hard to follow.

(A) vacuous

(B) enervating

(C) tortuous

(D) captivating

(E) bellicose

The road sign *made* is a subtle Straight Ahead clue. The keywords "hard to follow" give us a synonym for the contents of the blank, but the deceptive *tortuous* (meaning "full of plot twists") may not at first strike you as the correct answer, because it is easily mistaken for the similarly spelled word *torturous,* meaning "painful". Let's examine some of the wrong answers.

While those who are not fans of spy movies may find them to be *vacuous,* or empty, that word would not fit with the keywords; nor would *enervating,* meaning "weakening or debilitating," do the job. Although the movie might be *captivating,* or fascinating, this is another word that does not fit with the keywords. And finally, while *bellicose,* meaning "aggressively hostile," could apply to some of the characters in the spy movie, it does not imply that the movie would be confusing. So the correct answer is (C).

To achieve a superior score on the GRE, you must be diligent in discovering deceptive words and recording them for study in a way that clearly indicates their deceptive nature. For instance, you may use color-coded flash cards or highlight items on your word lists to make them easier to review.

Be Systematic: Use the Kaplan Method

As with every other part of the GRE, the best way to approach Sentence Completions is strategically. Learning and using the step-by-step method that follows ensures that you will answer every question as efficiently as possible while avoiding as many pitfalls and trap answers as possible.

❶ Read the whole sentence.

  • Look for road signs and keywords to help you determine what type of word you're looking for.

  • If the sentence is long or clumsy, rephrase it in your own words.

❷ Predict an answer.

  • Use the road signs, keywords, and logic you found in step 1 to determine the direction in which the sentence is heading.

  • In two-blank questions, pick the easiest blank and predict its answer first.

❸ Scan the answer choices, choosing the one that best fits your prediction.

- Look for a match with your prediction.

- Eliminate choices that don't come close to your prediction.

- On two-blank sentences, eliminate choices that don't match your first prediction; then repeat steps 2 and 3 (Predict and Scan) for the other blank.

❹ Read your selected answer choice back into the sentence.

- If it makes sense, you have a winner.

- If it doesn't make sense, go back to the answer choices and find a better one.

- If you get stuck, eliminate the choices you know are wrong and guess among the remaining choices.

CHAPTER TWO

Text Completions

Like Sentence Completion questions with more than one blank, Text Completions require the test taker to find more than one word to complete them. However, they can be a bit more complex and challenging than two-blank Sentence Completions because of what they require of you.

THE NEWEST QUESTION TYPE ON THE GRE: TEXT COMPLETIONS

In this new question type, you will be asked to select one entry for each blank from the corresponding column of choices, and you may need to fill in as many as three blanks within one question. In addition, Text Completions are often longer than Sentence Completions, and one question can consist of as many as five sentences.

And a few additional wrinkles: In Text Completion questions, you must choose each word individually and independently of the other words, and there is no partial credit for these questions; you need to pick every word correctly to get credit for a correct answer. As this book goes to press, the GRE website states that test takers will get a maximum of one of this question type on their tests; please check www.gre.org for the latest information.

Just as with the Sentence Completion question, this new question type tests your vocabulary and your ability to understand context. The principles and strategies you use for Sentence Completion problems can be applied to this question type. Try this sample question:

As a result of the ___(i)___ pace of life, urban living ___(ii)___ many young professionals the opportunity to ___(iii)___ their lives with a sense of constant excitement.

Blank (i)	Blank (ii)	Blank (iii)
(A) intrinsic	(D) instigates	(G) eschew
(B) ephemeral	(E) affords	(H) inter
(C) frenetic	(F) arrogates	(I) imbue

Answers: (C), (E), and (I)

Use the clues in the sentence to determine which word belongs in each blank. In the first blank, you are looking for an adjective that would best describe urban living and that is similar to "constant excitement." Choice (A) means "inherent," which doesn't fit the context of the phrase, and (B) means "fleeting or brief"—again, an unsuitable description of the pace of urban life; answer (C) fits perfectly.

The second blank requires a word that means to be made available or to give the opportunity. Since one meaning of *afford* is to offer or impart, choice (E) is correct.

The final blank requires a word that tells what young professionals have the opportunity to do. Choice (G) means "to avoid," and choice (H) means "to bury," so they are incorrect. Young professionals are not likely to choose urban living to avoid constant excitement; therefore, (I), which means "to permeate," is the correct answer.

In general, the hardest Text Completion questions will be difficult for reasons similar to what we have seen in tough Sentence Completions: challenging or deceptive vocabulary, subtle clues, and the need to use word charge or relate the blanks to one another. Another challenge peculiar to Text Completions: although it is natural to try to fill in earlier blanks before later ones, it may be impossible to predict what goes in an earlier blank without the clues found in the later part of the sentence, including later blanks, forcing students to "work backwards" to achieve success.

CHAPTER THREE

Sentence and Text Completions Practice Set

ONE-BLANK COMPLETIONS

Question 1

1. Because Marissa had always been a staunch supporter of animal rights, her audience was confounded by her _____ stance during the debate.

   (A) radiant

   (B) vacillating

   (C) ingenuous

   (D) credulous

   (E) unwavering

Explanation: Question 1

1. The sentence seems to begin with a Straight Ahead road sign, so you may have been tempted by (E) (the 180°), but a careful read reveals the context clue "confounded by," which actually signals a contrast between the blank and a "staunch supporter." That's (B).

Question 2

2. The modest attire and ascetic lifestyle of the medieval monk portrayed by ancient manuscripts uncovered in the early 1940s would lead one to believe that becoming a monk a few centuries ago required a rather _____ nature to match their everyday routines.

   (A) flamboyant

   (B) esoteric

   (C) uncanny

   (D) spartan

   (E) oblique

Explanation: Question 2

2. This sentence is made difficult by excess verbiage, so take a moment to paraphrase the important parts first. The sentence really boils down to "a monk with modest attire and an ascetic lifestyle would have a _____ nature." Only (D) works. Beware of (B), the Close Second: while *esoteric* can often be used in the context of groups such as monks on the GRE, there are no clues in this problem that would warrant this choice.

Question 3

3. After several critics lambasted the novel for its abhorrent material, the author completely _____ the text before releasing an updated edition.

   (A) expurgated
   (B) rebuked
   (C) muddled
   (D) eulogized
   (E) desecrated

Explanation: Question 3

3. With no road signs at all in this sentence, we'll need to hunt for other types of clues. The author's action comes after the critics *lambasted* the novel for *abhorrent* material, both of which carry a negative charge, so the blank needs to be a positive term. That eliminates everything but (A) and (D). If you didn't know the meanings of those words, you may have recognized the root *purge* from (A), the correct answer.

Question 4

4. Originally intended as a euphonious instrument, the minstrel's poorly tuned lute would actually produce sounds that could only be described as _____ in nature.

   (A) sonorous
   (B) noisome
   (C) laconic
   (D) cacophonic
   (E) gushy

Explanation: Question 4

4. Begin by eliminating (E), the Clunker. While the standard road signs seem to be missing, the keywords *Originally* and *actually* indicate that the blank is an antonym of *euphonious*, or pleasant sounding. The Sound-Alike (B) may have been tempting as *noisome* looks like it comes from the root *noise*. Be wary of such deceptive vocabulary on the GRE: *noisome* actually refers to a foul odor and has nothing to do with sound. The harsh-sounding word you seek is *cacophonic*.

Question 5

5. Upon her arrival, the inquisitive diplomat was quite surprised to find the Mongolian noble to be rather _____ in person, for the tales from her countrymen described him as an extremely ponderous fellow.

    (A) innocuous
    (B) gaunt
    (C) simpleminded
    (D) whimsical
    (E) prudent

Explanation: Question 5

5. While we might think of nobles as *simpleminded* or *whimsical*, nothing in the sentence would suggest either of these two Close Seconds, so begin by eliminating them. The diplomat was "quite surprised" when she met the noble because she heard that he was "extremely ponderous." This may have led you to (C), the Sound-Alike, as *ponderous* looks like "thinking." This is deceptive vocabulary as *ponderous* actually means heavy in weight. The contrast you are looking for is *skinny*, not *thoughtless*. That's (B).

Question 6

6. Mary Shelley, famous for her creation of the immensely popular *Frankenstein* novels, played a prominent role in Britain's literary revolution during the 19th century, which was in part aimed at revamping the _____ novels of that day in an effort to entice more people to develop an interest in popular literature.

    (A) jejune
    (B) prestigious
    (C) rancid
    (D) sensational
    (E) agnostic

Explanation: Question 6

6. Wordiness and a lack of road signs make this Sentence Completion a bit more difficult, so paraphrase the sentence before trying to predict the blank. The first half may be interesting to know, but the second half is what you should focus on to answer the question. The sentence basically boils down to "revamping _____ novels to get more people interested in literature." This allows you to immediately eliminate (C), the Clunker in the bunch. While novels might be *sensational*, this is actually a 180°, as the sentence implies that people *weren't* interested in the literature (hence the need to revamp). Your prediction might be *bland* or *dull*, and that's what (A) means.

Question 7

7. After decades of archaeological excavation and research, the society has finally learned of the true cause of a public outcry against free speech in the middle of the 15th century: The newly unearthed arcane manuscripts revealed the pope's remonstrations against a certain collection of art that the church had deemed _____ in nature at the time.

   (A) divine
   (B) salacious
   (C) limpid
   (D) mercurial
   (E) protean

Explanation: Question 7

7. This is a wordy sentence completion made difficult by a lack of clues. While the first half of the sentence may seem unimportant at first, it is important that you do not dismiss it too early as the clue you seek is actually buried there. Since the public outcry is "against free speech," the blank must deal with the art's subject matter with regard to that. This eliminates all but (A) and (B). The pope would not remonstrate against art he considered *divine* (the 180°), so (B) is correct.

Question 8

8. That _____ habits are responsible for higher health-care costs for society does not explain why a significant number of patients in most hospitals today lead rather active lifestyles.

   (A) cantankerous
   (B) sedentary
   (C) petulant
   (D) cavalier
   (E) niggardly

Explanation: Question 8

8. When a sentence does not contain a clear road sign, it is important to check for subtle ones. In this case, the phrase "does not explain why" indicates that the blank will contrast "active lifestyle," so look for a choice that refers to an inactive one. That's (B).

TWO-BLANK COMPLETIONS

Question 9

9. Tales of the _____ deeds of ancient despotic leaders have contributed greatly to society's distaste for _____ government.

   (A) magnanimous...democratic
   (B) insipid...referendum
   (C) pernicious...authoritarian
   (D) sacrosanct...tyrannical
   (E) bombastic...egalitarian

Explanation: Question 9

9. Keywords in a sentence are not necessarily near their respective blanks, as this problem illustrates. Society's distaste is the clue to the first blank, so look for a choice with a negative charge. That eliminates (A) and (D). The second blank results from "tales of...ancient *despotic* leaders," so you may have predicted something that means *dictatorship*. That's (C).

Question 10

10. The aging engineer found it strange that the _____ etching process she studied as a student of technology was considered _____ today.

    (A) interesting...exotic

    (B) porous...translucent

    (C) innovative...antiquated

    (D) implausible...oblique

    (E) cutting-edge...progressive

Explanation: Question 10

10. This seemingly straightforward sentence is actually quite deceptive. While the word *strange* might at first indicate a contrast between the two blanks, such as (C) (the 180°) has it, an engineer would actually *not* find it strange if the etching process she studied as a student was currently considered *antiquated*. She would, however, find (E) quite strange.

Question 11

11. When the public accused the museum director of malingering, his staff members were quick to point out that their own _____ attitude toward work was a direct reflection of the director's _____ for his.

    (A) distasteful...fervor

    (B) assiduous...torpor

    (C) garrulous...capriciousness

    (D) sedulous...zeal

    (E) precocious...lethargy

Explanation: Question 11

11. The director's staff is quick to point something out but without any context clues, it is difficult to predict whether the prediction should be positive or negative. The only thing we *do* know is that the staff's attitude was a "direct reflection" of the director, so the two blanks are both either positive or negative. (A) and (B) have one of each and can quickly be eliminated as 180° choices. *Lethargy* in (E) is certainly negative and possibly fitting, but *precocious* does not work in the context, so (E) is a Close Second. The two words in (C) have nothing to do with work ethic, making that our Clunker. That leaves (D), the correct answer.

Question 12

12. Although her opponents _____ her with their incendiary remarks, Mason resisted the urge to respond to the _____ comments during the ceremony.

   (A) berated...belligerent
   (B) lauded...insipid
   (C) assaulted...salubrious
   (D) redressed...consanguineous
   (E) aggrandized...irascible

Explanation: Question 12

12. The Detour road sign *although* may have initially had you looking for a contrast between the two blanks, but a careful look reveals that the two blanks actually go in the same vein. The one clue we get are the "incendiary remarks," so look for a choice with a negative charge in the second blank. Of the remaining choices only (A), (B), and (E) seem negative for that blank. Incendiary remarks are generally delivered in a negative sense, so the first blank should be negative as well, making (A) correct, while (B) and (E) are 180° choices.

TEXT COMPLETION

Question 13

13. That teachers are grossly underpaid, while not ___(i)___, may nevertheless still be ___(ii)___. While their ___(iii)___ compensation is rather low, they do receive excellent fringe benefits to more than make up for this deficiency.

Blank (i)	Blank (ii)	Blank (iii)
completely palpable	somewhat perverted	pecuniary
quite hyperbole	partially spurious	pellucid
entirely salacious	a bit of a stretch	penurious

Explanation: Question 13

13. As with many tough Text Completion problems, it is difficult to make a solid prediction for either of the first two blanks. We know that the two are related, with the first being more extreme than the second, but that alone gets us nowhere, as there is more than one combination that works. To crack this problem, we must therefore begin with the last blank. The "excellent fringe benefits" are meant to make up for a type of compensation. Of the choices, only *pecuniary* (relating to money) makes any sense for Blank (iii). Since the author believes the excellent fringe benefits "more than make up for" the low pay, he must be of the opinion that teachers are not grossly underpaid in the least. For Blank (i), *completely palpable* would imply that the author finds *some* truth in the statement. Since that isn't the case it must be our 180°. Blank (i) is therefore *quite hyperbole,* and Blank (ii) is (literally!) *a bit of a stretch.*

Blank (i) quite hyperbole   **Blank (ii) a bit of a stretch**   **Blank (iii) pecuniary**

Question 14

14. In some countries, there is a common misconception that the ___(i)___ are ___(ii)___. However, this is clearly contradicted by Frederick Barbarossa's time. In his day, the ___(iii)___ were credited with most of the work, yet progress was not impeded in the least.

Blank (i)	Blank (ii)	Blank (iii)
esurient	insolent	patricians
philanthropic	indolent	paeans
impoverished	indigent	plebeians

Explanation: Question 14

14. A difficult to navigate Text Completion with few clues. While most of it is vague, we do get one solid clue in "yet progress was not impeded in the least." This is meant to contrast something in the first sentence as signaled by the Detour road sign *However*. In that sentence, Blank (ii) is our most likely candidate. While the three choices are Sound-Alikes for each other, *indolent* (lazy) is the word we are looking for. For Blank (iii), either the *patricians* or the *plebeians* may have received credit for most of the work, but to contradict the first sentence, Blank (i) and Blank (iii) need to be synonyms of sorts. While a patrician may or may not have been the Close Second *philanthropic* (or *esurient* for that matter), plebeians were by definition impoverished (good practice for the Analogies section!), so Blank (i) is *impoverished* and Blank (iii) is *plebeians*.

Blank (i) impoverished **Blank (ii) indolent** **Blank (iii) plebeians**

Question 15

15. While historians once regarded Saladin as a rather ___(i)___ fellow, the findings of many modern archaeologists have since proven otherwise. Though he was a military genius who triumphed over many a foe, never once did Saladin ___(ii)___ those he vanquished in battle.

Blank (i)	Blank (ii)
truculent	abase
erudite	venerate
aberrant	expatiate

Explanation: Question 15

15. In this difficult problem, the second blank seems easier at first glance, but it is actually the first that is easier to fill. A military genius who triumphs over many foes might either never *abase* or never *venerate* his foes. A glance back at Blank (i) reveals that only *truculent* (cruel) works in such a context. (If you were tempted by the Sound-Alike *aberrant* (divergent), you may have been thinking of the word *abhorrent* (detestable) instead.) If Saladin was thought of as truculent at one time yet not anymore, he must not *abase* his defeated foes.

Blank (i) truculent **Blank (ii) abase**

CHAPTER FOUR

Analogies

Analogies are a type of Short Verbal question that test your reasoning ability as much as they test your vocabulary. Analogies require you to recognize the relationship between a pair of words, called the *stem pair*, and then find a corresponding pair of words among the answer choices that has that same relationship. You will see around eight of these questions on the test and should spend no more than 45 seconds answering each one. The directions for this section are as follows:

> **Directions:** In each of the sample questions, a related pair of words or phrases is followed by five lettered pairs of words or phrases. Click on the lettered pair that best expresses a relationship similar to that expressed in the original pair.

On the GRE CAT, the more questions you get right, the harder the Analogies you will see. If you perform well, toward the end of your test, you can expect to see Analogies that contain very difficult, esoteric vocabulary.

On Analogies, as with other question types in the GRE Verbal section, **predicting an answer** is the best strategy for success. Skillful GRE test takers will be able to rapidly spot and precisely articulate the relationship between the stem pair and find a match among the answer choices. And as with other question types, learning to identify and eliminate wrong answers will be an important tool in your toolbox.

The four basic principles of Analogies questions will be your guide to achieving a superior score on this question type.

Principle 1

GRE Analogy questions consist of two words.

These two words, called the stem pair, will be separated by a colon and will be followed by five answer choices, each consisting of two words separated by a colon. Here's an example:

MAP : ATLAS ::

(A) key : lock
(B) street : sign
(C) ingredient : cookbook
(D) word : dictionary
(E) theory : hypothesis

Principle 2

There will always be a direct and necessary relationship between the words in the stem pair (but not necessarily in the answer choices).

You can express the relationship between the words in the stem pair by constructing a short sentence that contains both stem words. To be useful, this sentence, called a bridge, must express a necessary and direct relationship between the stem words.

For example, for the stem pair above, a strong bridge would be "An ATLAS is a collection of MAPS." The test for constructing such a bridge is that we can insert the phrase "by definition" into the bridge. Strong bridges often contain an unequivocal word, such as *always, never,* or *must.*

Notice that you may reverse the order of the stem words (as long as you remember that you did this) and even slightly change them—in this example, MAP became MAPS—but you should avoid more radical changes such as changing a noun to a verb.

Bridges that are not useful in answering GRE Analogies express relationships between the words in the stem pair that are not necessary or direct. For instance, in the above example, weak bridges include the following:

- A MAP might be found in an ATLAS.

- A MAP is usually smaller than an ATLAS.

- MAPS and ATLASES have to do with geography.

- A page in an ATLAS is usually a MAP.

Words such as *might, usually, can, seldom, sometimes, some, may,* and *may not* are diagnostic of weak bridges.

Principle 3

Articulate this relationship before looking at the answer choices.

This practice will do two things for you: it will allow you to recognize the correct answer more quickly and easily, and it will allow you to avoid getting tempted by wrong answers. Let's start by discussing answer recognition strategies. (The savvy test taker will recognize this approach as a variation on the "predict-an-answer" strategy that works so effectively on many other GRE Verbal questions.)

Since the GRE is a standardized test, each test question is a variation on a theme, and many aspects of the test are predictable. In the case of the Analogies question, we can distinguish a handful of "classic bridges" that, when recognized, allow us to more quickly identify a correct answer. Learn these classic bridges and you will make it easier for yourself to achieve a superior score!

Bridge 1: Function/purpose

AIRPLANE : HANGAR ::

(A) grain : mill
(B) money : vault
(C) finger : hand
(D) tree : farm
(E) insect : ecosystem

A HANGAR is a place to store an AIRPLANE.

(**Answer:** B)

Bridge 2: Definition

PLATITUDE : TRITE ::

(A) riddle : unsolvable
(B) axiom : geometric
(C) omen : portentous
(D) syllogism : wise
(E) circumlocution : concise

A PLATITUDE is, by definition, TRITE.

(**Answer:** C)

Bridge 3: Lack

RENEGADE : LOYALTY ::

(A) recluse : privacy
(B) thief : charity
(C) chauvinist : patriotism
(D) libertine : restraint
(E) mime : artistry

A RENEGADE lacks LOYALTY.

(**Answer:** D)

Bridge 4: Characteristic actions or items

COBBLER : LEATHER ::

(A) chandler : wax
(B) executrix : paper
(C) actor : words
(D) cartwright : wheels
(E) prosthetist : limbs

LEATHER is the raw material used by a COBBLER.

(**Answer:** A)

Bridge 5: Part/whole

OVERTURE : OPERA ::

(A) caboose : train
(B) quotation : interview
(C) rhyme : limerick
(D) preamble : constitution
(E) stage : play

The OVERTURE is music that comes just before an OPERA.

(**Answer:** D)

Bridge 6: Type

LINEN : FABRIC ::

(A) ditty : ballad
(B) square : polygon
(C) jacket : suit
(D) scale : fish
(E) necklace : bracelet

LINEN is a type of FABRIC.

(**Answer:** B)

Bridge 7: Degree (often going to an extreme)

ATTENTIVE : RAPT ::

(A) ecstatic : happy
(B) critical : derisive
(C) inventive : innovative
(D) jealous : envious
(E) kind : considerate

RAPT means extremely ATTENTIVE.

(**Answer:** B)

Principle 4

Avoid falling for common wrong answer types.

Once you have come up with an accurate and strong bridge, it is time to examine the answer choices. Recognizing correct answers is, of course, the best and quickest way to get correct answers. However, there will be times when you encounter words you just don't know or words used in an unfamiliar context—and these are especially common on the harder test questions that advanced students typically encounter. What can you do in those cases? A classic Kaplan strategy is to attack the answer set, using a process of elimination to get rid of wrong answers and narrow down the choices. So learning to recognize typical wrong answer types is always an important test-taking skill.

On the GRE Analogies section, wrong answers fall into two general categories: weak bridges and strong-but-wrong bridges. We've established that a strong bridge expresses a direct and necessary relationship. However, word pairs that may at first glance seem related may turn out to have a weak or ambiguous relationship to one another. Another type of wrong answer on Analogies questions is one that contains a strong-but-wrong bridge: the words have a direct and necessary relationship, but it does not match the relationship of the stem pair.

Let's examine some of these wrong answer types in more detail.

Unrelated Words

A pair of words with no strong relationship is a common wrong answer. *Unlikely : know* is an example of this.

Cliché Trap or Context Trap

These are words that often appear together in context, but don't have any logical relationship. For instance, *alcohol : tolerance* and *compulsive : gambler* are examples of this type.

"Both Are" Bridges

This type of wrong answer includes words that are not directly related to each other, but are both related to a third word.

salt : pepper   These are both condiments.
jazz : folk   These are both types of music.

Same Subject Trap

The words are in the same subject area as the stem pair, but they don't have the same bridge. For example, the stem pair might be ABSTRACT : ARTICLE (bridge: an ABSTRACT is a summary of an ARTICLE); a Same Subject trap answer might be *journal : publication* (bridge: a journal is a type of publication).

Reverse Direction Trap

Finally, the Reverse Direction trap is a strong-but-wrong answer that would be correct if only the words were reversed. If the stem pair were JOY : ECSTASY, a reverse direction wrong answer might be *terror : fear*.

THE KAPLAN 4-STEP METHOD FOR ANALOGIES

Now that you know some of the things to watch out for on GRE Analogies, it's time to put everything together into a step-by-step, strategic approach. Learning and using the following step-by-step method ensures that you will answer every question as efficiently as possible while avoiding as many pitfalls and trap answers as possible.

❶ Find a strong bridge between the stem words.

- The stem pair will always have a strong bridge, and the more precisely you can express it, the easier it will be for you to identify an answer with the same bridge.

❷ Try out the bridge with each answer choice.

- Look for an answer in which the words have the same relationship as the stem pair. Be sure to keep the same word order you used with the stem pair.

- Immediately eliminate answers that do not fit the bridge, including weak bridges and strong-but-wrong bridges.

- Always try all the answer choices, since you may find that more than one answer choice works with your bridge.

- If only one answer choice works with your bridge, select it.

❸ Adjust the bridge if necessary.

- If more than one answer choice works with your bridge, you will need to narrow it—make it more precise.

- If none of the answer choices works, you will probably need to expand it—make it more general.

- Consider alternate definitions for the stem words. You may have used the wrong definition of a word when you created your bridge.

❹ If stuck, build bridges between answer choice pairs and work backwards.

- Eliminate all answer choice pairs that do not have a strong bridge.

- Eliminate all answer choice pairs that have the same bridge as another answer choice pair.

- Beware of answer choices that reverse the bridge.

WORKING BACKWARDS

Working backwards is a strategy we have not yet seen in action, so let's try an example. Imagine you encountered the problem below, but you were not able to articulate the relationship between the stem pair. (We won't reveal the stem pair for the moment to avoid becoming distracted by it.)

XXXXXXX : XXXXX ::

(A) applause : approval
(B) buttress : support
(C) alcohol : tolerance
(D) antiseptic : infection
(E) embrace : affection

Looking at the answer choice pairs one by one, we find:

(A) *Applause* is a manifestation of *approval*—a strong bridge
(B) A *buttress* is used to provide *support*—a strong bridge
(C) There is no strong logical relationship between *alcohol* and *tolerance*—a cliché trap, so eliminate it.
(D) An *antiseptic* is used to prevent *infection*—a strong bridge.
(E) An *embrace* is a manifestation of *affection*—a strong bridge.

Since the bridges for (A) and (E) are identical, we can eliminate both of them. So, at this point, we have two possibilities: (B) and (D). If we were completely unable to create a bridge for the stem pair, our odds of guessing right between the two remaining choices would still be 50 percent! But if we knew one of the words, that might improve the odds of guessing further. Let's imagine that the second word is one we know:

XXXXXXX : RELIEF ::

(A) applause : approval
(B) buttress : support
(C) alcohol : tolerance
(D) antiseptic : infection
(E) embrace : affection

So could the mystery word be something that *provides* support or something that *prevents* it? It seems much more likely that the missing word is something that is used to provide support (as in answer choice (B)) rather than to prevent support (answer choice (D)), and we would pick (B). (In case you are curious, the mystery word is ANODYNE.)

You can see that there are many Kaplan strategies that can help you improve your performance on GRE Analogies. By practicing the strategies you have just learned and using the suggested approaches when you find yourself stuck, you will be able to unlock some of the very hardest Analogies questions and answer them with confidence. There may still be problems whose answers you cannot be sure of, but even in those problems, using Kaplan techniques and elimination strategies will allow you to make the best possible guesses and have the best chance of choosing the correct answers. Now it's time to use what you have learned, practice diligently, and turn these strategic approaches to GRE Analogies into habits!

CHAPTER FIVE

Analogies Practice Set

1. DILETTANTE : EXPERTISE ::

   (A) ascetic : austerity
   (B) connoisseur : aptitude
   (C) loafer : idleness
   (D) misanthrope : compassion
   (E) charlatan : indifference

A DILETTANTE, by definition, lacks EXPERTISE; likewise, a MISANTHROPE, by definition, lacks COMPASSION. Of the wrong answers, choice (B) is a Same Subject trap, designed to tempt you by reminding you of the subject of expert skill or knowledge. Choices (A) and (C) can be eliminated because they contain the same wrong bridge: an ASCETIC is marked by AUSTERITY, and a LOAFER is marked by IDLENESS. Choice (E) can be eliminated because it contains a weak bridge.

2. CASUAL : CAVALIER ::

   (A) stubborn : recalcitrant
   (B) disparaging : encomiastic
   (C) corpulent : fleshy
   (D) sparse : scant
   (E) daft : vivacious

Someone who is CAVALIER is excessively CASUAL; likewise, someone who is RECALCITRANT is excessively STUBBORN. If you chose (C), you fell for the Reverse Direction trap. Someone who is CORPULENT is excessively FLESHY; that's the correct bridge, but the order of the words has been reversed. Someone who is ENCOMIASTIC is praising, not DISPARAGING, so choice (B) can be eliminated. SPARSE and SCANT are synonyms, and since neither the stem words nor the right answer choice will ever be a pair of synonyms, choice (D) can be eliminated. Someone who is VIVACIOUS may or may not be DAFT, so choice (E) can be eliminated because it contains a weak bridge.

3. VAGRANT : PEREGRINATE ::

   (A) magistrate : collaborate
   (B) skeptic : believe
   (C) debaucher : seduce
   (D) tyrant : persuade
   (E) hedonist : abstain

A VAGRANT, by definition, PEREGRINATES, meaning "travels or journeys"; likewise, a DEBAUCHER, by definition, SEDUCES. Of the wrong answer choices, (A) and (D) can be eliminated because they contain weak bridges; a MAGISTRATE may or may not COLLABORATE, and a TYRANT may or may not PERSUADE. Choices (B) and (E) can be eliminated because they share the same wrong bridge: a SKEPTIC does not BELIEVE, and a HEDONIST does not ABSTAIN.

4. SOLECISM : GRAMMAR ::

   (A) equation : arithmetic
   (B) neologism : term
   (C) anthology : literature
   (D) sophism : reasoning
   (E) exposition : grammar

A SOLECISM uses incorrect GRAMMAR; likewise, a SOPHISM uses incorrect REASONING. Choice (A) can be eliminated because it contains a weak bridge: an EQUATION may or may not use incorrect ARITHMETIC. Choice (B) can be eliminated because it employs the wrong bridge: a NEOLOGISM is a new TERM. Choice (C) also uses a wrong bridge: an ANTHOLOGY is a collection of pieces of LITERATURE. Choice (E) EXPOSITION: PUNCTUATION has a weak bridge but may have been distracting because GRAMMAR and PUNCTATION are often discussed as a pair.

5. DOWNWARD : PRONE ::

   (A) skyward : limber
   (B) horizontal : recumbent
   (C) upward : supine
   (D) outward : erect
   (E) upright : prostrate

One lying down and facing DOWNWARD, by definition, is PRONE; likewise, one lying down and facing UPWARD is SUPINE. If you first tried to build the bridge "One who is PRONE faces DOWNWARD," both choices (C) and (D) would have fit, and you would have had to adjust your bridge by making it more specific; one who is ERECT faces OUTWARD, but that person is standing, not lying down. Choice (A) can be eliminated because it contains a weak bridge:

one lying down and facing SKYWARD may or may not be LIMBER. Choice (B) uses the wrong bridge: if one's body is HORIZONTAL, he or she is RECUMBENT. Choice (E) also uses the wrong bridge: one standing UPRIGHT is not PROSTRATE.

6. COMESTIBLE : EAT ::

   (A) potable : breathe
   (B) alimental : wear
   (C) salubrious : drink
   (D) mephitic : consume
   (E) functional : use

Something COMESTIBLE is fit to EAT; likewise, something FUNCTIONAL is fit to USE. Of the wrong answers, choices (A) and (B) are clearly wrong: something POTABLE is fit to drink, which has nothing to do with BREATHING; similarly, something ALIMENTAL is fit to eat, which has nothing to do with WEARING. Choice (C) also has a weak bridge: something SALUBRIOUS, meaning "healthful," may or may not be fit to drink. Finally, choice (D) uses the wrong bridge: something MEPHITIC, meaning "poisonous," will kill or injure if CONSUMED.

7. PHILANDERER : LOVER ::

   (A) activist : environment
   (B) fanatic : team
   (C) apostate : religion
   (D) patriot : homeland
   (E) chauvinist : military

A PHILANDERER is not faithful to his LOVER; likewise, an APOSTATE is not faithful to his RELIGION. Choices (A) and (B) may have been tempting because those pairs of words are often seen together. Nevertheless, both can be eliminated because of their weak bridges: an ACTIVIST does not necessarily advocate for the ENVIRONMENT, nor does a FANATIC necessarily support a TEAM. Choice (D) uses the wrong bridge: a PATRIOT is devoted to his HOMELAND. Choice (E) also uses a wrong bridge: a CHAUVINIST has blind enthusiasm for the MILITARY.

8. COMPASS : CIRCLE ::

   (A) caliper : diameter
   (B) spline : curve
   (C) odometer : distance
   (D) line : straightedge
   (E) pencil : contour

A COMPASS is used to draw a CIRCLE; likewise, a SPLINE is used to draw a CURVE. Choice (D) employs the Reverse Direction trap: a STRAIGHTEDGE is used to draw a LINE. That's the right bridge, but the order of the words has been reversed. Choices (A) and (C) can be eliminated because they use the same wrong bridge: a CALIPER is used to measure DIAMETER, and an ODOMETER is used to measure DISTANCE. Choice (E) can be eliminated because of its weak bridge: a PENCIL may or may not be used to draw a CONTOUR.

9. ANODYNE : OPIATE ::

   (A) athlete : pugilist
   (B) pundit : comic
   (C) soporific : sleep
   (D) conifer : tree
   (E) solitude : seclusion

An OPIATE is a type of ANODYNE, meaning "a medicine that relieves pain"; likewise, a PUGILIST, meaning "boxer," is a type of athlete. It is very important to ascertain the correct direction of this bridge, as choice (D) is a Reverse Direction trap: a CONIFER is a type of TREE, but the word order is the opposite of the order of the stem words. Choice (B) contains a weak bridge and can be eliminated. A SOPORIFIC causes SLEEP, which is the wrong bridge, so choice (C) can be eliminated. The stem words will never be perfect synonyms, so the correct answer choice will never contain a pair of synonyms; since SOLITUDE and SECLUSION are synonyms, choice (E) can be eliminated.

10. NARTHEX : CHURCH ::

   (A) antechamber : parlor
   (B) stern : barge
   (C) nave : cathedral
   (D) cabin : airplane
   (E) foyer : theater

The NARTHEX is the front part of a CHURCH; likewise, a FOYER is the front part of a THEATER. If you first tried the bridge: a NARTHEX is part of a CHURCH, choices (B), (C), (D), and (E) would have worked, and you would have had to make your bridge more specific. Any time the bridge for a pair of words involves the words "both are," it is a weak bridge; so choice (A) can be eliminated because an ANTECHAMBER and a PARLOR both are rooms in a house. Choice (C) may have been tempting because it involves a religious building, just like the stem pair; but a NAVE is the main part, not the front part, of a CATHEDRAL.

11. FOUNDER : FAIL ::

   (A) peruse : read
   (B) satisfy : sate
   (C) extirpate : destroy
   (D) mar : gawk
   (E) inundate : provoke

This analogy is difficult not only because it uses a secondary definition of the word FOUNDER, but because once you discern that definition, the stem words may appear to be synonyms. When the two stem words seem like synonyms, figure out which word is the harsher or more extreme version of the other word. In this case, the first word is more extreme: to FOUNDER is to FAIL completely; likewise, to EXTIRPATE is to DESTROY completely. Choice (B) contains a Reverse Direction trap: to SATE is to SATISFY completely; it is incorrect because the order of the words has been reversed. Choice (A) can be eliminated because it uses the wrong bridge: to PERUSE is to READ carefully, not completely. The last two choices, (D) and (E), can be eliminated because they contain weak bridges.

12. PUNCTILIOUS : ETIQUETTE ::

    (A) lackadaisical : ambition

    (B) capricious : whim

    (C) quixotic : practicality

    (D) pietistic : doctrine

    (E) vacuous : contentment

Someone who is PUNCTILIOUS is strict in his or her observance of ETIQUETTE; likewise, someone who is PIETISTIC is strict in his or her observance of DOCTRINE. Choices (A) and (C) can be eliminated because they share the same wrong bridge: someone who is LACKADAISICAL, meaning "unmotivated and lazy," lacks AMBITION; and someone who is QUIXOTIC, meaning "impulsive and overly idealistic," lacks PRACTICALITY. Choice (B) uses the bridge "Someone who is CAPRICIOUS is guided by WHIM." If you were working backwards you might have noticed that this bridge works for the stem words, but it also works for choice (D); adjusting the bridge would have allowed you to eliminate choice (B). Choice (E) contains a weak bridge and can be eliminated.

13. URSINE : BEAR ::

    (A) piscine : fish

    (B) apian : monkey

    (C) simian : cat

    (D) equine : cow

    (E) vulpine : wolf

Something URSINE, by definition, is of or pertaining to BEARS; likewise, something PISCINE, by definition, is of or pertaining to FISH. If you are familiar with astrological signs, your knowledge of Pisces may have led you to the correct answer. The remaining answer choices are wrong, for they all mismatch the qualities with the animals they describe. Something APIAN is of or pertaining to bees, not MONKEYS. Something SIMIAN is of or pertaining to apes, not CATS. Something EQUINE is of or pertaining to horses, not COWS. Finally, something VULPINE is of or pertaining to foxes, not WOLVES.

14. DECENT : SCURRILOUS ::

    (A) coy : diminutive

    (B) generous : estimable

    (C) disobedient : froward

    (D) active : indolent

    (E) clever : oracular

Someone who is SCURRILOUS, meaning "obscene," is not DECENT; likewise, someone who is INDOLENT, meaning "lazy," is not ACTIVE. Even if you did not know the definition of

SCURRILOUS, you might have determined that it sounds more like an opposite of DECENT than similar to it. This would have led you to eliminate choice (B), GENEROUS : ESTIMABLE, and choice (C), DISOBEDIENT : FROWARD, which sound more similar in meaning than opposite. Of the remaining answer choices, both (A) and (E) contain weak bridges: someone who is DIMINUTIVE, meaning "small in stature," may or may not be COY; and someone who is ORACULAR, meaning "prophetic," may or may not be CLEVER.

15. RAMIFY : BRANCH ::

(A) unravel : knot

(B) molt : feather

(C) propound : analysis

(D) dismantle : garment

(E) bisect : half

To RAMIFY is to divide into BRANCHES; likewise, to BISECT is to divide into HALVES. Choice (A) can be eliminated because it contains a weak bridge. Choices (B) and (D) are incorrect because they employ the same wrong bridge: to MOLT is to shed FEATHERS, and to DISMANTLE is to shed GARMENTS. Choice (C) can also be eliminated because it uses a wrong bridge: to PROPOUND is to put forth for ANALYSIS.

CHAPTER SIX

Antonyms

For many GRE test takers, Antonyms are the hardest type of Short Verbal question, since they are the most vocabulary intensive and provide little in the way of clues to finding the correct answer. However, if you approach these questions strategically, you will find that you can get many questions right even if you don't know the exact definitions of the tested words.

Antonyms require you to identify an answer choice that is most opposite in meaning to the stem word. You will see around nine of these questions on the test and should spend no more than 30 seconds answering each one. The directions for this section are as follows:

> **Directions:** Each question in this section consists of a word printed in capital letters followed by five lettered words or phrases. Choose the lettered word or phrase that is most nearly opposite in meaning to the word in capital letters. Since some of the questions require you to distinguish fine shades of meaning, be sure to consider all the choices before deciding which one is best.

On the GRE CAT, the more questions you get right, the harder the Antonym questions you will see. If you perform well, toward the end of your test, you can expect to see Antonyms that contain very difficult, esoteric vocabulary, and using Kaplan strategies will become increasingly important.

For Antonyms, as with many other question types in the GRE Verbal section, **predicting an answer** is the best strategy for success. Skillful GRE test takers will be able to mentally define the stem word, predict its opposite, and find a match among the answer choices. And as with other question types, learning to identify and eliminate wrong answers will be an important tool in your toolbox.

The following five basic principles of Antonyms questions will be your guide to achieving a superior score on this question type.

Principle 1

Use Kaplan's strategies for unlocking the meaning of difficult vocabulary words.

High-difficulty Antonyms questions may seem impenetrable at first glance. However, just a small amount of information can go a long way toward helping you answer the question correctly. Remember, you do not need to write a definition of this word, but just pick out an antonym from a list of five choices, so an approximate sense of its meaning can be sufficient.

Think of a Context in Which You Have Heard the Word Before

You might be able to figure out the meaning of a word by recalling a familiar phrase containing the word. What's your best guess as to the meaning of the italicized words in these phrases? A *formidable* foe; *abject* poverty; salary will be *commensurate* with experience; *mitigating* circumstances.

Look for Word Roots, Stems, Prefixes, and Suffixes

This is another way to get a sense of a word's meaning. For example, even if you don't know the meaning of *benevolent*, the prefix *bene* (which means "good," and is found in such familiar words as *benefit*) tells you that its opposite will probably be something bad. And if you see the prefix *mal* (meaning "bad") in one of the answer choices, you have probably found the antonym (in this case, *malevolent*).

Use Your Knowledge of a Romance Language

Guessing a word's meaning based on its similarity to another word in a foreign language can lead to correct answers on GRE Antonyms questions. For instance, you may be able to guess that *moratorium* has something to do with an ending or stoppage, based on its similarity to the French word *morte*, meaning "death"; you may speculate that *credulous* is related to belief based on its similarity to the Italian word *credere*; and you could get a sense of the meaning of *mundane* based on its similarity to the Spanish word *mundo*, meaning "world."

Principle 2

Use word "charge" to help you guess.

Even if you don't have much of a clue about a word's meaning, when you can get a sense of the word's charge—is it positive or negative?—you can make surprisingly good progress toward getting a correct answer, even when other vocabulary-decoding strategies fail. If a stem word sounds positive, you know its antonym must have a negative charge, and vice versa. Here is a sample of a tough Antonyms question:

SCABROUS:

(A) thorny
(B) unblemished
(C) perplexing
(D) blank
(E) examined

Notice that SCABROUS sounds harsh; it has a negative charge. Looking at the answer choices, we only find one answer with a positive charge: answer (B), *unblemished*. All the other answers here couldn't be an antonym of *scabrous*, since they are either negative (answers (A) and (C)) or neutral (answers (D) and (E)). And answer (B), *unblemished*, works; *scabrous* means "rough or scaly."

Principle 3

On difficult Antonyms questions, use a process of elimination.

If unlocking the stem word is just not working, take a look at the answer set. Eliminating obvious wrong answers and avoiding trap answers and misleading choices can allow you to narrow down the answer set and give you a good chance of guessing the right answer. So learning to recognize typical wrong answers is an important test-taking skill on Antonyms questions (as it is on many other GRE Verbal questions), especially for the harder Antonyms questions that advanced test takers are most likely to see.

On the GRE Antonyms section, there are several categories of wrong answer types. Let's examine some of these wrong answer types in more detail.

Words That Have no Clear Opposites

Words such as *attitude*, *equine*, *deserve*, *priority*, and *birthright* have no clear opposite and can be eliminated from consideration.

Words That Are Synonyms of Other Answer Choices

The antonyms of such words will be the same. For instance, if *serene* and *tranquil* both appear in an Antonyms answer set, you can eliminate them both; since they are synonyms of each other, neither could be the correct answer—if they were correct, there would be two correct answers, which cannot happen on the GRE.

Au Contraire, or Opposite, Answers

When you are able to define the stem word, you can always eliminate answer choices that are the opposite of what you are looking for. Get rid of any synonyms for the stem word, since you are looking for its antonym.

Principle 4

Work backwards from the answer choices when you don't know the meaning of the stem word.

This can be an effective way of getting right answers on very difficult Antonyms questions. Keep in mind that this is a last resort, since the target time for Antonyms questions is 30 seconds each, and working backwards can be time-consuming. However, when you are clueless about the stem word, it's a viable option for being able to make a reasonable guess, when combined with the process of elimination (described above, in Principle 3) and with any other relevant Kaplan strategies.

Working backwards involves going through the answer set and finding an antonym for each of the answer choices. If you are having trouble coming up with an antonym, don't waste more than five seconds trying. Many words don't have clear opposites, so you can just get rid of those words. After eliminating answer choices that do not have an antonym, and choices that are synonyms for each other and thus have the same antonym, consider the antonyms you have come up with for each of the answers that remains. You can ask yourself, "How likely is it that the stem word means _____?" If you are totally stuck, just pick the answer choice that has the clearest opposite. Here is an example.

Imagine you do not know the meaning of the stem word, *unequivocal*. What would you do?

UNEQUIVOCAL

(A) volatile

(B) serious

(C) ambiguous

(D) somber

(E) ruddy

First, try to find an antonym for each answer choice.

(A)	volatile	Antonym: stable
(B)	serious	Antonym: lighthearted
(C)	ambiguous	Antonym: definite, explicit
(D)	somber	Antonym: lighthearted
(E)	ruddy	No antonym

First, since *ruddy*, meaning "red in color," has no antonym, eliminate it. Next, did you notice that answers (B) and (D) were synonyms for each other? If you didn't, you surely noticed that their antonyms are the same! Eliminate both of them. Now our answer set looks like this:

(A)	volatile	Antonym: stable
(B)	~~serious~~	~~Antonym: lighthearted~~
(C)	ambiguous	Antonym: definite, explicit
(D)	~~somber~~	~~Antonym: lighthearted~~
(E)	~~ruddy~~	~~no antonym~~

We can check each of the remaining choices—and there are only two!—to decide on an answer. How likely is it that the stem word means *stable*? How likely is it that the stem word means *definite* or *explicit*? Returning to a strategy mentioned earlier (Principle 1, above), we might use context to help make this decision. Have you ever heard *unequivocal* used in a sentence? How about the phrase, "unequivocal evidence"? So which one makes more sense, "stable evidence" or "definite evidence"? The latter sounds much better, leading us to the correct answer, (C), *ambiguous*.

Principle 5

Watch out for deceptive vocabulary.

On the high-difficulty questions likely to be seen by advanced test takers, the test maker will sometimes include words that don't sound like what they mean. The best defense against such words is taking note of them as you study (perhaps by means of color-coded flash cards) so you will not be fooled on Test Day. Here's a quick quiz on some typical deceptive GRE vocabulary words.

1. A *restive* person is (A) relaxed or (B) on edge.

2. A *noisome* crowd is (A) loud or (B) foul smelling.

3. A *prolix* speech is (A) to the point or (B) rambling and wordy.

4. A *tortuous* movie is (A) full of plot twists or (B) painful to watch.

5. To *obviate* is (A) to make clear or (B) to make unnecessary.

6. A *disinterested* person is (A) unbiased or (B) indifferent.

Answers: 1 B, 2 B, 3 B, 4 A, 5 B, 6 A.

Another way the test maker can make the test more difficult is by testing less common meanings of words or unexpected parts of speech. For instance, you may think you know the meaning of this common word, PROMPT, but when you look for its obvious antonyms, *late* or *tardy*, you discover that you are on the wrong track! Here is the question, including its answer set:

PROMPT

(A) refuse
(B) rest
(C) deceive
(D) discourage
(E) postpone

You notice that each of these answer choices consists of a verb, so *prompt* must be a verb, not an adjective as you had at first thought! So you must switch gears. What does *prompt* mean as a verb? It means to move or induce to action, and its antonym would be answer (D), to discourage.

USE THE KAPLAN 4-STEP METHOD FOR ANTONYMS

Now that you know some strategies for GRE Antonyms, it's time to put everything together into a step-by-step, strategic approach. Learning and using the following step-by-step method ensures that you will answer every question as efficiently as possible while avoiding as many pitfalls and trap answers as possible.

❶ **Define the stem word.**

- Even if you don't know the precise definition of the word, a general sense of the word can be adequate.

- Use Kaplan vocabulary strategies, such as looking for roots, thinking about context, and noticing word charge, to get a rough definition of the word.

❷ **Predict the word's opposite.**

- This is the most powerful thing you can do, since it helps you avoid tempting trap answers.

❸ **Find an answer that matches your prediction.**

- Sometimes more than one answer choice will be close to your prediction. Check them all to find the best fit.

- Consider alternate definitions for the stem word. You may have used the wrong definition of a word when you created your prediction.

❹ **If stuck, work backwards.**

- Eliminate all answer choices that have no clear opposite.

- Eliminate all answer choices that have the same opposite as another answer choice.

- Beware of answer choices that are synonyms for the stem word.

Now it's time to get some practice. By using the Kaplan strategies and techniques that you have just learned and by continuing to improve your vocabulary, you will be on your way to a superior score on the GRE Verbal section!

CHAPTER SEVEN

Antonyms Practice Set

1. INTRANSIGENCE:

   (A) exuberance
   (B) solemnity
   (C) compliance
   (D) desperation
   (E) acrimony

INTRANSIGENCE means "stubbornness or an unwillingness to change," so a good prediction for its opposite would be "willingness to compromise." Thus, the closest match is choice (C), COMPLIANCE. If you spotted the prefix *in*, meaning "not," and the word root *trans*, meaning "across," you might have guessed the word had something to do with not moving. Using word charge also might have helped if you recognized that INTRANSIGENCE has a negative connotation; searching for an answer choice with a positive connotation would have allowed you to eliminate choices (B) SOLEMNITY, (D) DESPERATION, and (E) ACRIMONY.

2. PROLIFERATE:

   (A) wane
   (B) conjure
   (C) mesmerize
   (D) recur
   (E) rectify

If you have heard the phrase "nuclear proliferation," you might have used the word's context to figure out that PROLIFERATE means "to increase in number" or "spread rapidly." A good prediction for the opposite would have been "decrease." Choice (A) WANE fits this prediction. Choices (B) CONJURE and (D) RECUR don't have clear opposites and thus can be eliminated.

3. DEFERENCE:

   (A) apprehension
   (B) turbulence
   (C) insubordination
   (D) trepidation
   (E) consensus

DEFERENCE means "respectful submission," so a good prediction for its opposite would be "disobedience." This matches choice (C) INSUBORDINATION. Had you not known the definition of choice (C), you could have used the prefix *in*, meaning "not," and the word root *sub*, meaning "under," to deduce that the meaning had something to do with not being under someone or something. Choice (A) APPREHENSION and choice (D) TREPIDATION are synonyms and thus can be eliminated.

4. CHECK:

   (A) enrage
   (B) revert
   (C) negate
   (D) unleash
   (E) promote

The stem word CHECK has multiple meanings, which increases the difficulty of this problem. Nevertheless, the meaning with the most clear opposite is "to restrain" (secondary definitions, like "to investigate" and "to mark" do not have opposites). A good prediction for the opposite would have been "to release," which makes (D) UNLEASH the correct answer. You also could have worked backwards; making opposites from the answer choices you get the following: (A) DELIGHT, (B) no clear opposite, (C) AFFIRM, (D) RESTRAIN, and (E) DENOUNCE. From there, you would have seen that (D) RESTRAIN is a definition of CHECK and therefore the correct answer.

5. GARRULOUS:

   (A) reticent
   (B) dilapidated
   (C) mottled
   (D) billowing
   (E) derelict

GARRULOUS means "excessively talkative," so a good prediction for its opposite would be "uncommunicative." Choice (A) RETICENT, which means "reserved" or "prone to silence," fits this prediction. Choices (C) MOTTLED (meaning "spotted") and (D) BILLOWING do not have clear opposites and thus can be eliminated. Because choices (B) DILAPIDATED and (E) DERELICT are synonyms, they too can be eliminated.

6. EBULLIENT

    (A) festive

    (B) lustrous

    (C) oblivious

    (D) pristine

    (E) apathetic

The stem word EBULLIENT means "overflowing with enthusiasm," so a good prediction for its opposite would be "unenthusiastic," which matches choice (E) APATHETIC. If you realized that EBULLIENT has a positive connotation, you could have used word charge to seek out an answer choice with a negative connotation, thus eliminating (A) FESTIVE, (B) LUSTROUS, and (D) PRISTINE. You then would have had to decide whether EBULLIENT better matches the opposite of (C) OBLIVIOUS, which is "aware," or (E) APATHETIC, which is "passionate."

7. IMPERIOUS:

    (A) platonic

    (B) assiduous

    (C) servile

    (D) craven

    (E) innocuous

The stem word IMPERIOUS means "overbearing" or "domineering." If you noticed that this word is very similar to the word "imperial," you might have guessed IMPERIOUS has something to do with ruling or having power over people. Thus, a logical prediction for its opposite would have been "servantlike." With this prediction, choice (C) SERVILE should have immediately stood out as the correct answer.

8. CONCESSION:

    (A) vindication

    (B) disputation

    (C) appellation

    (D) profusion

    (E) unanimity

A CONCESSION is "the act of yielding." Using the word root *cess*, which means "to yield," or connecting CONCESSION with its relative "to concede," would have led you to predict an opposite that has something to do with arguing against or protesting. Answer choice (B) DISPUTATION is the best match. If you know the French word *appelle*, you could have eliminated (C) APPELLATION (a name or title), which has no clear opposite. You might have been sidetracked by oddball answer choice (E) UNANIMITY, which is the only choice that doesn't end in *-ion*; beware of visually distracting answer choices.

9. FREQUENT:

(A) degrade
(B) curtail
(C) eradicate
(D) avoid
(E) sustain

Upon seeing FREQUENT in the stem, you might have assumed that it was an adjective, meaning "constant, habitual, or regular" and predicted the opposite, "infrequent." In this instance, however, the answer choices let us know that FREQUENT is a verb. As a verb, FREQUENT means "to visit often," so the opposite would be "to stay away from." This matches choice (D) AVOID.

10. VERACIOUS:

(A) mendacious
(B) improbable
(C) gregarious
(D) confrontational
(E) belligerent

The stem word VERACIOUS means "truthful," so a good prediction for its opposite would be "untruthful," which matches choice (A) MENDACIOUS. Recognizing the word root *ver*, meaning "true," would have helped you define the stem word. You might have found its opposite with your knowledge of the French word *mensonge* or Spanish word *mendira*, both meaning "lie." Choices (D) CONFRONTATIONAL and (E) BELLIGERENT are synonyms and thus can be eliminated.

11. APPROPRIATE:

(A) offend
(B) masticate
(C) relinquish
(D) glean
(E) confiscate

You might have assumed the stem word APPROPRIATE was an adjective, meaning "proper," but a scan of the answer choice reveals verbs. In its verb form, APPROPRIATE means "to take possession of," so a good prediction for its opposite would be "to give up possession of." Choice (C) RELINQUISH matches this prediction. While choices (B) MASTICATE and (D) GLEAN can be eliminated because they do not have clear opposites, the other wrong answer choices may have been tempting. Choice (A) OFFEND might have been appealing because *offensive* is a near opposite of the adjective form of APPROPRIATE. Choice (E) CONFISCATE might also have been distracting, as it is a synonym of APPROPRIATE.

12. ABNEGATION:

    (A) slothfulness

    (B) intemperance

    (C) sustenance

    (D) euphoria

    (E) reconciliation

The stem word ABNEGATION means "self-denial," so a good prediction for its opposite would have been "self-indulgence." Thus, the closest match is (B) INTEMPERANCE, which means "excessive indulgence of appetite or passion." If you spotted the word root *neg*, meaning "to deny," you might have guessed that ABNEGATION has something to do with denying oneself. Using the prefix *in*, meaning "not," and context for the word *temperance* (such as "temperance movement"), you might have deduced that INTEMPERENCE has something to do with not abstaining. Choice (C) SUSTENANCE can be eliminated because it has no clear opposite.

13. TRUCULENT:

    (A) jocose

    (B) generic

    (C) eloquent

    (D) pernicious

    (E) amiable

TRUCULENT means "aggressively hostile," so a good prediction for its opposite would be *friendly*, which matches choice (E) AMIABLE. Using word charge might have helped if you recognized that TRUCULENT has a negative connotation; searching for an answer choice with a positive connotation would have allowed you to eliminate choices (B) GENERIC and (D) PERNICIOUS. Choice (A) JOCOSE, meaning "given to joking," does not have a clear opposite and thus can be eliminated.

14. BENISON:

    (A) supplicant

    (B) rancor

    (C) anathema

    (D) virulence

    (E) opposition

A BENISON is a blessing, so a good prediction of its opposite would be a curse, which is the definition of (C) ANATHEMA. Recognizing the word root *ben*, meaning "good," in the stem word might have led you to look for something "bad" or "evil" in the answer choices; this would have led you to (C) ANATHEMA, after synonyms (B) RANCOR and (D) VIRULENCE were eliminated. Answer choice (A) SUPPLICANT does not have a clear opposite and thus can be eliminated.

15. OBFUSCATE:

    (A) accrue

    (B) enlighten

    (C) ossify

    (D) circumvent

    (E) perpetuate

The stem word OBFUSCATE means "to confuse" or "to make unclear," so a good prediction for its opposite would have been "to make clear." Choice (B) ENLIGHTEN is the best match. You may have been able to figure out the meaning of OBFUSCATE by noticing the similarities it shares with the words *confuse* and *obscure*. You also could have worked backwards; making opposites from the answer choices, you get the following: (A) DECREASE, (B) OBSCURE, (C) no clear opposite, (D) no clear opposite, and (E) STOP. From there, you would have seen the similarities between (B) OBSCURE and the stem word.

READING COMPREHENSION

Roses are red. Violets are blue.

The passage suggests that which of the following is a distinctive feature of a flower?

(A) size
(B) aroma
(C) beauty
(D) color
(E) petals

Ever since you learned to read, you've been tested on your comprehension of written material, so it's no surprise that Reading Comprehension is the most familiar section in all of standardized testing. Medicine, law, archaeology, psychology, dentistry, teaching, business—the exams that stand at the entrance to study in these and other fields have one thing in common: Reading Comprehension passages. No matter what academic area you pursue, you have to make sense of dense, even unfamiliar prose, and graduate school is no exception.

If you're looking to get an advanced Verbal score on the GRE, then you shouldn't expect to see too many easy Reading Comp passages. For the purposes of this book, we've compiled for your test-taking pleasure a group of the densest, nastiest passages we could find. If you can ace these in a reasonable amount of time, it's safe to say that you have absolutely nothing to fear from Reading Comp questions come Test Day.

Oh, and as for that gem of modern poetry above, the correct choice is (D)—but you already knew that, didn't you?

CHAPTER EIGHT

Reading Comprehension

The Verbal section of the GRE CAT will contain two or three Reading Comprehension passages, drawn from three areas: social sciences, natural sciences, and the arts and humanities, accompanied by anywhere from two to five questions per passage. Reading Comp will account for around 7 questions out of the 30 total Verbal questions you will face, although you will probably spend the biggest chunk of your Verbal time allotment on these questions—15 minutes, which is half of the 30 minutes you get to work on the Verbal section. The directions for this section are as follows:

> **Directions:** Each passage in this section is followed by questions based on its content. After reading the passage, choose the best answer to each question. Answer all questions following the passage on the basis of what is stated or implied in the passage.

Simple, right? "Choose the best answer," huh? Well, when you put it that way, I know just what to do! Perhaps it's not really so obvious how to ace the Reading Comprehension section. Let's take a closer look. What are the typical barriers to gaining the highest possible score in this area?

"I can't understand all this technical information—this is not my area of expertise." "I get lost in the details." "These passages put me to sleep!" "Reading Comp just takes too much time!" All of these are common complaints about Reading Comprehension on standardized tests such as the GRE. What kind of a reader are you? Do you tend to get lost in the details? Do you become overwhelmed by highly technical passages? Knowing your personal weaknesses can go a long way toward helping you improve your performance on the Reading Comprehension section. On the other hand, if you are already performing well in RC, you are probably already doing some of what is suggested here. Even so, you can improve your performance further by becoming more conscious and deliberate about your approach to reading and by incorporating any strategies that you have not already implemented.

First of all, it's important to think about your goals in reading a GRE Reading Comp passage. In everyday life, you may have a variety of goals when reading: to get specific information; to learn something or satisfy your curiosity; to get an overview of a field of study or a concept; to prepare for a test or a quiz; to consider someone else's ideas and see whether you agree; to be entertained. However, most of these goals are completely irrelevant to success on GRE Reading

Comprehension! **In the GRE Reading Comp section, you have one and only one goal: to get the highest score possible.** So how can you maximize your score and minimize the time and stress it takes to do so?

You need to commit yourself to relentlessly focusing on the Big Picture, and absolutely refuse to get involved with the details, until and unless there are questions that require you to do so. For the duration of the test, you must throw away your intellectual curiosity and become a mercenary GRE student, only interested in gaining points for your efforts. Anything less than this will interfere with your mastery of this section and cause you to waste time and to clutter your mind with useless information. To be successful, you must have a pragmatic, single-minded focus on your goal. You cannot let your opinions, preferences, or fears get in the way of accomplishing your mission: maximizing your score. And the way to do this is to completely redesign the way you approach reading a Reading Comp passage.

> An advanced test taker does not read the first question before reading the passage.

Remember, when reading in everyday life, your goals are completely different than they are in the GRE Reading Comp section. In everyday life, you may be trying to learn something, but on the GRE, your interest is purely mercenary. If you are tempted to try to learn or understand something during the first pass through a passage, ask yourself, "How will this improve my score?" If you don't yet know, then do not spend your time contemplating it. If and when you have a question to answer about that point or that idea, you will return to it.

So what does this look like in practice? On the GRE, your first goal is to construct a Passage Map: an overview of the passage designed to allow you to easily locate and understand the nitty-gritty details, if and when you have questions that require such an understanding. It is therefore crucial that you focus only on the parts of the passage that allow you to get an overview of it, skimming (not skipping) the details until you need them to answer questions. This approach is called reading critically, and there are four principles to guide you.

> An advanced test taker knows that a good road map doesn't include every detail of a passage, but recaps the points of each paragraph and reminds him or her where the evidence to support these points can be found.

READING CRITICALLY

Principle 1

Focus on the Big Picture: identify the topic, scope, and purpose.

Use the first minute or so after you begin reading a new passage to orient yourself. Read the first paragraph (or a bit more, or a bit less—roughly the first one-third) of a passage carefully, paraphrasing if necessary, in order to determine the **topic** and **scope** of the passage. While you will not be tested on either of these, they are helpful in keeping your focus where it needs to be—on the whole forest rather than down in the trees—and identifying the scope can be helpful in eliminating wrong answers to GRE RC questions, many of which are wrong because they are out of scope.

Write a word or a phrase to describe the topic—that is, the broad subject matter—and the scope—the specific focus of this passage—on your Passage Map, for later reference. If the author has revealed his or her purpose at this point, write that down, too, but don't worry if you cannot identify it yet. Many authors don't reveal their purpose until later in the passage.

A note on author purpose: While we have determined that **your** purpose is quite simple (to get the highest possible score!), GRE authors may have a variety of purposes, which we can group into half a dozen rough categories. The first three are the most opinionated, while the remaining categories are further down on the spectrum toward neutrality:

- **Convince, persuade, argue for, argue that**—the author agrees with an idea, theory, etc.

- **Rebut, refute, argue against**—the author disagrees with an idea.

- **Assess, critique, evaluate**—the author discusses how well someone else has expressed an idea, analyzing both the strengths and the weaknesses of his/her presentation.

- **Compare/contrast**—the author must discuss two things: two ideas, theories, etc. This passage type could be opinionated or neutral in tone.

- **Explain**—this type of passage answers the question "Why...?" or "How...?"

- **Describe**—this completely neutral passage just gives information.

You will need to identify the author's purpose in writing the passage in order to answer Global questions, and you'll need the author's purpose for including a detail or for writing a particular paragraph in order to answer Logic questions.

> An advanced test taker uses his road map to answer Global (primary purpose or main idea) questions.

Principle 2

Focus on the Big Picture: use the clues.

Certain words, phrases, and even sentences can provide you with the information you need to stay focused on the Big Picture in Reading Comprehension, and they allow you to avoid getting lost in the details. They include the following:

- Road signs

- Traffic signals

- Topic sentences

Road Signs

Road signs, as you will recall from your Sentence Completions studies, are transition words that help you understand prose and help you anticipate what should be coming next. The road signs you learned to identify and benefit from in Sentence Completions are helpful in Reading Comprehension for the same reasons. In addition to the road signs you learned for that section of the test, there are some additional categories of road signs that you should pay attention to. Here is a complete list:

- **Continuation road signs** (Straight Ahead road signs) such as *and, in addition, in the same way, moreover, plus,* and *also* tell you that you are about to get more of the same.

- **Contrast road signs** (Detour road signs) such as *but, however, instead, in contrast,* and *on the other hand* tell you that the author is about to make a shift.

- **Conclusion road signs** such as *therefore, thus, hence, in conclusion,* and *so* tell you that the author is about to make a point.

- **Evidence road signs** such as *because, for, since,* and *due to* tell you that the author is about to explain why something is true or why it happened.

- **Author emphasis road signs** such as *most importantly* tell you what the author considers important.

- **Sequence road signs** such as *first, second, third, next, after this,* and *finally* tell you the sequence of events.

Traffic Signals

Unlike ordinary road signs, which are 100 percent reliable indicators of where a passage is going, **traffic signals** are transition words and phrases that usually—but not always—signal where the author is going next. For instance, when you see one of the following words, *many* or *most* or *some,* you are likely to see a contrast later in the sentence, although that will not happen 100 percent of the time. So it is predictable (but not certain) that the sentence "Many people think that X is Y" will be followed by a sentence like "However, other people think X is Z" or possibly even one like "However, those of us who are smart realize that X is really A!" Here is a partial list of some traffic signals. You will notice that most of them indicate some sort of contrast:

When I see . . .	I should expect . . .
many, most, some	a contrast
a word with a clear opposite	the opposite
a word that is in a clear category	another word in that category
the mention of a problem	(a) solution(s)
something confusing, puzzling, surprising	(an) explanation(s)
tried, aimed, attempted, intended	failed!
usually, ordinarily, most commonly	. . . but not this time! (an exception)

As you begin to tune into traffic signals and the information they give you, you will find that your ability to anticipate where a passage is going almost magically improves. This will greatly improve your speed and efficiency in getting an overview of a Reading Comp passage.

Topic Sentences

Characteristic of well-written and well-edited passages is the **topic sentence**, a sentence (or sometimes just a phrase) found early in a body paragraph of an essay that provides the alert reader with the information he or she needs to anticipate the contents of the paragraph.

For instance, what would you expect if you read the following topic sentence?

There are three main reasons for this.

You would expect this paragraph to describe the three reasons for whatever-it-is, right? (Topic sentences are not rocket science!) And you would hope to see a sequence road sign such as *first* pretty close to that topic sentence, and words such as *second* or *next* and *third* or *finally* later in the paragraph.

Once you have confirmed what a paragraph contains, stop and jot a brief note for that paragraph on your Passage Map.

Topic sentences should be read carefully and paraphrased if necessary; the test taker must then confirm his or her idea of what that particular paragraph contains, by skimming. Which brings us, conveniently enough, to Principle 3.

Principle 3

Focus on the Big Picture: skim, don't read!

Most test takers complain that Reading Comprehension passages take way too much time. And most test takers read every word of every Reading Comp passage, some of those words more than once. Coincidence? We think not! Reading is, believe it or not, the very least efficient—or helpful—thing you can do when you have made your way to the heart of an RC passage. Instead, you need to skim, skim, skim (not skip!)—skim those details to avoid getting caught up in them or trying to understand or remember them. When you skim, you have two goals: to confirm your guesses and to watch for "surprises." And what exactly are "surprises"? you ask. Well, sometimes the writer does not do what you anticipated. This could be because you made one or more unwarranted assumptions in the process of guessing or because the writer failed to deliver on something a reader could reasonably expect.

Let's return to the example sentence given above for topic sentences:

There are three main reasons for this.

"Confirming your guesses" here means checking to make sure that all three reasons appear in this paragraph. Once you have confirmed that they do, note this fact in your Passage Map and move on. On the other hand, if it turns out that they do not (perhaps because one of the reasons is so involved and detailed that it takes up the remainder of the paragraph, pushing the other two reasons into later paragraphs), note that fact in your Passage Map. And of course, under no circumstances should you try to summarize, remember, or even understand what those three reasons are!

Principle 4

Read (and paraphrase) as appropriate.

So you may be wondering, when do I actually **read**? I mean, this is **Read**ing Comprehension, after all, right? Well, certainly there is a time and a place for reading in Reading Comp. For one thing, you will read the first paragraph as you first start a passage, during the first minute of the process, as you try to identify the topic, scope, and possibly even the purpose of the passage. In addition, you should read all topic sentences, paraphrasing as necessary to make sure you really understand them. And you should slow down to actually read, even when you are skimming, any time you encounter road signs (especially the types that indicate contrast), traffic signals, or "surprises."

But the very most important time to read (and paraphrase as necessary) is when answering GRE test questions! After all, you cannot answer from memory when you never even read a sentence or a paragraph to begin with. Using your Passage Map to locate specific information, go back into the passage and do research to answer Detail questions; check the passage to confirm your answer for Inference questions; review the relevant text to predict an answer to, and then to answer, Logic questions... there is hardly a question type for which checking the passage would not be appropriate. So these four principles, when used faithfully, will allow you to read actively, anticipate where the passage is going, avoid getting lost in the details, and ultimately, get the highest score you can get. You may have noticed that there is one more thing we have yet to discuss, and that is the actual questions—which should be the true focus of our attention, as the mercenary test takers we are!

ANSWERING GRE READING COMPREHENSION QUESTIONS

Since the GRE is a standardized test, both question types and wrong answer types are predictable. The most common Reading Comprehension questions are (in order of frequency) Inference questions, Detail questions, Global questions, and Logic questions. Let's discuss each of these briefly, covering how to recognize them and what to do in order to answer them correctly. Finally, we will close with a discussion of the most common wrong answer types, allowing you to eliminate your way to a correct answer, or at least a better guess, on the most difficult Reading Comp questions.

Inference Questions

An inference is something that is true, or almost certainly true, based on the information in the passage, but don't expect to find the answer stated in the passage. Inferences require you to read between the lines, coming up with something that the author strongly hints at or a conclusion that the author all but states.

Common wording for Inference questions is vague and indirect, using words such as *suggests, most likely, most probably,* and *implies.* While predicting answers is generally recommended for most GRE Verbal questions, we recommend that you do not try to predict answers for Inference questions. Instead, do research in the passage if possible, and use a process of elimination on the answer choices to identify which answer must be true based on the passage. You might also ask yourself which answer, if denied, would contradict or significantly weaken the passage.

Detail Questions

Detail questions ask about information that is directly stated in the passage, so their wording is definite and direct, really the opposite of the wording found in Inference questions. Look for phrases such as *According to the passage* and *The author states...* In answering these questions, it is imperative that you do research in the passage itself, using your Passage Map to locate the relevant detail and then reading around the detail (especially the material that precedes the detail) to get a thorough understanding of the detail's background. Then you should predict an answer before checking the answer choices.

Global Questions

This question type will ask you to sum up an author's overall intentions or ideas. The wording of Global questions makes them easy to identify. You'll see phrases such as *primary purpose, main concern,* or *best title.* What do you do? Go to your Passage Map and look at the words you used to describe the topic, scope, and purpose. You're especially interested in the author's purpose here, so if you have not yet articulated it, this would be a great time to do so—**before** you look at the answer choices, so you aren't swayed by tempting wrong answer choices! Remember the purpose words we discussed (under Principle 1), and pick one of these categories to describe the author's purpose. Then you can do a verb scan—run down through the answer choices, reading the first word or two and checking for a match with your prediction. Of course, you should read the answer choices with matching verbs in their entirety before selecting an answer.

Logic Questions

This type of question is similar to the Global question in asking "why?" However, it encompasses a smaller portion of the passage than does the Global question, focusing on the purpose of a detail or a paragraph. In fact, the wording of the question will usually be pretty explicit: *Why did the author...?* or phrases such as *What is the purpose/function of _____?* You could also see an incomplete sentence ending with the phrase *in order to* that you will need to complete with an answer from the list of choices. What to do? Review the referenced material, predict an answer, and look for your answer among the choices. As in Global questions, the answer choices are about the author's purpose in doing something, so you may be able to do a verb scan to narrow the choices down.

Common Wrong Answer Types

If you are stuck on a Reading Comprehension section, see if you can identify and eliminate some of these typical wrong answer types:

Out of scope: raises a point that was never mentioned in the passage.

Distortion: takes words and phrases from the passage and recombines them in a way that distorts what the passage actually says.

Extreme: a type of out-of-scope answer that goes further than the passage actually does; typically uses wording such as *always, all, every, never, no,* or *none.*

180 degrees or au contraire: does the opposite of what the question asks or directly contradicts information in the passage.

Misplaced detail: accurately summarizes information that is actually in the passage but that does not answer the specific question asked.

Half-right, half-wrong: sounds good at first but suddenly falls off a cliff!

Another thing to be cautious about is your own outside knowledge of the subject matter. Since answers to all GRE Reading Comp questions must necessarily be based on the passage and only on the passage, you must leave at the door any information you may happen to know about the topic of the passage. Answers based on outside knowledge alone are wrong answers!

So there you have it, in a nutshell—the Kaplan approach to GRE Reading Comprehension. Of course, the rest is up to you—you must practice, practice, practice to make these approaches a habit and to become skillful at them. If you practice and use the Kaplan approach and strategies, read actively, avoid getting caught up in details, skim your brains out, and predict an answer to most Reading Comp questions, you will be well on your way to GRE Reading Comp success!

CHAPTER NINE

Reading Comprehension Passage 1

Directions: Each passage in this group is followed by questions based on its content. After reading a passage, choose the best answer to each question. Answer all questions following a passage on the basis of what is stated or implied in that passage.

It was the publication of Hans Baron's
magnum opus *The Crisis of the Early Italian
Renaissance: Civic Humanism and Republican
Liberty in an Age of Classicism and Tyranny*
(5) in 1955 that first put republicanism on the
modern political map. Up until that point,
the field of political theory during the 20th
century had been dominated, by and large,
by studies of authoritarianism, liberalism,
(10) socialism, and Marxism. Yet from the 1970s
onward, communitarians such as Charles
Taylor and Alasdair MacIntyre came to see
in classical republicanism (or, as it is perhaps
more commonly known, civic humanism)
(15) a live alternative to liberalism on the one
hand and to communism on the other; for
communitarians, it was a remedy to the
"possessive individualism" embodied in
Lockean liberalism as well as a bulwark against
(20) the failed experiments of state socialism on
view in the USSR, Eastern Europe, and China.
Concomitantly, however, the neo-republican
Quentin Skinner (as well as Philip Pettit more
recently) sought to show how republicanism,
(25) one committed to nondomination, could indeed
be squared with liberalism.
What, then, is the chief difference between
classical republicanism and neo-republicanism?
There are not one but two differences in fact,
(30) the first historical, the second conceptual in
nature. J. G. A. Pocock, an apologist for civic
humanism, argues that the republics that
sprang up during the Italian Renaissance were
inspired principally by the classical tradition—in
(35) particular, by Aristotle's conception of man
as a being whose nature or essence can be
fully realized only by virtue of his participation
in the city-state (*polis*). It is for this reason
that Aristotle calls man a *bios politicos*, a
(40) being who is fundamentally a political or
social animal. In his voluminous writings,
Quentin Skinner, by contrast, has stressed the
Ciceronian juridical influence on the republican
thought of the Italian Renaissance. Traveling
(45) down this path, Skinner insists, leads one to
neo-republicanism.
To be sure, the very different historical
accounts civic humanists and neo-republicans
give us are not unrelated to the very different
(50) conceptualizations of liberty they separately
defend. The former, it seems, throw their
weight behind positive liberty whereas the
latter tie their fate to negative liberty. To be
free, civic humanists maintain, is to participate
(55) in civic life (*vivere civile*), to play an active
and essential role in self-government. Thus,
in order for the *res publica* to flourish, citizens

must not only cultivate civic virtues such as
courage, truthfulness, and friendship, they must
(60) also vigorously oppose corruption and tyranny
wherever and whenever it arises.
Neo-republicans think instead that liberty, at
its best, is synonymous with nondomination.
In their view, negative liberty ensures
(65) individuals that they are free from the exercise
of arbitrary state power. To this extent, neo-
republicanism is undoubtedly compatible with
the liberal principle of neutrality, a principle
that says that the state must remain agnostic
(70) about individual and group conceptions of the
good life. Accordingly, neo-republicans are
concerned less with persons acting as citizens
intimately involved in self-governance and
more with individuals endowed with rights that
(75) protect them from state power and that allow
them to pursue their own ends in the private
sphere as they see fit.

1. All of the following can be inferred from the
passage *EXCEPT* the claim that

(A) civic humanism is opposed to liberalism.
(B) after 1970 republicanism became a subject
of interest among scholars working in the
field of political theory.
(C) both classical republicans and neo-
republicans find support for their theories
in the Italian Renaissance.
(D) Aristotle's view that man is a political
animal is similar to the liberal view that
persons are primarily private individuals.
(E) neo-republicans think that state power
should be limited.

2. In the context of the passage, *agnostic* (line
69) is mostly closely synonymous with

(A) skeptical
(B) unknowable
(C) uncommitted
(D) disbelieving
(E) unsupportive

3. With which of the following would the author most likely agree?

   (A) Historical models can be the basis for latter-day political theories.
   (B) Important political theories generally have historical antecedents.
   (C) Negative liberty is not compatible with positive liberty.
   (D) If Hans Baron's book had not been published, modern republicanism would not have arisen.
   (E) On balance, classical republicanism is preferable to neo-republicanism.

4. The author alludes to communitarians in line 17 with the end of

   (A) drawing a contrast between liberalism and state socialism.
   (B) pointing out the failures of liberalism and socialism as political models.
   (C) bringing into relief the changes that republicanism had undergone since 1955.
   (D) alluding to future developments in republicanism on the horizon.
   (E) showing how the focus of political theorists had changed since 1955.

5. The principal assumption underlying the author's discussion of neo-republicanism is that

   (A) individuals have no interest in participating in politics.
   (B) individuals are inherently vulnerable.
   (C) the state can only be a force for ill.
   (D) each citizen's conception of the good life is as valid as any other's.
   (E) individuals value their own interests over those of the community.

6. Which of the following most accurately summarizes the organization of the passage?

   (A) The passage begins by explaining the origin of a phenomenon and then proceeds to classify various species of the phenomenon based on new evidence.
   (B) The passage starts out by exploring how a particular phenomenon came into existence and then points out how we can distinguish between its two species.
   (C) In the opening paragraph, the passage contrasts two competing theories but later explains how they can be unified.
   (D) From the outset, the passage highlights the differences between two recent views.
   (E) The passage details the basic features of two theories and then introduces two criteria by which they can be evaluated.

7. In her analysis of classical republicanism, the author implies that positive liberty

   (A) requires that one think of oneself as a member of a community.
   (B) is tantamount to doing what one wants to do.
   (C) cannot be conceived without negative liberty.
   (D) fosters in citizens an ideal of self-sacrifice.
   (E) belies the dimension of self-rule in the lives of a community's citizens.

8. According to the passage, the historical criterion that helps distinguish civic humanism from neo-republicanism is

   (A) a necessary precursor to the conceptual criterion.
   (B) similar in kind to the conceptual criterion.
   (C) not related to the conceptual criterion.
   (D) reinforced by the conceptual criterion.
   (E) incommensurable with the conceptual criterion.

ANSWERS AND EXPLANATIONS

What Makes It Difficult

Three things in particular make this passage challenging. First, the subject matter (political philosophy) naturally tends to be conceptually "top heavy." Second, the language the passage is written in is abstract, general, and dense. Finally, in order to grasp the meaning of the passage, you need to keep track of a number of distinctions.

Passage Map

Category: Social Sciences

Field: Political Science

Subfield: Political Theory

Topic: Republicanism

Scope: Two kinds of republicanism

Purpose: To provide a brief historical overview of the emergence of republicanism (paragraph 1); and to distinguish between classical republicanism and neo-republicanism (paragraphs 2–4)

¶1: emergence of modern republicanism

¶2: historical criterion applied to classical republicanism and neo-republicanism

¶3: positive liberty in classical republicanism

¶4: negative liberty in neo-republicanism

1. **D**

This question is especially difficult not only because it requires us to work through a number of heady concepts but also because it requires us to go through four valid inferences in order to get to the one invalid inference. Not an easy thing to do—especially under Test Day conditions.

Let's try to get the big picture in front of us. Recall that the author has two aims in the passage: first, to provide a brief historical overview of the emergence of republicanism (this she does in the opening paragraph); and, second, to draw a line between one kind of republicanism—namely, classical republicanism or civic humanism—and another—neo-republicanism. Consider how she draws that line. In paragraph 2, she tells us that there are two ways of doing so (a historical way and a conceptual way); she then goes on to show, in paragraphs 2–4, how the historical and conceptual distinctions apply to these two different kinds of republicanism. At the end of paragraph 2, she claims that civic humanists are committed to the Aristotelian view, which states that human beings have to be actively engaged in the life of the city in order for them to thrive. Apparently, neo-republicans are not. Later on, at the tail end of paragraph 4 when she is discussing how neo-republicanism is compatible with liberalism, she distinguishes between "citizens intimately involved in self-governance" (read: Aristotle's view) and private individuals being protected from the state (read: the liberal view). The implication, then, is that Aristotle's view of man is *distinct from* the liberal view of the private individual. Hence, **D** is an invalid inference because it says just the opposite.

A can be inferred from the passage. In paragraph 1, the author states that civic humanism is a "live alternative" (line 15) to liberalism and that, according to communitarians, it was a "remedy" (line 17) to liberalism. The author thus implies that the kind of civic humanism endorsed by communitarians is opposed to liberalism. This by itself is sufficient for **A** to be inferable.

B can also be inferred from the passage. The author states in paragraph 1 that civic humanists were writing after 1970. A few sentences later, she says that neo-republicans writing "concomitantly" (line 22)—that is, concomitant with the communitarians who threw their support behind civic humanism after 1970. So it must be the case that after 1970, republicanism did become a subject of interest in this discipline.

As can **C**. Here, the author is drawing our attention to the historical dimension. Pocock, who defends classical republicanism, points to the Italian Renaissance; so does Skinner, the theorist who backs neo-republicanism. So two prominent republicans, each of whom represents one branch of republicanism, point to the same period in order to support their views.

Likewise, **E**. Neo-republicans believe that liberty should be understood in negative terms. In the last paragraph, we learn that a free person is free just in virtue of the fact that the state is not always looking over his shoulder. From this and from the claim in the final line that individuals have rights that guarantee that they won't be interfered with, we can infer that the state is not everywhere. But if it's not everywhere, then it has to be limited.

2. **C**

What's tricky about the meaning of *agnostic* in this context is that it does not mean what we typically think when we hear the term being employed in everyday life. By *agnostic*, we usually mean a recognition that we can't know something about a certain issue or topic before us. So someone who professes to being agnostic about the existence of God is implying that he doesn't know whether God exists.

In *this* context, though, we need to key into the less familiar sense of the term. Fortunately, there are clues earlier in the same sentence in which *agnostic* appears. Note, first, the gist of the sentence in question: the state isn't supposed to impose its own view of how people should live their lives. Note, second, that the author mentions the principle of neutrality and then goes on to say what this means. It behooves us, then, to draw the inference that *agnostic*, which figures prominently in the definition of neutrality, will have a good deal in common with our commonsensical understanding of what it means for something to be neutral. To be neutral is to stand back, keep out of things, and state no opinion about the present issue. The answer that most closely captures this sense is **C**.

At first blush, **A** and **D** look attractive because in other contexts we tend to associate agnosticism with skepticism (doubting that something is the case) and atheism (denying that God exists). Not so here. As we observed above, we have no good reason to believe that the state doubts that we can have our own conceptions of the good life—quite the contrary. On this view, it simply has no business in stepping into the fray. The takeaway? Here's another example that vividly shows that we can get into trouble when we rely on outside information to answer the questions.

B gives us the most literal gloss of the primary sense of *agnostic*—namely, unknowable. But, once again, we're looking for the secondary sense in this context. For this reason, we should rule out **B**.

E comes closest in meaning to the correct answer. However, *unsupportive* is simply too strong. Not stating an opinion either way on the matter at hand (that is, being agnostic in this context) is not quite the same thing as not standing behind something or someone (that is, being unsupportive). Still unclear about the difference? Consider, for instance, that I may be *agnostic* about your love of clamming, having no opinion about it either way, and at the same time I could conceivably neither support you nor refuse to support you in this hobby of yours. I'm, well, noncommittal about the whole thing. The upshot is that **E** is a distortion.

3. **A**

Recall that this question type is not concerned with what the author explicitly *says* or even what she *implies*; rather, it is concerned with what, based on the argument she makes in the passage, she would *have* to endorse. In this case, the only thing that the author would have to endorse would be **A**. The chief aim of paragraphs 2–4 is to show how a historical model—the republics that popped up during the Italian Renaissance—could be seen as inspirations for, or backdrops to, current political views.

B is a distortion. Note the logic here: There *could* be important historical antecedents for *some* political theories. Nevertheless, it would not be valid to infer that the author has to endorse the claim that this is "generally" the case.

C is outside of scope. There's not enough information in the passage for us to decide whether negative liberty is compatible with positive liberty or not. We just don't know.

D is certainly very tempting. According to the author, Baron's book was as a matter of fact sufficient for bringing modern republicanism into being. However (and this is the telling point), it doesn't follow from this that Baron's book is an absolutely necessary condition for modern republicanism to come about. Let's try to understand the line of argument here by thinking about a simple example. If the fact that it's raining outside is sufficient for you to put on your raincoat, isn't it at least possible that you could have put on your raincoat on occasions when it wasn't raining? Well, yes, of course. The same kind of thing holds for **D**.

Throughout the passage, the author is silent about whether classical republicanism is preferable to neo-republicanism. In fact, at no point in the passage does the author make any evaluative judgments of either theory. Consequently, **E** can't be correct.

4. **E**

In the opening sentence, the author tells us that Baron's book, which appeared in 1955, helped to make republicanism look appealing in the field of political science. In subsequent sentences, she first looks *backwards* to the kind of work political theorists had been doing and then looks *forward* to the work inspired by republicanism. Communitarians were one such prominent group of political thinkers who took up the republican cause. In the context in which we read about communitarians, the author is trying to point out how things have changed in the field of political theory after 1955. Thus, **E** is the correct choice.

True, communitarians did draw a line between liberalism and state socialism, but the *author's point* in bringing up communitarians is *not* to show just this. So **A** is out.

The same line of reasoning applies to **B**. Communitarians believed that liberalism and socialism hadn't worked out, but the author does not invoke communitarianism for this express purpose.

The field of political theory had undergone changes since 1955. Had republicanism undergone important changes? Possibly, but we don't know because this doesn't come up in paragraph 1. **C**, accordingly, is outside of scope.

Don't be fooled by **D** or by answers like **D**—it's just a fishing expedition. The author makes no mention of "future developments" in the context of paragraph 1. For this reason, **D**'s fate is the same as **C**'s: it's outside of scope.

5. **B**

Here, it's best to work backwards. Why would neo-republicans be interested in defining freedom in terms of nondomination? What makes them so worried about the power of the state? It must be that they think that the state is big and powerful and that individuals are small and weak. Individual rights thereby serve to curtail the power of the state. Summing things up, we can conclude that the main motivation behind neo-republicanism is the assumption that individuals are intrinsically susceptible to harm. And that leads us to pick **B**.

The allure of **A** is that it seems to be an "argument by association." We've read about participating in politics in the context of classical republicanism. We've also learned that neo-republicanism is distinct from classical republicanism. So we're led to believe that anything that falls under classical republicanism (like participating in politics) has to also be distinct from neo-republicanism. But that conclusion doesn't follow. It's perfectly conceivable that, in a neo-republican view, some individuals may have an interest in participating in politics. The truth is that we just don't know either way. Thus, we do well to avoid the "argument by association" illusion (it's a common Test Day trick) and count **A** as being outside of scope.

Consider **C**. The author asserts that the state can be a force for ill. Hence the move to construe freedom in terms of nondomination. But is that *all* that the state is? We can't be sure. **C**, therefore, is outside of scope.

D, likewise, is outside of scope. It is true that in the eyes of neo-republicans, the state should remain neutral on the question of how individuals should live their lives. It should neither endorse nor condemn views of the good life. However, being neutral does not entail the relativist conclusion that any view is just as good as any other view. The conclusion—that is, **D**—doesn't come up in the passage; nor does it necessarily follow from what neo-republicans believe.

Take another look at the final line of the passage. There, the author says that being given certain rights allows individuals "to pursue their own ends in the private sphere as they see fit." Pursuing one's own ends doesn't invariably mean that individuals have to put what they want above what others want. After all, some individuals may be interested in being good fathers and mothers, good employers, good volunteers in their communities, and the like. Nothing about the neo-republican view implies that **E** has to be the case. For this reason, **E** is a straightforward case of distortion.

6. **B**

Our strategy should be to call to mind *what* the passage is about and *how* the author put it together. We've already noted that the author's purpose is twofold. She wants to provide a brief historical overview of the emergence of republicanism (paragraph 1), and she wants to distinguish between classical republicanism and neo-republicanism (paragraphs 2–4). Having this much before us already gives us pretty good guidelines about what we should be looking for in the correct answer. The correct answer, that is, should say something about how the thing came about and then something else about how it gets cut in two, so to speak.

Which answer choice hits on both of these things? Only **B**.

Not **A**. The first part of the answer looks good, but the bit about new evidence at the end puts **A** out of the running. This is because at no point in the passage does the author say anything about new evidence.

Not **C** either. The giveaway is the last word—*unified*. Nowhere does the author make this claim.

D might have caught your eye. If we bracket for a moment the opening prepositional phrase ("from the outset"), then what we're left with does have something going for it. Certainly, it captures what goes on in paragraphs 2–4. And yet **D** is insufficient, for it misses what goes on in paragraph 1. What's more, once we take our finger off the prepositional phrase we'd covered up (again, "from the outset"), we notice that the statement is not entirely accurate either. So we should cross off **D**. Think about the larger lesson here: on Test Day, it's worth remembering that close reading counts.

The telltale sign that **E** is incorrect is the word *evaluated*. The author remains impartial throughout. From beginning to end, she neither praises one theory nor criticizes the other; in a word, she doesn't weigh in. So, while she does introduce two criteria in order to distinguish between the two views, she does not introduce either criterion with the goal of making an evaluation of the two theories.

7. **A**

We're being asked to think again about valid inferences—this time about valid inferences that follow from the author's discussion of positive liberty. Recall that positive liberty is equated with the freedom that comes from active participation in self-rule. Why am I free? Because I take part in deciding how all of us live together. It looks as if a logical precondition for self-rule is that one think of oneself as a member of a group (instead of, say, thinking of oneself as being an island unto oneself). It would be silly to talk about positive liberty if one didn't think of oneself this way from the get-go. The correct answer, therefore, is **A**.

Doing what one wants to do looks a lot like the sort of freedom one would enjoy under the neo-republican regime. This doesn't mean that it might not show up under classical republicanism, but positive liberty in any event certainly wouldn't be *equivalent* to doing what one wants to do. We have no reason to hold onto **B**.

C is opposite. In fact, the author assumes that positive and negative liberty can be conceived separately. We know this because she bases her argument on this very distinction and so on the assumption that the first can be discussed without being dependent in any way on the second.

D might give us pause. On the face of things, it may seem that this kind of polity would value self-sacrifice. But soon enough we're confronted with an important question—namely, does the author really assume this in order to get her argument off the ground? No. Courage, friendship, and trustworthiness may at times lead to self-sacrifice, but it hardly seems *necessary* for the author to assume out of the box that this is an ideal that classical republicanism *fosters*. Because self-sacrifice is *not* a necessary assumption, **D** should be ruled out.

For all intents and purposes, **E** is a vocabulary question. *Belies* means contradicts. Does positive liberty contradict self-rule? No, positive liberty encourages this. Hence, **E** is opposite.

8. **D**

The question is drawing our attention to the opening sentence of paragraph 3. We're being asked to think about the relationship between the first (historical) criterion and the second (conceptual) criterion. We read that the first is "not unrelated" (line 49) to the second. But "not unrelated" more simply means that they are somehow related. From what we read in the rest of paragraph 3 and in paragraph 4, the relationship seems to be a rather intimate one indeed. With this in mind, let's take a look at the options before us.

Well, we should immediately conclude that **C** is just the opposite of the correct answer. Take a look at **E**. *Incommensurable* means that one thing cannot be put with (or has nothing in common with) another thing. Not true here, so get rid of **E**. Now **B**. Yes, there is some similarity between the historical and the conceptual criterion. But the words that tell against **B** are "in kind." The historical and the conceptual are not similar *in kind*. By definition, they are *dissimilar* in kind: the first is historical whereas the second is conceptual. Perhaps we can clarify the relationship between the historical and the conceptual criterion if we get a concrete example before us. A mammal and a reptile are not similar in kind (one is warm-blooded while the other is not); but they could still have inessential things that they share (both, for instance, have skin). At the very least, the same thing could be said of the historical and the conceptual. **B**, in sum, is opposite.

We're thus left with **A** and **D**. **A**, however, is too strong: the historical may lead to the conceptual but not, or so the author implies, of necessity. Good thing too because **D** gives us just what we're looking for. The historical criterion is not only consistent with the conceptual criterion; the latter, it turns out, enhances—which is to say, reinforces—the former. Go with **D** then.

CHAPTER TEN

Reading Comprehension Passage 2

Directions: Each passage in this group is followed by questions based on its content. After reading a passage, choose the best answer to each question. Answer all questions following a passage on the basis of what is stated or implied in that passage.

Surveying paradigmatic works of tragic literature from antiquity to the present alongside the immense and ever-growing body of secondary literature on the subject,

(5) the literary critic Terry Eagleton arrived at the pat judgment that not only had no satisfactory definition of tragedy been offered to date but also that none besides the admittedly vacuous "very sad" could ever be offered. Overly broad

(10) definitions, which for all intents and purposes equate the tragic with seriousness, lead invariably to Scylla; overly narrow ones such as the Renaissance-inspired struggle theory to Charybdis. Notwithstanding this definitional

(15) dilemma, Eagleton's conclusion, as clear a case of defeatism as any heretofore advanced, leaves much to be desired.

In *A Definition of Tragedy*, Oscar Mandel, who is decidedly more sanguine than Eagleton

(20) on this score, discerns in Aristotle's *De Poetica* the rudiments of a substantive definition of the tragic. Following the spirit, albeit not the letter, of Aristotle's text, Mandel sets forth three requirements for any work to be counted as

(25) tragic, the third weighing most heavily in his account. First, it must have a protagonist whom we highly (or at least moderately) esteem. Second, it must show how the protagonist comes to suffer greatly. And, third, it must

(30) reveal how the protagonist's downfall was inevitably but unwittingly brought about by his own action. It is plain to see that, of the three requirements, the third (call this the *inevitability requirement*) is beyond question the most

(35) contentious as well as the most dubious.

The truth is that the inevitability requirement is entirely too stringent. While it may be a sufficient condition, it is not, *pace* Mandel's assertions, the *sin qua non* of tragic literature.

(40) One need look no further than Anton Chekhov's *Three Sisters*, a quintessential work of modern tragedy, to see why this is so. In a provincial capital quite remote from cosmopolitan Moscow, the well-educated,

(45) tireless, but spiritually drained sisters are ground down by the inexorable forces of time and fortune. Their failure to leave for Moscow, the childhood home they yen for, their failure, that is, to extricate themselves from

(50) the tedious and insufferable life brought on by their workaday habits, can only suggest a certain acknowledgement on their part of their powerlessness at the hands of fate.

In the final analysis, the question of whether

(55) the protagonist's fate is sealed in consequence of tragic action, a characteristic common among Greek and Renaissance tragic dramas,

or of inaction, a distinguishing feature of many modern tragedies, has very little to do with

(60) one of the absolutely essential ingredients of tragic literature: to wit, that profound sense of insurmountable powerlessness or, what is the same thing, that unnamable, implacable feeling expressing alienation from life itself.

(65) For one in the grips of tragedy, there are, I suppose, no words truer than Silenus's: The best thing is not to be born; second best to die soon.

1. In the middle of his discussion of Terry Eagleton's work, the author alludes to Scylla and Charybdis in order to

   (A) point out the principal faults with Eagleton's ideas about tragedy.

   (B) argue for the importance of understanding myths in our investigation into the nature of tragedy.

   (C) establish that a dilemma pertaining to the essence of tragedy has its origin in myth.

   (D) illustrate how a dilemma common to other intellectual inquiries also applies to our understanding of tragedy.

   (E) delineate the potential problems that lie in wait for anyone who wishes to define tragedy.

2. The author suggests that which of the following are important considerations in any satisfactory definition of tragedy?

   I. The protagonist's lack of control over her life

   II. The scope of the definition

   III. The hero's recognition that he has brought about his demise

   (A) I only

   (B) III only

   (C) I and II only

   (D) II and III only

   (E) I, II, and III

3. The primary purpose of the passage is to

   (A) criticize Eagleton's view that the most adequate definition of tragedy is very sad.

   (B) cast doubt on Eagleton's and Mandel's views of tragic literature for failing to enumerate all the necessary conditions for tragedy.

   (C) conclude, after analyzing the views of two tragic theorists, that tragedy cannot be defined adequately.

   (D) criticize Eagleton's view that tragedy cannot be adequately defined and Mandel's view that tragedy requires tragic action and to offer up another condition indispensible for tragedy.

   (E) find fault with Eagleton's view that tragedy amounts to what is "very sad" and Mandel's view that tragedy requires great suffering in order to advance a new definition of tragedy in their place.

4. According to the passage, which of the following could be true of works of tragedy?

   I. They are general phenomena in that they have been written at and performed in many different times and places.

   II. They typically express the idea that human beings are hollow and incomplete.

   III. They are the artist's renderings of a world that is alienated from its essence.

   (A) I only
   (B) II only
   (C) I and II only
   (D) I and III only
   (E) I, II, and III

5. The author's attitude toward the protagonists in *Three Sisters* can best be characterized as

   (A) laudatory.
   (B) conciliatory.
   (C) despondent.
   (D) myopic.
   (E) diffident.

6. It can reasonably be inferred from the author's assessments of Eagleton's and Mandel's views of tragedy that

   (A) Mandel's and Eagleton's conceptions of tragedy can ultimately be dismissed.

   (B) both theorists fall short of the mark of what constitutes tragedy, but for different reasons.

   (C) the tragic has as much to do with what is very sad as it has to do with the inevitability requirement.

   (D) the fact that tragic heroes undergo great suffering is at the center of both accounts.

   (E) tragic literature is most fully understood when it combines the insights of many different thinkers.

7. The author voices dissatisfaction with the present conception of tragedy in lines 36–68 (i.e., all of paragraph 3) by

   (A) describing in some detail how a particular genre influences the way we think about tragic literature more generally.

   (B) analyzing a work of literature in order to help us better appreciate its supreme aesthetic value.

   (C) raising a pointed objection to Mandel's definition of tragedy and supporting the former with a counterexample.

   (D) quibbling with the main criteria in Mandel's definition, none of which is applicable to a particular work of literature.

   (E) cogently defending conclusions about works of tragedy that, on pain of contradiction, Mandel cannot accept.

8. Regarding the passage as a whole, the author's opinion of the first and second requirements spelled out in Mandel's definition of tragedy is most likely that

(A) neither the first nor the second requirement fits very easily with the condition of powerlessness that he defends in the final paragraph.

(B) the first but not the second requirement is essentially at odds with his claim that Chekhov's *Three Sisters* is a work that exemplifies the condition of powerlessness.

(C) the second but not the first requirement would have to be rejected on the grounds that it is ostensibly the case that the sisters in *Three Sisters* do not undergo great suffering.

(D) in light of the condition of powerlessness that he endorses, it can be concluded that both requirements should not figure prominently in any account of tragedy.

(E) neither the first nor the second requirement should be necessarily ruled out in our attempt to grasp the essence of tragedy, provided that neither is antithetical to the condition of powerlessness.

ANSWERS AND EXPLANATIONS

What Makes It Difficult

The first thing to note about this humanities passage is that the vocabulary is especially, well, esoteric. The fact that so many GRE words appear in the passages should give you added incentive to learn the ones that show up most often on Test Day (see Kaplan Word List, etc.). The second, and no less significant, thing to note here is that the author leaves a lot out of his argument. In particular, she doesn't make key conclusions in the argument explicit. Keep in mind that whatever is left unsaid but that can be validly derived from the passage may very well show up as Inference questions on Test Day. We found this to be the case with this passage, and it is most certainly true of many other passages as well.

Passage Map

Category: Humanities

Field: Literary Criticism

Subfield: Tragic Theory

Topic: Tragedy

Scope: Definition of tragedy

Purpose: To criticize two scholars' views of tragedy—the one for begging off providing a definition of tragedy (Eagleton in ¶1), the other for advancing too narrow of a definition (Mandel in ¶2).

¶1: criticism of Eagleton's view of tragedy

¶2: Mandel's definition of tragedy: three requirements

¶3: counterexample to third requirement: Chekhov's *Three Sisters*

¶4: generalization drawn from analysis of *Three Sisters*—namely, that tragedy has to do *essentially*—but *not entirely*—with powerlessness and alienation

1. **E**

The passage as a whole is concerned with how to come up with a good definition of tragedy. In lines 9–14, the author leads into Scylla and Charybdis by mentioning "overly broad definitions" and "overly narrow ones," respectively. Just afterward, she calls this situation a "definitional dilemma." From these clues, we're thus led to infer that Scylla and Charybdis are names for the dangers that may befall anyone who tries to come up with a good definition of tragedy. **E** is in line with this inference.

A cannot be correct because Terry Eagleton begs off providing a good definition in the first place. He seems to think that the task is simply impossible. So broad and narrow definitions, represented by Scylla and Charybdis, respectively, are not signs of Eagleton's principal faults. **B** is outside of scope. The author is making no larger claim about the significance of myth. Similarly, **C** is outside of scope. This we know from talk of "origin of myth"; the latter has no place in the author's account and so is irrelevant. Like **B** and **C**, **D** is also outside of scope. Because the author makes no reference to other intellectual inquiries, we have no reason for believing that those are in any way applicable to the case at hand.

2. **C**

Questions of the "which of the following" sort don't allow us to make any predictions about what, roughly speaking, the correct answer should look like. For this reason, we should simply look at each answer choice in turn. Notice that this is a Detail question, so the question we should raise about each should be something like the following: "Did this come up?" If it did, hold onto it; if it didn't, let it go. Let's ask that question of **I**: "Did the author talk about the protagonist's lack of control over her life?" Yes, she brings up lack of control—which is synonymous with powerlessness—at the end of paragraph 3 and in the latter half of paragraph 4. Hold onto **I**. So then: "Did the author talk about the scope of a definition?" Here too, the answer is yes. In the opening paragraph, the author is concerned with broad and narrow definitions—that is, with the proper scope of a good definition. Hold onto **II**. Finally, "Did the author speak about the hero's recognition that he has brought about his demise?" Tread lightly here. First, recall that at the heart of the question is *satisfactory* definition. Since **III** looks a lot like Mandel's conception of tragedy and the latter is something that the author finds unsatisfactory, we should be wary of **III**. Add to this the fact that the answer choice mentions that the hero *recognizes* that he has done this to himself; the hero's recognition is not mentioned anywhere in the passage as a necessary condition for tragedy. Rule out **III** then. We've held onto **I** and **II**. The correct answer, therefore, has to be **C**.

3. **D**

What is the main point of the passage? It is to criticize two authors' views of tragedy (paragraphs 1–3) and to generate a new necessary condition for tragedy (paragraph 4). The answer that most closely matches our understanding is **D**. Consider that **A** is too narrow: Mandel isn't even mentioned despite the fact that he is the "main character" in the passage. The problem with **B** is that it includes Eagleton in the author's criticism of Mandel. In other words, the author *does* criticize Mandel for not providing all the necessary conditions for tragedy. But she *does not* have anything explicit to say about whether Eagleton falls prey to the same problem. Consequently, **B** is a distortion. For its part, **C** is opposite. The author implies throughout the passage that tragedy can be definable. Though she pokes holes in both theorists' accounts, the author seems, if anything, more sympathetic to Mandel, who thinks that tragedy is definable, than she is to Eagleton, who does not.

E, finally, is too strong because of the bit that follows the "in order to." In the final paragraph, the author doesn't provide us with a new definition of tragedy; she simply tells us that there's at least one necessary ingredient in tragedy that Mandel fails to pick up on. Think about the point about necessary and sufficient conditions this way: To make a quiche, it's necessary to use eggs. But eggs aren't enough for something to be a quiche. After all, eggs can be used in a lot of other things—cake and omelets, just to name a few. The author is making the same point about powerlessness in the realm of tragedy: it's necessary (or "absolutely essential") but not sufficient for something to be tragic.

4. **A**

Did you pick up on one of the tricky things about this question—namely, that it's not asking us to look for what *is* true of tragic works but to look for what *could be* true of those works? This piece of information tells us that we're really looking at an Inference question here. Now, there's no way to predict this one off the bat, so let's evaluate **I**, **II**, and **III** each in turn.

I should strike us as being right. The opening sentence of paragraph 1 as well as the opening sentence of paragraph 4 suggest that works of tragedy have been written at least over the past 2,000 years: during antiquity, the Renaissance, and the modern age. Hence, not only *could* **I** be true, it *is* true.

By contrast, **II** and **III** can't be inferred from the information in the passage. In **II**, the adjectives "hollow and incomplete" are not very good synonyms for alienated and powerless. Whereas *incomplete* falls at least into the realm of possibility, *hollow* is too extreme and, as a result, should help us rule out **II**. In **III**, two things should catch our eye. The first is that the passage speaks about art throughout, not about the real world in itself—that is, the real world beyond the fictional world created by art. This should raise our suspicions. The second is that the author never speaks about the *world* being alienated from anything, only about *characters* being alienated from the fictional world they inhabit. By itself, this second point suffices to show that **III** can't be the case. Since we've managed to hold onto **I** and to rule out **II** and **III**, **A** has to be the correct answer.

5. **A**

This question tests your ability to identify GRE vocabulary words within the Reading Comprehension portion of the exam. Well, at the very least we should be thinking that the author *liked, esteemed,* and *pitied* these characters. She says as much when she describes them as being "well-educated, tireless, but spiritually drained" (lines 44–45). The only answer that comes close is *laudatory*, meaning worthy of praise. *Perspicacious* means especially keen or insightful. Nope. *Despondent* means very sad. It could be inferred that the characters themselves are despondent, but the author's *attitude* is surely not despondent. **C**, then, is opposite. *Myopic* means shortsighted, and that has nothing to do with the passage before us, let alone the author's attitude toward the protagonists in this work. So get rid of **D**. And *diffident* means being modest or timid, and that's not on target. In sum, none but **A** rings true.

6. **B**

This Inference question is essentially asking us to consider not just what Eagleton and Mandel have in common but also what they do not. What do they have in common? According to the author, they don't give us an adequate conception of tragedy. And now what are the main differences between them? They take different approaches to the task, Eagleton throwing his hands up and saying, in effect, that tragedy can't be defined and Mandel digging his heels in and saying that it can. **B** captures what they share (that is, failure) and what they differ on (that is, the reasons for their respective failures).

Regarding **A**, the author does not think that their ideas should be dismissed. Why would she have bothered methodically working through their ideas in the first place if this was her attitude toward their ideas? No, clearly she thinks that much can be learned from them. Thus, **A** is opposite.

And **C**? Read the "very sad" bit as a shorthand of Eagleton's view and the "inevitability requirement" bit as an *aspect* of Mandel's view. The author's ultimate assessment is that neither will do. What's more, she never says whether the first thing about sadness should be weighed *as heavily as* the second thing about inevitability. For both of these reasons, **C** can't be inferred.

D can't be correct either, and this for two reasons. First, it can't be validly inferred from the fact that a work is very sad that the heroes have necessarily suffered greatly. The fact of great suffering is, at best, probable and not certain. Second, great suffering is not at the center of Mandel's view—as we know, the inevitability requirement is.

The keyword in **E** is *combine*. The author does examine different thinkers' ideas, but her strategy is not to combine those ideas; her strategy is to criticize these ideas. Consequently, **E** can't be inferred.

7. C

In this question, we're *only* looking at paragraph 3. Make sure that by "present conception of tragedy" you understand Mandel's view. Think about what the opening sentence is doing: it's making clear to us the author's chief complaint with Mandel. And then consider what the rest of the paragraph is doing: it's trying to provide evidence for the complaint already mentioned. Thus, **C** is correct.

No such luck with **A**. Don't be fooled: all talk of genre and influence goes beyond the bounds of the passage. We run into a similar problem in **B**. Aesthetic value, supreme or otherwise, takes our eyes off the main focus of paragraph 3. The author, in short, has nothing to say about **B**. In sum, **A** and **B** are outside of scope. On the face of it, **D** looks pretty good. True, the author is worrying about something in Mandel's definition. However, she is not worrying about criteria—only about one criterion (the inevitability requirement, in fact). Consequently, **D** is opposite. Turning to **E**, we don't see much to recommend it. For one thing, the author is not defending conclusions (she is, as the question tells us, simply voicing dissatisfaction). For another, she is not pointing out a trap that Mandel is falling into.

8. E

To begin with, get the scope of the question squarely before you. The question has to do with the whole passage, not with one of its parts. Now let's think about the first two requirements. The first is that the protagonist is worthy of our esteem; the second that he or she suffers greatly. Ask yourself: What do you think the author's opinion about these two requirements is? Most likely likes them? Most likely doesn't like them? It's the first: she most likely thinks that they are good things. Evidence for the first part of this conclusion can be found in paragraph 3 where the author seems to look favorably on the characters in the modern tragedy *Three Sisters*. Evidence for the second part can be found in the final paragraph where the author quotes Silenus. From Silenus's thought that it's best not to be born, we can infer that the life of the tragic hero is full of suffering. **E** puts this point even more delicately by making us see that both requirements are OK so long as they don't contradict the condition of powerlessness. And that sounds right. Choose **E**.

A is just the opposite of the correct answer. From what we have said so far, the author gives us no reason to believe that these requirements would not fit with the condition of powerlessness. With respect to **B**, the first condition isn't at all at odds with the condition of powerlessness. The author implies as much in paragraph 3 when she shows that good characters in works of tragedy necessarily feel powerless. **C** is also opposite. From all that we read in paragraph 3, we can reasonably conclude that the sisters do suffer a good deal. That leaves us with **D** to consider. **D** is without question quite tempting. Yet that both requirements should not figure prominently is outside of scope. We do have reason to believe that they should figure *in some way*, but we *can't know* for sure *how prominently* they should figure. Because of this, **D** is outside of scope.

CHAPTER ELEVEN

Reading Comprehension Passage 3

Directions: Each passage in this group is followed by questions based on its content. After reading a passage, choose the best answer to each question. Answer all questions following a passage on the basis of what is stated or implied in that passage.

In the Scholium following the definitions to Book I of the *Principia*, the 18th-century physicist Isaac Newton presents a God's eye view of the universe, absolute space being
(5) nothing more than God's "sensorium." The latter's essential properties are immovability, indivisibility, uniformity, ontological independence, and infinity understood as totality. Corporeal bodies are not themselves
(10) parts of space; rather, they occupy regions of space, all motion and resting taking place therein.

G. W. Leibniz was none too pleased with Newton's absolutism. In defense of relationism,
(15) he insists that space consists solely of objects and the relations that are obtained between them and that absolutism is suspect on the theological grounds that it diminishes God's wisdom. In his third letter to Samuel Clarke,
(20) Leibniz establishes that absolute space violates the Principle of Sufficient Reason (PSR), arguing thusly: One of the essential properties of space, as Newton readily admits, is that it is everywhere uniform. It follows that a particular
(25) configuration of bodies (X) actually occupying one region of space (A) *could have* occupied another region of space (B). But then God could have had no reason for X's residing in A rather than in B. Consequently, absolute
(30) space violates the PSR.

It fell to the lot of one of Newton's friends, the aforementioned Clarke, to defend Newton against Leibniz's objection. Clarke reasoned that when there is no more perfection in one
(35) state of affairs than there is in another, the fact that God brings about the first rather than the second can be explained simply by appealing to God's will. Under such conditions of absolute indifference, there can be no further reason
(40) than that God elected to express his will in the act of creation.

In the same letter to Leibniz, Clarke attempted to turn the tables on Leibniz. Suppose, he says, that things related to each
(45) other were all transposed without destroying the definite order between them (call that order X) such that X were now placed near the fixed stars. Leibniz would have to conclude that X is the same thing, in effect, for it maintains
(50) the same relations among bodies, and that X is in the same place, which is absurd. Here we have a textbook case of circular reasoning, with Clarke presupposing what he wishes to conclude.

(55) Leibniz regarded Clarke's reply to his main objection as sheer nonsense. He wrote that in "absolutely indifferent things there is [no

foundation for] choice, and consequently no election or will, since choice must be found
(60) on some reason or principle." In a word, God "does nothing without reason." Concerning the PSR, Leibniz was of course right.

Seen from a distance, the Leibniz-Clarke debate has an uncanny resemblance to
(65) the medieval skirmish between nominalists and scholastics. Nominalists affirmed God's potency by arguing that, though he had elected not to do so, God could have created another world if he so desired. For their
(70) part, scholastics averred that God had to act solely in accordance with an internal reason for everything he did. Nominalists accused scholastics of limiting God's omnipotence while scholastics accused nominalists of challenging
(75) God's benevolence. Some 400 years later, Leibniz and Clarke found themselves saddled with the same theological baggage.

1. Implicit in the author's judgment that "Leibniz was of course right" (line 62) is the belief that

    (A) relationism is a more defensible view of space than absolutism.

    (B) appealing to God's will cannot be a sufficient reason for God's acting.

    (C) the Principle of Sufficient Reason is the foundation of Leibniz's theory of space.

    (D) Clarke's reply to Leibniz's objection illustrates Clarke's commitment to relationism.

    (E) everything that happens must be explicable in terms of God's will.

2. It can be reasonably inferred from the author's comparison of the Leibniz-Clarke dispute to the medieval debate that

   (A) theories of absolute space and relative space were also on the minds of scholastics and nominalists.

   (B) during the Middle Ages whatever one believed about space had ramifications for what one believed about theology.

   (C) Leibniz's and Clarke's views on space and God were influenced by the ideas of nominalists and scholastics, respectively.

   (D) there is an affinity between medieval theologians' thoughts about God's omnipotence and modern philosophers' ideas about God's wisdom.

   (E) Leibniz's arguments are similar to those made by the scholastics while Clarke's arguments resemble those made by the nominalists.

3. The author suggests that Clarke's argument against Leibniz's relational theory of space is an example of circular reasoning on the grounds that

   (A) Clarke assumes that space is a container for objects in order to conclude that Leibniz's relationism cannot be true.

   (B) Clarke assumes that the relations between objects can be maintained despite the fact that those objects are transposed from one region of space to another.

   (C) Clarke assumes that Leibniz actually held an absolutist theory of space in order to show that relationism is false.

   (D) Clarke assumes that there is a definite relation between bodies in order to conclude that such a relation is impossible.

   (E) Clarke assumes that space is equivalent to the totality of existing objects in order to conclude that Newtonian absolute space is true.

4. The central point of the passage is to

   (A) question the effects of natural theology on Leibniz's and Clarke's inquiries into the shape and substance of space.

   (B) provide evidence for the claim that Newton's account of space was the driving force behind scientific inquiry in the 18th century.

   (C) reveal how the scientific study of the universe was marred by religious issues more appropriately addressed by theologians.

   (D) show how Leibniz's and Clarke's dispute over the layout of space had important consequences for their understanding of the nature of God.

   (E) discuss the ways that God's power led Leibniz and Clarke to very different conclusions about the organization of space.

5. For which of the following statements does the passage provide support?

   I. Absolute space is an immense field that has an existence independent of objects.

   II. The principle of sufficient reason contests God's omnipotence.

   III. Indivisibility is an essential property of relative space.

   (A) I only

   (B) III only

   (C) I and III only

   (D) II and III only

   (E) I, II, and III

6. In his reply to Leibniz that Newton's theory of space can be reconciled with the Principle of Sufficient Reason, Clarke presupposes that

   (A) there are important exceptions to be made to the PSR.

   (B) divine will always trumps divine rationality.

   (C) from God's point of view absolutely identical situations can exist.

   (D) reason may be opposed to volition in humans but not in God.

   (E) the PSR can accommodate events that cannot be explained.

7. Based on the information in the passage, with which of the following would the author most likely agree?

    (A) Not all scientists living in the 18th century believed in God.

    (B) The study of the universe can conceivably go hand in hand with the study of theology.

    (C) Absolute space and relative space are the only models of space.

    (D) Scholarly debates are essential for advancing the cause of truth.

    (E) The Principle of Sufficient Reason is the foundation for all scholarly investigations.

8. The principal difference between the absolute theory of space and the relational theory of space is that

    (A) the relationship between objects in the latter cannot change whereas such relations can change in the former.

    (B) the latter can be conceived of as being independent of corporeal bodies whereas the former cannot.

    (C) objects occupy regions of space in the former while objects are defined in relation to other objects in the latter.

    (D) the former is the manifestation of God's senses while the latter bears no relation to God's senses.

    (E) in the former bodies can undergo motion and rest whereas in the latter they cannot undergo motion and rest.

ANSWERS AND EXPLANATIONS

What Makes It Difficult

This passage is as abstract as it is dense. The best strategy is to try to grasp the essential things about each position. Associating Newton and Clarke with absolutism and God's will and associating Leibniz with relationism and God's reason should hopefully put you in a position to answer the questions with confidence.

Passage Map

Category: Physical Sciences

Field: Physics/Astronomy

Subfield: Natural Religion (i.e., Natural Theology)

Topic: Space

Scope: The implications of theories of space for natural theology

Purpose: To illustrate how Newton's and Leibniz's theories of space carried certain theological implications

¶1: Newton's theory of space

¶2: Leibniz's objection to Newton

¶3: Clarke's defense of Newton

¶4: Clarke's objection to Leibniz

¶5: Leibniz's defense of PSR

¶6: Nominalist-scholastic debate

1. **B**

The line referred to in the question can be found at the end of paragraph 5. In this paragraph, Leibniz tries to show that Clarke's reply to Leibniz's original objection fails to meet the standard set by the Principle of Sufficient Reason (PSR). Well, what is the PSR anyway? Unfortunately, the author never explicitly tells us; what it is has to be inferred from information in the passage. In two different places (first in paragraph 2 and then in paragraph 5), the author mentions that God has to have a reason for everything he creates. This means that if anything exists, it has to have a reason for so existing. That's the PSR.

Now, let's see how the PSR applies to the case before us. In paragraph 5, Leibniz says that if someone is trying to explain the existence of something, he can only appeal to God's reason. He thinks that it would be absurd to appeal to anything else—such as the will. This is because appeals to God's will make it possible for us to see God as an arbitrary being, a being who could act without a reason for doing so. And that, as we read in paragraph 2, could be read as a challenge to God's wisdom. Thus, the basic idea behind the author's judgment that Leibniz was right is that making an appeal to God's will won't meet the standard of the PSR. So the correct answer choice is **B**.

Look at **A**. The author never says whether one theory of space is better or worse than another. Consequently, **A** is outside of scope. What about **C**? It may be that the PSR is the foundation of Leibniz's theory of space, but that thought has no relevance in the immediate context. Our focus should be on the PSR and its connection to God. So we can eliminate **C**. **D**, for its part, is the opposite: as a matter of fact, Clarke endorsed Newton's absolutist view of space, not Leibniz's relationist view of space. Similarly, **E** is the opposite. The answer choice looks like a real possibility until we get to the part about God's will. We're looking not for God's will but for God's reason. That rules out **E**.

2.   **E**

The trick with this question is to try to figure out what things are being compared. Let's begin with what we know. In paragraphs 2 and 5, Leibniz defends God's rationality. In paragraph 3, Clarke defends God's power. Now, turn to paragraph 6. The scholastics argue that God was a rational being whereas the nominalists believe that God is an omnipotent being. Where does this leave us? It looks as though Leibniz is on the scholastic "team," Clarke on the nominalist "team." Thus, we're led to pick **E**.

A makes an unwarranted comparison. The author doesn't say whether space played a role in medieval discussions, so theories of space can't be the basis for the larger comparison. Better get rid of **A**. **B** looks like a broad generalization that can't be drawn based on the information in the final paragraph. With some qualifications, we should be willing to grant that such an inference can be made of Leibniz and Clarke, but we'd be going off the deep end were we to speculate that the same thing applied to medieval theologians. **C** also goes off the deep end, but for a different reason. Were Leibniz and Clarke *influenced* by medieval thinkers? We can't say because the author remains absolutely quiet on this issue. **C**, therefore, is outside of scope. **D** doesn't line up the right terms in the right way. The comparison is *not* between medieval conceptions of God's will and modern conceptions of God's wisdom. God's will and God's rationality show up in *both* periods. Like **A**, then, **D** makes an unwarranted comparison.

3.   **A**

The author gives us a definition of circular reasoning: to argue circularly is to presuppose whatever you want to conclude from the get-go. Let's think about what Clarke wants to conclude. It has to be that Newton's view of space is true. (But he can't assume this.) Now, on Newton's view, things are not themselves space or spatial; things are *in* space. Space is like one long sheet upon which we put things. So far, so good. Clarke wants to get here, but he can't *start* here. Instead, he needs to start off with Leibniz's view and then show that his view leads to absurdity. Consider Leibniz's view. Leibniz, recall, thought that space consists only of things and the relations between things—and that's it. From this premise, though, Clarke would have us *transpose* objects *across space* so as to put them *somewhere else*—namely, near the fixed stars. But Leibniz wouldn't allow that because objects could only move in relation to each other and not across some homogeneous expanse. In other words, Clarke is *assuming* that objects (and the relations between them) are set against a larger backdrop—Newtonian homogeneous space—in order to conclude that Leibniz can't make sense of our intuitions that the objects in question are not in the same place. He's assuming, that is, that space is a container into which we put objects. But that's just **A**.

B is a slippery answer. Let's imagine that a server is carrying a large tray of food, a bottle of wine, wine glasses, and the like from the kitchen to a table. She assumes (or hopes) that the relations between all the things on the tray won't change as she walks toward the table. Clarke assumes pretty much the same thing about objects in space, but it's not a *flaw* in his argument. Remember that the flaw is assuming that there's something independent of and "below" these objects that we can move them across in the first place.

Hopefully, **C, D,** and **E** will give us less trouble than **B**. **C** can't be correct because Clarke did *not* assume that Leibniz was a closet Newtonian. So **C** is opposite. Now, with respect to **D**, Clarke has to assume that there's a definite relation between bodies if he is going to do justice to Leibniz's argument. After all, he can't refute Leibniz if he doesn't begin with claims that Leibniz would accept. **D**, therefore, is opposite. Finally, we should be able to rule out **E** for the same reasons we ruled out **D**: they're both saying just about the same thing, but they're using different words to do so.

4. **D**

We need to get clear in our minds what the passage is about. Let's think about the key ideas we read about and then make a generalization. In the opening paragraph, the author introduces us to Newton's absolute theory of space. In paragraph 2, we read that Leibniz opposes this theory; he thinks instead that a relational theory of space is the way things are. Why does he think this? Because the relational theory is more befitting the nature of God. From here on out, we learn a good deal about the relationship between space and God. Let's generalize: God and space will have to figure in the correct answer. But what is the relationship between these two? According to the author, Leibniz's and Clarke's views about space had to be consistent with their views about God: they couldn't hold something about space that led to an infringement of God's power or a lessening of God's rationality. Our take on it looks a lot like **D**.

You probably had your doubts about **B**. If so, good. Not only is it too narrow to be the main point of the passage insofar as it only mentions Newton, but it is also too broad insofar as it goes well beyond what we read in the passage. Also suspect is **A** for the reason that the author never *questions* (which is to say, *doubts*) the role that theology plays in Leibniz's and Clarke's inquiries. Consequently, **A** is the opposite of the correct answer. This leads us to **C**. Perhaps you worried about the verb *marred*—and for good reason. This word implies that the author does not think that religious issues and scientific issues should be combined. We don't get this impression from the author at any point in the passage, so it has to be outside of scope. Now to the most tempting choice—**E**. What helps us rule out **E** is talk of God's power. God's power was an *explicit* preoccupation for Clarke but *not* an explicit preoccupation for Leibniz. So **E** is opposite.

5. **A**

With this Detail question, we need to perform two tests. First, did it show up? And, second, is there anything further said about it? We need to consider each Roman numeral in turn.

Consider **I**. First, was absolute space thought to be utterly distinct from the objects that occupy it? Yes. And, second, was there some further discussion of this view throughout the passage? Yes, there was—at the end of paragraph 1 and throughout Clarke's defense of this view. We should hold onto **I** then.

Consider **II**. Was it mentioned that the principle of sufficient reason *contests* God's omnipotence? No. So we don't need to go through the second test.

Consider **III**. Was it mentioned that indivisibility is an essential property of relative space? No, it wasn't. No need to go any further.

Thus, **I** only—that is, **A**.

6. **C**

The question is referring to paragraph 3. There, Clarke defends Newton's theory of space against the charge that it violates the Principle of Sufficient Reason. It's implied in paragraphs 2 and 4 that the PSR is synonymous with the proposition that everything has to have a reason for its existence. Now, Clarke's response to Leibniz is that there may be certain situations that are exactly the same as well as absolutely perfect so that the only reason that God chooses either is in order to create something in the first place. His reason, in short, is just to create. So what's Clarke's main assumption? It is that there *exist* situations (at least in God's mind) that are exactly the same and absolutely perfect, something that Leibniz *denies* in the following paragraph. Hence, **C** is the correct answer choice.

Clarke is trying to defend the PSR, so the idea that he is limiting its scope is just the opposite. This line of thought leads us to eliminate **A**. **B** is too broad of a generalization; it is also opposite. We know that Clarke is attempting to show how will and rationality come together in God, not how one is more important than the other. What about **C**? Well, Clarke doesn't draw any distinctions between God and humans in his arguments; nor do his arguments trade on such a distinction. Because **D** is outside of scope, we'd do well to get rid of it. And **E** is self-refuting by definition: The PSR is supposed to say that everything can be explained, i.e., that everything has a reason for its existence. Therefore, it's not in the nature of the PSR to accommodate things that *can't* be explained.

7. **B**

The litmus test for this question is not what the author explicitly said but what she would have to give her rational assent to based on the argument she made in the passage. If we find anything that (1) *runs counter to* what she explicitly said, that (2) goes beyond what she would *have to* believe, or that (3) goes beyond what she would *likely* believe, then we have grounds for eliminating it.

Start with the most stringent test (the first test) and then go down to the least stringent (the third test). Do any answer choices run counter to what she explicitly said? No.

The second test states that we can eliminate an answer choice if it goes well beyond what she would *have to* believe. Well, based on what she wrote, she wouldn't have to believe **A**. That answer is an issue that she doesn't have to weigh in on. Nor would she have to believe **D**—namely, that debates are *essential*. She may grant that they're important, but she doesn't have to grant that they're essential. Any others? Nope.

The third test states that we can eliminate an answer choice if it goes beyond what she would *likely* believe. She wouldn't likely believe **B**. This is because she may willingly admit that there may be other models of space besides these two. Nor would she be likely to believe **E**. Might she? Yes. But is she *likely* to? No. She is not likely to believe that the PSR is the basis of *all* scholarly investigations.

Only **B** passes all three tests.

8. **C**

The main difference between the two is that the first is a "container" while the second one is not. Let's try to imagine what absolute space is like. Imagine a long black tarp that stretches indefinitely in all directions. Now begin "populating" that black surface with objects of whatever kinds—planets, trees, books, you name it. These objects can be said to be *in* space. The relational mode is much different. Let's imagine an immense sea, so immense that nothing is beyond it. Let's now imagine boats, ducks, whales, and so on. In this picture, everything is made up of objects and relations between them: boats are spatially related to whales, whales to ducks, and all of these to parts of the sea. Nothing is *on* the sea. Everything is simply connected to another. In sum, absolute space presents with a "container" while relational space does not. But that's just **C**.

In short order, we can eliminate the rest of the answer choices. Since we didn't read about motion in relation to these two theories, **A** and **E** can be jettisoned. **B** puts things in reverse: it's absolute space that is independent of bodies—not relative space. With respect to **D**, absolute space is not a *literal* manifestation of God's senses; "sensorium" in line 5 is a metaphor for the thing that God creates—namely, space. More to the point, we don't know whether God's "sensorium" bears any relation to relative space. In light of this, we can't determine that "sensorium" is the thing that distinguishes the first theory from the second.

CHAPTER TWELVE

Reading Comprehension Passage 4

Directions: Each passage in this group is followed by questions based on its content. After reading a passage, choose the best answer to each question. Answer all questions following a passage on the basis of what is stated or implied in that passage.

Few metaphysicians worry overly much anymore about the question of why there is something rather than nothing. However, most evolutionary biologists take the demand quite
(5) seriously to provide rock-solid evolutionary explanations for how a diversity of organisms and species could have come into existence, how complexity could have arisen out of simplicity, and how excellent design could
(10) have sprung from a mindless, random process. Proponents of Intelligent Design charge that evolutionary theory cannot account for the "irreducible complexity" of certain natural phenomena, while theists second Robert
(15) MacKenzie's 1868 review of Charles Darwin's *The Origin of Species,* which called patently false the proposition that "Absolute Ignorance [is] fully qualified to take the place of Absolute Wisdom in all the achievements of creative skill."
(20)   To come to some fuller understanding of the fundamental change in worldview inaugurated by evolutionary biology, we would do well to begin by analyzing the concept of teleology. *Telos* is that for which something is done or
(25) that toward which animate beings strive. Thus, an eye is for seeing, a walk for health, a house for shelter, and a book for reading. Little 't' teleology so conceived, though, mustn't be confused with big 'T' Teleology, according to
(30) which the whole of nature is either progressing, by virtue of some world-historical or cosmic force, toward some overarching purpose or is already the embodiment of some divine plan.
    That teleology needn't entail Teleology
(35) was evolutionary theory's great insight. From the moment that organic life first appeared on Earth some 4.5 billion years ago, natural selection has been an inexorable, unceasing, and entirely mindless process of winnowing
(40) and sifting through a set of design plans. The geological record is littered with plant and animal species falling extinct under the pressures of climatic and geographical changes. Only those designs that natural
(45) selection has blindly hit upon and that have worked, designs that are well-adapted to the specific environment and that therefore confer upon certain organisms or certain species some ostensible advantage, will be inheritable
(50) by their progeny. This implies that there is no Higher End, no Higher Purpose that governs the actions of intelligent and unintelligent life, only local purposes fitting into the materialist picture of "selfish genes" seeking to pass on
(55) genetic information to their descendants *ad infinitum*. There is therefore no Teleology from on high, only teleology all the way down. And there is no more need for what Daniel Dennett has called the "mind-first" hypothesis either.

(60) Nothing under the sun is exempt from the process of natural selection—not eyes or wings and certainly not minds. Thanks to research in evolutionary theory over the past 150 years, it is no longer mysterious how an ignorant,
(65) mindless machine, by means of chance, trial and error, and gradual modifications taking place over long swaths of time, could have produced sophisticated, cognizant machines able to reflect upon the process itself. What
(70) recommends the evolutionary story of the emergence of intelligent life is not just its plausibility; it is the fact, confirmed time and again by studies in geology, genetics, cell biology, zoology, and botany, that it is true.

1. The principal difference between teleology and Teleology could be understood in terms of the difference between

    (A) quality and quantity.

    (B) example and concept.

    (C) property and object.

    (D) cause and effect.

    (E) part and whole.

2. The main idea of the passage is that

    (A) new species come into being through a process called natural selection.

    (B) evolution represents a sea change in our comprehension of all forms of life.

    (C) natural selection shows us how evolution through a set of randomly generated but intelligent procedures is possible.

    (D) intelligent and sentient creatures are the inevitable results of natural selection.

    (E) absolute ignorance works to create living beings much in the same way that absolute wisdom does.

3. For which of the following topics does the passage provide supporting evidence?

    I.   The plurality of species

    II. The complex nature of some organisms

    III. The evolution of design

    (A) I only

    (B) III only

    (C) I and II only

    (D) II and III only

    (E) I, II, and III

4. The author's discussion of metaphysicians in the first paragraph is intended to

   (A) draw a parallel between philosophers' work on esoteric subject matter and evolutionary biologists' research into exoteric issues.

   (B) reveal how the answers given by evolutionary biologists will someday be just as self-evident as those given by metaphysicians.

   (C) sharpen the contrast between questions that used to be but are no longer relevant and those that are still the subject of lively debate.

   (D) lead us to see how progress in evolutionary biology has made research in metaphysics obsolete.

   (E) make the point that the questions metaphysicians once asked can now be answered by evolutionary biologists.

5. Based on information in the passage, it can be inferred from the author's statement that evolution has no need for the "mind-first" hypothesis that

   (A) the first appearance of living things did not involve an intelligent being.

   (B) unintelligent beings necessarily follow from an intelligent being.

   (C) in human beings our mental life came before our physical existence.

   (D) living beings had to have come from multicell organisms.

   (E) experiments in ordering organic life finally yielded intelligent design.

6. Which of the following best describes the organization of the passage?

   (A) Research questions are discussed, background information is provided, and a call for further research is made.

   (B) Important objections to the current theory are made, a measured defense is argued for, and minor revisions to the theory are offered.

   (C) A key issue is raised, a distinction is made, and the original issue is addressed to the author's satisfaction.

   (D) A number of problems are mentioned, and a solution to each of the problems is provided in turn.

   (E) A disagreement is discussed, an explanation for the disagreement is offered, and sympathy for one of the parties is expressed.

7. The author refers to "selfish genes" in the third paragraph in order to

   (A) establish that it is not possible for human beings to be altruistic.

   (B) point out a flaw in the idea that humans are more important than other sentient creatures.

   (C) clarify the close-knit relationship between intelligent and unintelligent life.

   (D) marshal support for the argument that the meaning of life is nothing but reproduction.

   (E) suggest that evidence for natural selection is found most conspicuously in genes.

8. Implicit in the statement that many species have become extinct is the idea that

   (A) some species are better than other species by virtue of their higher order complexity.

   (B) the diversity of species now in existence could have been derived from earlier species.

   (C) catastrophic events are the main cause of species going out of existence.

   (D) natural selection has the innate capacity to choose which species will live and which will die.

   (E) some species were unable to adapt sufficiently to survive certain changes in the environment.

ANSWERS AND EXPLANATIONS

What Makes It Difficult

You probably picked up on a few things that made reading this passage no easy task. Here's something you may have been puzzled about: it looks as if the author sends you on a wild goose chase in the opening paragraph. There we hear about three problems that evolutionary biology needs to solve (these are diversity, complexity, and design) and two objections to evolutionary biology (these are the "irreducible complexity" objection and—let's call it the "mind-first" objection). The rest of the passage, however, only touches on one of the problems—the design problem—in connection with the "mind-first" objection. In which case, a lot of what is mentioned in the opening paragraph remains largely unaddressed. It's worth keeping this in mind: many passages will introduce more topics than can reasonably be discussed throughout the passage.

I'm sure you also didn't enjoy wading through the long last paragraph. Maybe you thought that it could have been divided into two or three paragraphs. You're probably right. Even so, on Test Day, expect long paragraphs when you turn to the science passages. They tend to be quite common.

Passage Map

Category: Biological Sciences

Field: Evolutionary Biology

Subfield: Evolutionary Theory

Topic: Natural Selection

Scope: The change in worldview brought about by natural selection

Purpose: To tease out the important consequences of this change in worldview

¶1: main explanatory issues in evolutionary biology

¶2: difference between teleology and Teleology

¶3: two related implications of natural selection: the first that evolution keeps teleology but does away with Teleology; the second that evolution can explain how intelligent life could have arisen from a dumb, blind, mindless process (i.e., from natural selection)

1. **E**

This reads a lot like an analogy question where A : B :: C : D. First, then, we need to know a thing or two about teleology and Teleology. Little 't' teleology just means a goal that individuals aim for or a purpose for which something was made. In contrast, big 't' Teleology has to do with how *all of nature* is organized: with some larger plan or purpose in mind. In essence, teleology is concerned with finite things—*small* things with a determinate existence such as you and me—whereas teleology is concerned with the *totality* of all things—that is, *really big* things such as everything that exists. So finite things are what go into making up the whole of nature. This way of putting things should help us see that we're talking about the relationship between part and whole. In the form of an analogy, teleology : Teleology :: part : whole. Consequently, **E** is the correct answer choice. None of the other answer choices really makes sense here.

2. B

In broad strokes, the passage has to do with the role that natural selection plays in evolution. Natural selection, we learn, affirms teleology but does away with Teleology; it also does away with the "mind-first" hypothesis, a hypothesis that states that really smart things must come before and must create rather dumb things. Natural selection thus brings about a "fundamental change in worldview" (line 21). The right answer choice should therefore be in line with your understanding of the passage—but that's just **B**.

A falls outside the scope of the passage. The author does not speak at any length about "speciation," or the emergence of new species. **C** looks like a real possibility until we read the word *intelligent*. No, natural selection is not intelligent; it is blind and dumb. Hence, **C** is opposite. **D** goes too far. As we pointed out above, the author is concerned with showing how creatures with minds could have been produced from a mindless machine (natural selection). But the author does not imply that the results are *inevitable*. This leaves us with **E**, which we can quickly get rid of. The author never likens the *way* that natural selection operates to the *way* that a divine creator operates. If anything, they'd be opposite.

3. B

Read this question closely so as not to miss what it's driving at. The question is not asking us *simply* to pick out what we *saw* in the passage. Of course, if we *didn't* see something, then that answer choice *cannot* be correct. But if we did see something, this does not mean that the answer choice *has to be* correct. This is because we're looking to figure out whether I, II, or III was supported by evidence in the passage. As a general rule of thumb, "supported by evidence" just means that there is more stuff written about the thing in question after it is first mentioned. Keep this rule of thumb in mind on Test Day.

Let's use this rule of thumb to evaluate each answer choice. Note, first, that a plurality of species, the complex nature of some organisms, and the evolution of design were all mentioned in the opening paragraph. But which of these had more stuff written about it after first being mentioned? Not I: it's not discussed after line 7 in the opening paragraph. Ditto II. Only III, which is the subject of the third paragraph. So the correct answer is **B**.

4. C

The adverb *however* beginning in line 3 tells us that there is something that metaphysicians and evolutionary biologists don't have in common. So we can already eliminate **A**, which suggests that the two *do* have something in common. But on what issue or in what way do metaphysicians and evolutionary biologists differ? Well, the author informs us that not many metaphysicians think that a certain question is important these days while evolutionary biologists, it seems, have lots of questions that hold their attention. For this reason, the correct answer will have to say something about the difference between "dead" and "live" research questions. Do we find any answer choices that do? Yes, **C**.

In **B**, the adjective *self-evident* looks dubious: we don't know about whether metaphysicians think that the question before them is now self-evident or not. So **B** is outside of scope. **D** suggests that metaphysicians are the "loser," and evolutionary biology is the "victor"—or, better yet, the "usurper." But we have no reason to believe that is what the author is getting at; and we have no reason to believe that metaphysics, as a field of inquiry, is now obsolete. Like **D**, **E** suggests that evolutionary biologists have outstripped metaphysicians: what metaphysicians couldn't do very well evolutionary biologists can. Yet there is no concrete evidence in the passage to suggest that metaphysicians have *handed over* their questions to evolutionary biologists who have then answered them.

5. **A**

We need to get straight what the "mind-first" hypothesis is before we look at the answer choices. Unfortunately, the author doesn't explicitly say what this hypothesis is. Look at the next two sentences, though. Here, we read that "sophisticated, cognizant machines"—read: humans and other smart things—have been produced by a dumb, mindless machine—read: natural selection. So something mindless produced something with a mind. To keep things clear, let's go ahead and call this the "mind-last" hypothesis. Now we need to make a few inferences: first, that the "mind-first" hypothesis is the opposite of the "mind-last" hypothesis; and second, that the "mind-first" hypothesis involves a smart being (God) creating less smart beings (humans, animals, plants, and so on). Finally, let's put everything together: If evolution has no need for the "mind-first" hypothesis, then it follows that the process of creation doesn't require a smart being for organic life to come into being. Simply put, God's not necessary. So **A** is the correct answer choice.

B is opposite—it's simply a restatement of the "mind-first" hypothesis, the hypothesis that evolutionary theory is rejecting. **C** is a red herring. Whether our mental life comes before our physical existence can't be inferred from information in the passage. Given that the author makes no mention whatever of multicell organisms, **D** looks even more far-fetched than **C**. (A word of caution here: **D** is trying to get you to use information that you may have learned from biology classes to answer the question. Be aware that this is one ruse you may run into on Test Day.) The information in **E** is accurate, but the answer has nothing explicitly to do with the question being asked. Another lesson here: some answers may be true (insofar as they accurately pick out information from the passage) but not correct (insofar as they failed to answer the specific question before us).

6. **C**

By now, we should be pros at answering this type of question. Hopefully, you've been learning to read these passages not just for content but for also for form so that you're building the structure of the passage either in your head or on scratch paper as you go. Good thing too because in this passage, you probably noticed that in the first paragraph the author mentions some problems that evolutionary biology needs to solve and then goes on to raise two objections to evolutionary biology. In the second paragraph, the author draws a line between teleology and Teleology. In the final paragraph, he shows us *one* of the main problems discussed in the opening paragraph— namely, the problem of getting smart things out of dumb things—can be solved. Go with **C**: a key issue is raised (paragraph 1), a distinction made (paragraph 2), and that issue is addressed (paragraph 3).

Remember that we can rule out wrong answer choices by pinpointing their *weakest points*.

So what's the weakest point in **A**? That's easy enough: the author doesn't call for further research. The weakest point in **B**? Also easy enough: the author never makes any minor revisions to the theory. The weakest point in **D**? A little more difficult: the author doesn't provide solutions to *all* of the problems, only to *one* of the problems (how you get smart things out of a dumb process).

The weakest point in **E**? No *explanation* for the disagreement between theists and evolutionary biologists is provided. The author instead tries to show us that a reply to one of the theists' objections can be made.

7. D

Begin with what "selfish genes" are trying to do. According to the author, they're trying to get what they have into their descendants. They're selfish, then, in the sense that they're only interested in the kind of "immortality" that comes with passing what they have on to the next generation. All right, but what's the larger *point* of talking about "selfish genes"? The author clearly wants to show that there's no divine purpose (that is, no big 't' Teleology) in the world, and this lack of overarching purpose is evinced in "selfish genes." The answer that most closely matches our understanding of the passage is **D**.

A is trying to get you to think about the opposite of selfish behavior in the context of ethics. There, altruism is normally pitted against self-regarding behavior. But what's the relevance of that ethical distinction within the current context? Well, none, so **A** is out. **B** can be ruled out for two reasons. First, the author is not trying to point out any flaw. Second, he is not attempting to demonstrate that humans are on par with other sentient creatures (or that other sentient creatures are more important than humans). **B**, therefore, is opposite. **C** may be relevant in a discussion of natural selection, but it has no bearing on the question of Teleology, which is our present concern. **E** looks like something that we can have no opinion about based on information in the passage. For all we know, it could be correct (or it could be incorrect). Hence, **E** is a classic case of being outside of scope.

8. E

The lines relevant to this question are 41–44. Perhaps you thought of two assumptions underlying the thought that animals have become extinct. The first is that something must have caused these species to go extinct, and it looks as though changes in climate and geography may have led to this. The second is that natural selection may not have been "quick enough" to help certain species survive and adapt under adverse conditions. The first assumption we came up with pays off: it's a gloss of **E**.

We shouldn't have any problems with ruling out **A**. Complexity was only mentioned in the first paragraph, and it has played no role in the rest of the passage. So it is very unlikely to be an assumption that the author is making in the third paragraph. **B** seems to have no relevance to the question at hand. It is trivially true that later species came from earlier species, but what does that have to do with a question concerning extinction? **C** might at first look tempting, but it shouldn't be. We have no reason to believe that catastrophic events such as earthquakes and floods are the *main* cause of extinction. Strictly speaking, we have no reason to believe that catastrophic events are even *a* cause of extinction. For its part, **D** seems to compare the powers of natural selection with those of some divine being. From the information in the passage, we can conclude that **D** is simply false. Since it's false, it can't be an underlying assumption.

section three

GRE VERBAL RESOURCES

GRE Word Groups

The following lists contain a lot of common GRE words grouped together by meaning. Make flash cards from these lists and look over your cards a few times a week from now until the day of the test. Look over the word group lists once or twice a week for 30 seconds every week until the test. If you don't have much time until the exam date, look over your lists more frequently. Then, by the day of the test, you should have a rough idea of what most of the words on your lists mean.

Note: The categories in which these words are listed are *general* and should *not* be interpreted as the exact definitions of the words.

ABBREVIATED COMMUNICATION

abridge
compendium
cursory
curtail
syllabus
synopsis
terse

ACT QUICKLY

apace
abrupt
headlong
impetuous
precipitate

ASSIST

abet
advocate
ancillary
bolster
corroborate
countenance
espouse
mainstay
munificent
proponent
stalwart
sustenance

BAD MOOD

bilious
dudgeon
irascible
pettish
petulant
pique
querulous
umbrage
waspish

BEGINNER/AMATEUR

dilettante
fledgling
neophyte
novitiate
proselyte
tyro

BEGINNING/YOUNG

burgeoning
callow
engender
inchoate
incipient
nascent

BITING (AS IN WIT OR TEMPERAMENT)

acerbic
acidulous
acrimonious
asperity
caustic
mordacious
mordant
trenchant

BOLD

audacious
courageous
dauntless

BORING

banal
fatuous
hackneyed
insipid
mundane
pedestrian
platitude
prosaic
quotidian
trite

CAROUSAL

bacchanalian
debauchery
depraved
dissipated
iniquity
libertine
libidinous
licentious
reprobate
ribald
salacious

sordid
turpitude

CHANGING QUICKLY

capricious
mercurial
volatile

COPY

counterpart
emulate
facsimile
factitious
paradigm
precursor
quintessence
simulated
vicarious

CRITICIZE/CRITICISM

aspersion
belittle
berate
calumny
castigate
decry
defamation
denounce
deride/derisive
diatribe
disparage
excoriate
gainsay
harangue
impugn
inveigh
lambaste
objurgate
obloquy
opprobrium
pillory
rebuke
remonstrate
reprehend
reprove
revile
tirade
vituperate

DEATH/MOURNING

bereave
cadaver
defunct
demise
dolorous
elegy
knell
lament
macabre
moribund
obsequies
sepulchral
wraith

DENYING OF SELF

abnegate
abstain
ascetic
spartan
stoic
temperate

DICTATORIAL

authoritarian
despotic
dogmatic
hegemonic (hegemony)
imperious
peremptory
tyrannical

DIFFICULT TO UNDERSTAND

abstruse
ambiguous
arcane
bemusing
cryptic
enigmatic
esoteric
inscrutable
obscure
opaque
paradoxical
perplexing
recondite
turbid

DISGUSTING/OFFENSIVE

defile
fetid
invidious
noisome
odious
putrid
rebarbative

EASY TO UNDERSTAND

articulate
cogent
eloquent
evident
limpid
lucid
pellucid

ECCENTRIC/DISSIMILAR

aberrant
anachronism
anomalous
discrete
eclectic
esoteric
iconoclast

EMBARRASS

abash
chagrin
compunction
contrition
diffidence
expiate
foible
gaucherie
rue

EQUAL

equitable
equity
tantamount

FALSEHOOD

apocryphal
canard
chicanery
dissemble

duplicity
equivocate
erroneous
ersatz
fallacious
feigned
guile
mendacious/mendacity
perfidy
prevaricate
specious
spurious

FAMILY

conjugal
consanguine
distaff
endogamous
filial
fratricide
progenitor
scion

FAVORING/NOT IMPARTIAL

ardor/ardent
doctrinaire
fervid
partisan
tendentious
zealot

FORGIVE

absolve
acquit
exculpate
exonerate
expiate
palliate
redress
vindicate

FUNNY

chortle
droll
facetious
flippant
gibe
jocular

levity
ludicrous
raillery
riposte
simper

GAPS/OPENINGS

abatement
aperture
fissure
hiatus
interregnum
interstice
lull
orifice
rent
respite
rift

GENEROUS/KIND

altruistic
beneficent
clement
largess
magnanimous
munificent
philanthropic
unstinting

GREEDY

avaricious
covetous
mercenary
miserly
penurious
rapacious
venal

HARD-HEARTED

asperity
baleful
dour
fell
malevolent
mordant
sardonic
scathing
truculent
vitriolic
vituperation

HARMFUL

baleful
baneful
deleterious
inimical
injurious
insidious
minatory
perfidious
pernicious

HARSH-SOUNDING

cacophony
din
dissonant
raucous
strident

HATRED

abhorrence
anathema
antagonism
antipathy
detestation
enmity
loathing
malice
odium
rancor

HEALTHY

beneficial
salubrious
salutary

HESITATE

dither
oscillate
teeter
vacillate
waver

HOSTILE

antithetic
churlish
curmudgeon
irascible
malevolent
misanthropic

truculent
vindictive

INNOCENT/INEXPERIENCED

credulous
gullible
ingenuous
naive
novitiate
tyro

INSINCERE

disingenuous
dissemble
fulsome
ostensible
unctuous

INVESTIGATE

appraise
ascertain
assay
descry
peruse

LAZY/SLUGGISH

indolent
inert
lackadaisical
languid
lassitude
lethargic
phlegmatic
quiescent
slothful
torpid

LUCK

adventitious
amulet
auspicious
fortuitous
kismet
optimum
portentous
propitiate
propitious
providential
talisman

NAG

admonish
cavil
belabor
enjoin
exhort
harangue
hector
martinet
remonstrate
reproof

NASTY

fetid
noisome
noxious

NOT A STRAIGHT LINE

askance
awry
careen
carom
circuitous
circumvent
gyrate
labyrinth
meander
oblique
serrated
sidle
sinuous
undulating
vortex

OVERBLOWN/WORDY

bombastic
circumlocution
garrulous
grandiloquent
loquacious
periphrastic
prolix
rhetoric
turgid
verbose

PACIFY/SATISFY

ameliorate
appease

assuage
defer
mitigate
mollify
placate
propitiate
satiate
slake
sooth

PLEASANT-SOUNDING

euphonious
harmonious
melodious
sonorous

POOR

destitute
esurient
impecunious
indigent

PRAISE

acclaim
accolade
aggrandize
encomium
eulogize
extol
fawn
laud/laudatory
venerate/veneration

PREDICT

augur
auspice
fey
harbinger
portentous
presage
prescient
prognosticate

PREVENT/OBSTRUCT

discomfort
encumber
fetter
forfend
hinder

impede
inhibit
occlude

SMART/LEARNED

astute
canny
erudite
perspicacious

SORROW

disconsolate
doleful
dolor
elegiac
forlorn
lament
lugubrious
melancholy
morose
plaintive
threnody

STUBBORN

implacable
inexorable
intractable
intransigent
obdurate
obstinate
recalcitrant
refractory
renitent
untoward
vexing

TERSE

compendious
curt
laconic
pithy
succinct
taciturn

TIME/ORDER/DURATION

anachronism
antecede
antedate
anterior

archaic
diurnal
eon
ephemeral
epoch
fortnight
millennium
penultimate
synchronous
temporal

Timid/Timidity

craven
diffident
pusillanimous
recreant
timorous
trepidation

Truth

candor/candid
fealty
frankness
indisputable
indubitable
legitimate
probity
sincere
veracious
verity

Unusual

aberration
anomaly
iconoclast
idiosyncrasy

Walking About

ambulatory
itinerant
peripatetic

Wandering

discursive
expatiate
forage
itinerant
peregrination
peripatetic
sojourn

Weaken

adulterate
enervate
exacerbate
inhibit
obviate
stultify
undermine
vitiate

Wisdom

adage
aphorism
apothegm
axiom
bromide
dictum
epigram
platitude
sententious
truism

Withdrawal/Retreat

abeyance
abjure
abnegation
abortive
abrogate
decamp
demur
recant
recidivism
remission
renege
rescind
retrograde

GRE Root List

Kaplan's Root List can boost your knowledge of GRE-level words, and that can help you get more questions right. No one can predict exactly which words will show up on your test, but there are certain words that the test makers favor. The Root List gives you the component parts of many typical GRE words. Knowing these words can help you because you may run across them on your GRE. Also, becoming comfortable with the types of words that pop up will reduce your anxiety about the test.

Knowing roots can help you in two more ways. First, instead of learning one word at a time, you can learn a whole group of words that contain a certain root. They'll be related in meaning, so if you remember one, it will be easier for you to remember others. Second, roots can often help you decode an unknown GRE word. If you recognize a familiar root, you could get a good enough grasp of the word to answer the question.

A: WITHOUT

amoral: neither moral nor immoral
atheist: one who does not believe in God
atypical: not typical
anonymous: of unknown authorship or origin
apathy: lack of interest or emotion
atrophy: the wasting away of body tissue
anomaly: an irregularity
agnostic: one who questions the existence of God

AB/ABS: OFF, AWAY FROM, APART, DOWN

abduct: to take by force
abhor: to hate, detest
abolish: to do away with, make void
abstract: conceived apart from concrete realities, specific objects, or actual instances
abnormal: deviating from a standard
abdicate: to renounce or relinquish a throne
abstinence: forbearance from any indulgence of appetite
abstruse: hard to understand; secret, hidden

AC/ACR: SHARP, BITTER

acid: something that is sharp, sour, or ill-natured
acute: sharp at the end; ending in a point
acerbic: sour or astringent in taste; harsh in temper
acrid: sharp or biting to the taste or smell
acrimonious: caustic, stinging, or bitter in nature
exacerbate: to increase bitterness or violence; aggravate

ACT/AG: TO DO; TO DRIVE; TO FORCE; TO LEAD

agile: quick and well-coordinated in movement; active, lively
agitate: to move or force into violent, irregular action
litigate: to make the subject of a lawsuit
prodigal: wastefully or recklessly extravagant
pedagogue: a teacher
synagogue: a gathering or congregation of Jews for the purpose of religious worship

AD/AL: TO, TOWARD, NEAR

adapt: adjust or modify fittingly
adjacent: near, close, or contiguous; adjoining
addict: to give oneself over, as to a habit or pursuit
admire: to regard with wonder, pleasure, and approval

address: to direct a speech or written statement to
adhere: to stick fast; cleave; cling
adjoin: to be close or in contact with
advocate: to plead in favor of

AL/ALI/ALTER: OTHER, ANOTHER

alternative: a possible choice
alias: an assumed name; another name
alibi: the defense by an accused person that he was verifiably elsewhere at the time of the crime with which he is charged
alien: one born in another country; a foreigner
alter ego: the second self; a substitute or deputy
altruist: a person unselfishly concerned for the welfare of others
allegory: figurative treatment of one subject under the guise of another

AM: LOVE

amateur: a person who engages in an activity for pleasure rather than financial or professional gain
amatory: of or pertaining to lovers or lovemaking
amenity: agreeable ways or manners
amorous: inclined to love, esp. sexual love
enamored: inflamed with love; charmed; captivated
amity: friendship; peaceful harmony
inamorata: a female lover
amiable: having or showing agreeable personal qualities
amicable: characterized by exhibiting goodwill

AMB: TO GO; TO WALK

ambient: moving freely; circulating
ambitious: desirous of achieving or obtaining power
preamble: an introductory statement
ambassador: an authorized messenger or representative
ambulance: a wheeled vehicle equipped for carrying sick people, usually to a hospital
ambulatory: of, pertaining to, or capable of walking
ambush: the act of lying concealed so as to attack by surprise
perambulator: one who makes a tour of inspection on foot

AMBI/AMPH: BOTH, MORE THAN ONE, AROUND

ambiguous: open to various interpretations

amphibian: any cold-blooded vertebrate, the larva of which is aquatic and the adult of which is terrestrial; a person or thing having a twofold nature

ambidextrous: able to use both hands equally well

ANIM: OF THE LIFE, MIND, SOUL, SPIRIT

unanimous: in complete accord

animosity: a feeling of ill will or enmity

animus: hostile feeling or attitude

equanimity: mental or emotional stability, especially under tension

magnanimous: generous in forgiving an insult or injury

ANNUI/ENNI: YEAR

annual: of, for, or pertaining to a year; yearly

anniversary: the yearly recurrence of the date of a past event

annuity: a specified income payable at stated intervals

perennial: lasting for an indefinite amount of time

annals: a record of events, esp. a yearly record

ANTE: BEFORE

anterior: placed before

antecedent: existing, being, or going before

antedate: precede in time

antebellum: before the war (especially the American Civil War)

antediluvian: belonging to the period before the biblical flood; very old or old-fashioned

ANTHRO/ANDR: MAN, HUMAN

anthropology: the science that deals with the origins of mankind

android: robot; mechanical man

misanthrope: one who hates humans or mankind

philanderer: one who carries on flirtations

androgynous: being both male and female

androgen: any substance that promotes masculine characteristics

anthropocentric: regarding man as the central fact of the universe

ANTI: AGAINST

antibody: a protein naturally existing in blood serum, that reacts to overcome the toxic effects of an antigen

antidote: a remedy for counteracting the effects of poison, disease, etc.

antiseptic: free from germs; particularly clean or neat

antipathy: aversion

antipodal: on the opposite side of the globe

APO: AWAY

apology: an expression of one's regret or sorrow for having wronged another

apostle: one of the 12 disciples sent forth by Jesus to preach the gospel

apocalypse: revelation; discovery; disclosure

apogee: the highest or most distant point

apocryphal: of doubtful authorship or authenticity

apostasy: a total desertion of one's religion, principles, party, cause, etc.

ARCH/ARCHI/ARCHY: CHIEF, PRINCIPAL, RULER

architect: the devisor, maker, or planner of anything

archenemy: chief enemy

monarchy: a government in which the supreme power is lodged in a sovereign

anarchy: a state or society without government or law

oligarchy: a state or society ruled by a select group

AUTO: SELF

automatic: self-moving or self-acting

autocrat: an absolute ruler

autonomy: independence or freedom

BE: TO BE; TO HAVE A PARTICULAR QUALITY; TO EXIST

belittle: to regard something as less impressive than it apparently is

bemoan: to express pity for

bewilder: to confuse or puzzle completely

belie: to misrepresent; to contradict

BEL/BEL: WAR

antebellum: before the war

rebel: a person who resists authority, control, or tradition

belligerent: warlike, given to waging war

BEN/BON: GOOD

benefit: anything advantageous to a person or thing

benign: having a kindly disposition

benediction: act of uttering a blessing

benevolent: desiring to do good to others

bonus: something given over and above what is due

bona fide: in good faith; without fraud

BI: TWICE, DOUBLE

binoculars: involving two eyes

biennial: happening every two years

bilateral: pertaining to or affecting two or both sides

bilingual: able to speak one's native language and another with equal facility

bipartisan: representing two parties

CAD/CID: TO FALL; TO HAPPEN BY CHANCE

accident: happening by chance; unexpected

coincidence: a striking occurrence of two or more events at one time, apparently by chance

decadent: decaying; deteriorating

cascade: a waterfall descending over a steep surface

recidivist: one who repeatedly relapses, as into crime

CANT/CENT/CHANT: TO SING

accent: prominence of a syllable in terms of pronunciation

chant: a song; singing

enchant: to subject to magical influence; bewitch

recant: to withdraw or disavow a statement

incantation: the chanting of words purporting to have magical power

incentive: that which incites action

CAP/CIP/CEPT: TO TAKE; TO GET

capture: to take by force or stratagem

anticipate: to realize beforehand; foretaste or foresee

susceptible: capable of receiving, admitting, undergoing, or being affected by something

emancipate: to free from restraint

percipient: having perception; discerning; discriminating

precept: a commandment or direction given as a rule of conduct

CAP/CAPIT/CIPIT: HEAD, HEADLONG

capital: the city or town that is the official seat of government

disciple: one who is a pupil of the doctrines of another

precipitate: to hasten the occurrence of; to bring about prematurely

precipice: a cliff with a vertical face

capitulate: to surrender unconditionally or on stipulated terms

caption: a heading or title

CARD/CORD/COUR: HEART

cardiac: pertaining to the heart

encourage: to inspire with spirit or confidence

concord: agreement; peace, amity

discord: lack of harmony between persons or things

concordance: agreement, concord, harmony

CARN: FLESH

carnivorous: eating flesh

carnage: the slaughter of a great number of people

carnival: a traveling amusement show

reincarnation: rebirth of a soul in a new body

incarnation: a being invested with a bodily form

CAST/CHAST: CUT

cast: to throw or hurl; fling

caste: a hereditary social group, limited to people of the same rank

castigate: to punish in order to correct

chastise: to discipline, esp. by corporal punishment

chaste: free from obscenity; decent

CED/CEED/CESS: TO GO; TO YIELD; TO STOP

antecedent: existing, being, or going before

concede: to acknowledge as true, just, or proper; admit

predecessor: one who comes before another in an office, position, etc.

cessation: a temporary or complete discontinuance

incessant: without stop

CENTR: CENTER

concentrate: to bring to a common center; to converge, to direct toward one point

eccentric: off center

concentric: having a common center, as in circles or spheres

centrifuge: an apparatus that rotates at high speed that separates substances of different densities using centrifugal force

centrist: of or pertaining to moderate political or social ideas

CERN/CERT/CRET/CRIM/CRIT: TO SEPARATE; TO JUDGE; TO DISTINGUISH; TO DECIDE

discrete: detached from others, separate

ascertain: to make sure of; to determine

certitude: freedom from doubt

discreet: judicious in one's conduct of speech, esp. with regard to maintaining silence about something of a delicate nature

hypocrite: a person who pretends to have beliefs that she does not

criterion: a standard of judgment or criticism

CHRON: TIME

synchronize: to occur at the same time or agree in time

chronology: the sequential order in which past events occurred

anachronism: an obsolete or archaic form

chronic: constant, habitual

chronometer: a timepiece with a mechanism to adjust for accuracy

CIRCU: AROUND, ON ALL SIDES

circumference: the outer boundary of a circular area

circumstances: the existing conditions or state of affairs surrounding and affecting an agent

circuit: the act of going or moving around

circumambulate: to walk about or around

circuitous: roundabout, indirect

CIS: TO CUT

scissors: cutting instrument for paper

precise: definitely stated or defined

exorcise: to seek to expel an evil spirit by ceremony

incision: a cut, gash, or notch

incisive: penetrating, cutting

CLA/CLO/CLU: SHUT, CLOSE

conclude: to bring to an end; finish; to terminate

claustrophobia: an abnormal fear of enclosed places

disclose: to make known, reveal, or uncover

exclusive: not admitting of something else; shutting out others

cloister: a courtyard bordered with covered walks, esp. in a religious institution

preclude: to prevent the presence, existence, or occurrence of

CLAIM/CLAM: TO SHOUT; TO CRY OUT

exclaim: to cry out or speak suddenly and vehemently

proclaim: to announce or declare in an official way

clamor: a loud uproar

disclaim: to deny interest in or connection with

reclaim: to claim or demand the return of a right or possession

CLI: TO LEAN TOWARD

decline: to cause to slope or incline downward

recline: to lean back

climax: the most intense point in the development of something

proclivity: inclination, bias

disinclination: aversion, distaste

CO/COL/COM/CON: WITH, TOGETHER

connect: to bind or fasten together

coerce: to compel by force, intimidation, or authority

compatible: capable of existing together in harmony

collide: to strike one another with a forceful impact

collaborate: to work with another, cooperate

conciliate: to placate, win over

commensurate: suitable in measure, proportionate

COUR/CUR: RUNNING; A COURSE

recur: to happen again

curriculum: the regular course of study

courier: a messenger traveling in haste who bears news

excursion: a short journey or trip

cursive: handwriting in flowing strokes with the letters joined together

concur: to accord in opinion; agree

incursion: a hostile entrance into a place, esp. suddenly

cursory: going rapidly over something; hasty; superficial

CRE/CRESC/CRET: TO GROW

creation: the act of producing or causing to exist

increase: to make greater in any respect

increment: something added or gained; an addition or increase

accretion: an increase by natural growth

CRED: TO BELIEVE; TO TRUST

incredible: unbelievable

credentials: anything that provides the basis for belief

credo: any formula of belief

credulity: willingness to believe or trust too readily

credit: trustworthiness

CRYP: HIDDEN

crypt: a subterranean chamber or vault

apocryphal: of doubtful authorship or authenticity

cryptology: the science of interpreting secret writings, codes, ciphers, and the like

cryptography: procedures of making and using secret writing

CUB/CUMB: TO LIE DOWN

cubicle: any small space or compartment that is partitioned off

succumb: to give away to superior force; yield

incubate: to sit upon for the purpose of hatching

incumbent: holding an indicated position

recumbent: lying down; reclining; leaning

CULP: BLAME

culprit: a person guilty of an offense

culpable: deserving blame or censure

inculpate: to charge with fault

mea culpa: through my fault; my fault

DAC/DOC: TO TEACH

doctor: someone licensed to practice medicine; a learned person

doctrine: a particular principle advocated, as of a government or religion

indoctrinate: to imbue a person with learning

docile: easily managed or handled; tractable

didactic: intended for instruction

DE: AWAY, OFF, DOWN, COMPLETELY, REVERSAL

descend: to move from a higher to a lower place

decipher: to make out the meaning; to interpret

defile: to make foul, dirty, or unclean

defame: to attack the good name or reputation of

deferential: respectful; to yield to judgment

delineate: to trace the outline of; sketch or trace in outline

DEM: PEOPLE

democracy: government by the people

epidemic: affecting at the same time a large number of people, and spreading from person to person

endemic: peculiar to a particular people or locality

pandemic: general, universal

demographics: vital and social statistics of populations

DI/DIA: APART, THROUGH

dialogue: conversation between two or more persons

diagnose: to determine the identity of something from the symptoms

dilate: to make wider or larger; to cause to expand

dilatory: inclined to delay or procrastinate

dichotomy: division into two parts, kinds, etc.

DIC/DICT/DIT: TO SAY; TO TELL; TO USE WORDS

dictionary: a book containing a selection of the words of a language

predict: to tell in advance

verdict: judgment, decree

interdict: to forbid; prohibit

DIGN: WORTH

dignity: nobility or elevation of character; worthiness

dignitary: a person who holds a high rank or office

deign: to think fit or in accordance with one's dignity

condign: well deserved; fitting; adequate

disdain: to look upon or treat with contempt

DIS/DIF: AWAY FROM, APART, REVERSAL, NOT

disperse: to drive or send off in various directions

disseminate: to scatter or spread widely; promulgate

dissipate: to scatter wastefully

dissuade: to deter by advice or persuasion

diffuse: to pour out and spread, as in a fluid

DOG/DOX: OPINION

orthodox: sound or correct in opinion or doctrine

paradox: an opinion or statement contrary to accepted opinion

dogma: a system of tenets, as of a church

DOL: SUFFER, PAIN

condolence: expression of sympathy with one who is suffering

indolence: a state of being lazy or slothful

doleful: sorrowful, mournful

dolorous: full of pain or sorrow, grievous

DON/DOT/DOW: TO GIVE

donate: to present as a gift or contribution

pardon: kind indulgence, forgiveness

antidote: something that prevents or counteracts ill effects

anecdote: a short narrative about an interesting event

endow: to provide with a permanent fund

DUB: DOUBT

dubious: doubtful

dubiety: doubtfulness

indubitable: unquestionable

DUC/DUCT: TO LEAD

abduct: to carry off or lead away

conduct: personal behavior, way of acting

conducive: contributive, helpful

induce: to lead or move by influence

induct: to install in a position with formal ceremonies

produce: to bring into existence; give cause to

DUR: HARD

endure: to hold out against; to sustain without yielding

durable: able to resist decay

duress: compulsion by threat, coercion

dour: sullen, gloomy

duration: the length of time something exists

DYS: FAULTY, ABNORMAL

dystrophy: faulty or inadequate nutrition or development

dyspepsia: impaired digestion

dyslexia: an impairment of the ability to read due to a brain defect

dysfunctional: poorly functioning

E/EF/EX: OUT, OUT OF, FROM, FORMER, COMPLETELY

evade: to escape from, avoid

exclude: to shut out; to leave out

extricate: to disentangle, release

exonerate: to free or declare free from blame

expire: to come to an end, cease to be valid

efface: to rub or wipe out; surpass, eclipse

EPI: UPON

epidemic: affecting at the same time a large number of people, and spreading from person to person

epilogue: a concluding part added to a literary work

epidermis: the outer layer of the skin

epigram: a witty or pointed saying tersely expressed

epithet: a word or phrase, used invectively as a term of abuse

EQU: EQUAL, EVEN

equation: the act of making equal

adequate: equal to the requirement or occasion

equidistant: equally distant

iniquity: gross injustice; wickedness

ERR: TO WANDER

err: to go astray in thought or belief, to be mistaken

error: a deviation from accuracy or correctness

erratic: deviating from the proper or usual course in conduct

ESCE: BECOMING

adolescent: between childhood and adulthood

obsolescent: becoming obsolete

incandescent: glowing with heat, shining

convalescent: recovering from illness

reminiscent: reminding or suggestive of

EU: GOOD, WELL

euphemism: pleasant-sounding term for something unpleasant

eulogy: speech or writing in praise or commendation

eugenics: improvement of qualities of race by control of inherited characteristics

euthanasia: killing a person painlessly, usually one who has an incurable, painful disease

euphony: pleasantness of sound

EXTRA: OUTSIDE, BEYOND

extraordinary: beyond the ordinary

extract: to take out, obtain against a person's will

extradite: to hand over (person accused of crime) to state where crime was committed

extrasensory: derived by means other than known senses

extrapolate: to estimate (unknown facts or values) from known data

FAB/FAM: SPEAK

fable: fictional tale, esp. legendary

affable: friendly, courteous

ineffable: too great for description in words; that which must not be uttered

famous: well known, celebrated

defame: attack good name of

FAC/FIC/FIG/FAIT/FEIT/FY: TO DO; TO MAKE

factory: building for manufacture of goods

faction: small dissenting group within larger one, esp. in politics

deficient: incomplete or insufficient

prolific: producing many offspring or much output

configuration: manner of arrangement, shape

ratify: to confirm or accept by formal consent

effigy: sculpture or model of person

counterfeit: imitation, forgery

FER: TO BRING; TO CARRY; TO BEAR

offer: to present for acceptance, refusal, or consideration

confer: to grant, bestow

referendum: to vote on political question open to the entire electorate

proffer: to offer

proliferate: to reproduce; produce rapidly

FERV: TO BOIL; TO BUBBLE

fervor: passion, zeal

fervid: ardent, intense

effervescent: with the quality of giving off bubbles of gas

FID: FAITH, TRUST

confide: to entrust with a secret

affidavit: written statement on oath

fidelity: faithfulness, loyalty

fiduciary: of a trust; held or given in trust

infidel: disbeliever in the supposed true religion

FIN: END

final: at the end; coming last

confine: to keep or restrict within certain limits; imprison

definitive: decisive, unconditional, final

infinite: boundless; endless

infinitesimal: infinitely or very small

FLAG/FLAM: TO BURN

flammable: easily set on fire

flambeau: a lighted torch

flagrant: blatant, scandalous

conflagration: a large destructive fire

FLECT/FLEX: TO BEND

deflect: to bend or turn aside from a purpose

flexible: able to bend without breaking

inflect: to change or vary pitch of

reflect: to throw back

genuflect: to bend knee, esp. in worship

FLU/FLUX: TO FLOW

fluid: substance, esp. gas or liquid, capable of flowing freely

fluctuation: something that varies, rising and falling

effluence: flowing out of (light, electricity, etc.)

confluence: merging into one

mellifluous: pleasing, musical

FORE: BEFORE

foresight: care or provision for future

foreshadow: be warning or indication of (future event)

forestall: to prevent by advance action

forthright: straightforward, outspoken, decisive

FORT: CHANCE

fortune: chance or luck in human affairs

fortunate: lucky, auspicious

fortuitous: happening by luck

FORT: STRENGTH

fortify: to provide with fortifications; strengthen

fortissimo: very loud

forte: strong point; something a person does well

FRA/FRAC/FRAG/FRING: TO BREAK

fracture: breakage, esp. of a bone

fragment: a part broken off

fractious: irritable, peevish

refractory: stubborn, unmanageable, rebellious

infringe: to break or violate (law, etc.)

FUS: TO POUR

profuse: lavish, extravagant, copious

fusillade: continuous discharge of firearms or outburst of criticism

suffuse: to spread throughout or over from within

diffuse: to spread widely or thinly

infusion: infusing; liquid extract so obtained

GEN: BIRTH, CREATION, RACE, KIND

generous: giving or given freely

genetics: study of heredity and variation among animals and plants

gender: classification roughly corresponding to the two sexes and sexlessness

carcinogenic: producing cancer

congenital: existing or as such from birth

progeny: offspring, descendants

miscegenation: interbreeding of races

GN/GNO: KNOW

agnostic: person who believes that the existence of God is not provable

ignore: to refuse to take notice of

ignoramus: a person lacking knowledge, uninformed

recognize: to identify as already known

incognito: with one's name or identity concealed

prognosis: to forecast, especially of disease

diagnose: to make an identification of disease or fault from symptoms

GRAD/GRESS: TO STEP

progress: forward movement

aggressive: given to hostile act or feeling

degrade: to humiliate, dishonor, reduce to lower rank

digress: to depart from main subject

egress: going out; way out

regress: to move backward, revert to an earlier state

GRAT: PLEASING

grateful: thankful

ingratiate: to bring oneself into favor

gratuity: money given for good service

gracious: kindly, esp. to inferiors; merciful

HER/HES: TO STICK

coherent: logically consistent; having waves in phase and of one wavelength

adhesive: tending to remain in memory; sticky; an adhesive substance

inherent: involved in the constitution or essential character of something

adherent: able to adhere; believer or advocate of a particular thing

heredity: the qualities genetically derived from one's ancestors and the transmission of those qualities

(H)ETERO: DIFFERENT

heterosexual: of or pertaining to sexual orientation toward members of the opposite sex; relating to different sexes

heterogeneous: of other origin: not originating in the body

heterodox: different from acknowledged standard; holding unorthodox opinions or doctrines

(H)OM: SAME

homogeneous: of the same or a similar kind of nature; of uniform structure of composition throughout

homonym: one of two or more words spelled and pronounced alike but different in meaning

homosexual: of, relating to, or exhibiting sexual desire toward a member of one's own sex

anomaly: deviation from the common rule

homeostasis: a relatively stable state of equilibrium

HYPER: OVER, EXCESSIVE

hyperactive: excessively active

hyperbole: purposeful exaggeration for effect

hyperglycemia: an abnormally high concentration of sugar in the blood

HYPO: UNDER, BENEATH, LESS THAN

hypodermic: relating to the parts beneath the skin

hypochondriac: one affected by extreme depression of mind or spirits often centered on imaginary physical ailments

hypocritical: affecting virtues or qualities one does not have

hypothesis: assumption subject to proof

IDIO: ONE'S OWN

idiot: an utterly stupid person

idiom: a language, dialect, or style of speaking particular to a people

idiosyncrasy: peculiarity of temperament; eccentricity

IM/IN/EM/EN: IN, INTO

embrace: to clasp in the arms; to include or contain

enclose: to close in on all sides

intrinsic: belonging to a thing by its very nature

influx: the act of flowing in; inflow

implicit: not expressly stated; implied

incarnate: given a bodily, esp. a human, form

indigenous: native; innate, natural

IM/IN: NOT, WITHOUT

inactive: not active

innocuous: not harmful or injurious

indolence: showing a disposition to avoid exertion; slothful

impartial: not partial or biased; just

indigent: deficient in what is requisite

INTER: BETWEEN, AMONG

interstate: connecting or jointly involving states

interim: a temporary or provisional arrangement; meantime

interloper: one who intrudes in the domain of others

intermittent: stopping or ceasing for a time

intersperse: to scatter here and there

JECT: TO THROW; TO THROW DOWN

inject: to place (quality, etc.) where needed in something

dejected: sad, depressed

eject: to throw out, expel

conjecture: formation of opinion on incomplete information

abject: utterly hopeless, humiliating, or wretched

JOIN/JUNCT: TO MEET; TO JOIN

junction: the act of joining; combining

adjoin: to be next to and joined with

subjugate: to conquer

rejoinder: to reply, retort

junta: (usually military) clique taking power after a coup d'état

JUR: TO SWEAR

perjury: willful lying while on oath

abjure: to renounce on oath

adjure: to beg or command

LAV/LUT/LUV: TO WASH

lavatory: a room with equipment for washing hands and face

dilute: to make thinner or weaker by the addition of water

pollute: to make foul or unclean

deluge: a great flood of water

antediluvian: before the biblical flood; extremely old

ablution: act of cleansing

LECT/LEG: TO SELECT; TO CHOOSE

collect: to gather together or assemble

elect: to choose; to decide

select: to choose with care

eclectic: selecting ideas, etc. from various sources

predilection: preference, liking

LEV: LIFT, LIGHT, RISE

relieve: to mitigate; to free from a burden

alleviate: to make easier to endure, lessen

relevant: bearing on or pertinent to information at hand

levee: embankment against river flooding

levitate: to rise in the air or cause to rise

levity: humor, frivolity, gaiety

LOC/LOG/LOQU: WORD, SPEECH

dialogue: conversation, esp. in a literary work

elocution: art of clear and expressive speaking

prologue: introduction to poem, play, etc.

eulogy: speech or writing in praise of someone

colloquial: of ordinary or familiar conversation

grandiloquent: pompous or inflated in language

loquacious: talkative

LUC/LUM/LUS: LIGHT

illustrate: to make intelligible with examples or analogies

illuminate: to supply or brighten with light

illustrious: highly distinguished

translucent: permitting light to pass through

lackluster: lacking brilliance or radiance

lucid: easily understood, intelligible

luminous: bright, brilliant, glowing

LUD/LUS: TO PLAY

allude: to refer casually or indirectly

illusion: something that deceives by producing a false impression of reality

ludicrous: ridiculous, laughable

delude: to mislead the mind or judgment of, deceive

elude: to avoid capture or escape defection by

prelude: a preliminary to an action, event, etc.

MAG/MAJ/MAX: BIG

magnify: to increase the apparent size of

magnitude: greatness of size, extent, or dimensions

maximum: the highest amount, value, or degree attained

magnate: a powerful or influential person

magnanimous: generous in forgiving an insult or injury

maxim: an expression of general truth or principle

MAL/MALE: BAD, ILL, EVIL, WRONG

malfunction: failure to function properly

malicious: full of or showing malice

malign: to speak harmful untruths about, to slander

malady: a disorder or disease of the body

maladroit: clumsy, tactless

malapropism: humorous misuse of a word

malfeasance: misconduct or wrongdoing often committed by a public official

malediction: a curse

MAN: HAND

manual: operated by hand

manufacture: to make by hand or machinery

emancipate: to free from bondage

manifest: readily perceived by the eye or the understanding

mandate: an authoritative order or command

MIN: SMALL

minute: a unit of time equal to one-60th of an hour, or 60 seconds

minutiae: small or trivial details

miniature: a copy or model that represents something in greatly reduced size

diminish: to lessen

diminution: the act or process of diminishing

MIN: TO PROJECT; TO HANG OVER

eminent: towering above others; projecting

imminent: about to occur; impending

prominent: projecting outward

preeminent: superior to or notable above all others

minatory: menacing, threatening

MIS/MIT: TO SEND

transmit: to send from one person, thing, or place to another

emissary: a messenger or agent sent to represent the interests of another

intermittent: stopping and starting at intervals

remit: to send money

remission: a lessening of intensity or degree

MISC: MIXED

miscellaneous: made up of a variety of parts or ingredients

miscegenation: the interbreeding of races, esp. marriage between white and nonwhite persons

promiscuous: consisting of diverse and unrelated parts or individuals

MON/MONIT: TO REMIND; TO WARN

monument: a structure, such as a building, tower, or sculpture, erected as a memorial

monitor: one that admonishes, cautions, or reminds

summon: to call together; convene

admonish: to counsel against something; caution

remonstrate: to say or plead in protect, objection, or reproof

premonition: forewarning, presentiment

MORPH: SHAPE

amorphous: without definite form; lacking a specific shape

metamorphosis: a transformation, as by magic or sorcery

anthropomorphism: attribution of human characteristics to inanimate objects, animals, or natural phenomena

MORT/MOR: DEATH

immortal: not subject to death

morbid: susceptible to preoccupation with unwholesome matters

moribund: dying, decaying

MUT: CHANGE

commute: to substitute; exchange; interchange
mutation: the process of being changed
transmutation: the act of changing from one form into another
permutation: a complete change; transformation
immutable: unchangeable, invariable

NAT/NAS/NAI: TO BE BORN

natural: present due to nature, not to artificial or man-made means
native: belonging to one by nature; inborn; innate
naive: lacking worldliness and sophistication; artless
cognate: related by blood; having a common ancestor
renaissance: rebirth, esp. referring to culture
nascent: starting to develop

NIC/NOC/NOX: HARM

innocent: uncorrupted by evil, malice, or wrongdoing
noxious: injurious or harmful to health or morals
obnoxious: highly disagreeable or offensive
innocuous: having no adverse effect; harmless

NOM: RULE, ORDER

astronomy: the scientific study of the universe beyond the earth
economy: the careful or thrifty use of resources, as of income, materials, or labor
gastronomy: the art or science of good eating
taxonomy: the science, laws, or principles of classification
autonomy: independence, self-governance

NOM/NYM/NOUN/NOWN: NAME

synonym: a word having a meaning similar to that of another word of the same language
anonymous: having an unknown or unacknowledged name
nominal: existing in name only; negligible
nominate: to propose by name as a candidate
nomenclature: a system of names; systematic naming
acronym: a word formed from the initial letters of a name

NOUNC/NUNC: TO ANNOUNCE

announce: to proclaim
pronounce: to articulate
renounce: to give up, especially by formal announcement

NOV/NEO/NOU: NEW

novice: a person new to any field or activity
renovate: to restore to an earlier condition
innovate: to begin or introduce something new
neologism: a newly coined word, phrase, or expression
neophyte: a recent convert
nouveau riche: one who has lately become rich

OB/OC/OF/OP: TOWARD, TO, AGAINST, OVER

obese: extremely fat, corpulent
obstinate: stubbornly adhering to an idea, inflexible
obstruct: to block or fill with obstacles
oblique: having a slanting or sloping direction
obstreperous: noisily defiant, unruly
obtuse: not sharp, pointed, or acute in any form
obfuscate: to render indistinct or dim; darken
obsequious: overly submissive

OMNI: ALL

omnibus: an anthology of the works of one author or of writings on related subjects
omnipresent: everywhere at one time
omnipotent: all powerful
omniscient: having infinite knowledge

PAC/PEAC: PEACE

appease: to bring peace to
pacify: to ease the anger or agitation of
pacifier: something or someone that eases the anger or agitation of
pact: a formal agreement, as between nations

PAN: ALL, EVERYONE

panorama: an unobstructed and wide view of an extensive area
panegyric: formal or elaborate praise at an assembly
panoply: a wide-ranging and impressive array or display
pantheon: a public building containing tombs or memorials of the illustrious dead of a nation
pandemic: widespread, general, universal

PAR: EQUAL

par: an equality in value or standing

parity: equally, as in amount, status, or character

apartheid: any system or caste that separates people according to race, etc.

disparage: to belittle, speak disrespectfully about

disparate: essentially different

PARA: NEXT TO, BESIDE

parallel: extending in the same direction

parasite: an organism that lives on or within a plant or animal of another species, from which it obtains nutrients

parody: to imitate for purposes of satire

parable: a short, allegorical story designed to illustrate a moral lesson or religious principle

paragon: a model of excellence

paranoid: suffering from a baseless distrust of others

PAS/PAT/ PATH: FEELING, SUFFERING, DISEASE

sympathy: harmony or agreement in feeling

empathy: the identification with the feelings or thoughts of others

compassion: a feeling of deep sympathy for someone struck by misfortune, accompanied by a desire to alleviate suffering

dispassionate: devoid of personal feeling or bias

impassive: showing or feeling no emotion

sociopath: a person whose behavior is antisocial and who lacks a sense of moral responsibility

pathogenic: causing disease

PAU/PO/POV/PU: FEW, LITTLE, POOR

poverty: the condition of being poor

paucity: smallness of quantity; scarcity; scantiness

pauper: a person without any personal means of support

impoverish: to deplete

pusillanimous: lacking courage or resolution

puerile: childish, immature

PED: CHILD, EDUCATION

pedagogue: a teacher

pediatrician: a doctor who primarily has children as patients

pedant: one who displays learning ostentatiously

encyclopedia: book or set of books containing articles on various topics, covering all branches of knowledge or of one particular subject

PED/POD: FOOT

pedal: a foot-operated lever or part used to control

pedestrian: a person who travels on foot

expedite: to speed up the progress of

impede: to retard progress by means of obstacles or hindrances

podium: a small platform for an orchestra conductor, speaker, etc.

antipodes: places diametrically opposite each other on the globe

PEN/PUN: TO PAY; TO COMPENSATE

penal: of or pertaining to punishment, as for crimes

penalty: a punishment imposed for a violation of law or rule

punitive: serving for, concerned with, or inflicting punishment

penance: a punishment undergone to express regret for a sin

penitent: contrite

PEND/PENS: TO HANG; TO WEIGHT; TO PAY

depend: to rely; to place trust in

stipend: a periodic payment; fixed or regular pay

compensate: to counterbalance, offset

indispensable: absolutely necessary, essential, or requisite

appendix: supplementary material at the end of a text

appendage: a limb or other subsidiary part that diverges from the central structure

PER: COMPLETELY

persistent: lasting or enduring tenaciously

perforate: to make a way through or into something

perplex: to cause to be puzzled or bewildered over what is not understood

peruse: to read with thoroughness or care

perfunctory: performed merely as routine duty

pertinacious: resolute

perspicacious: shrewd, astute

PERI: AROUND

perimeter: the border or outer boundary of a two-dimensional figure

periscope: an optical instrument for seeing objects in an obstructed field of vision

peripatetic: walking or traveling about; itinerant

PET/PIT: TO GO; TO SEEK; TO STRIVE

appetite: a desire for food or drink

compete: to strive to outdo another for acknowledgment

petition: a formally drawn request soliciting some benefit

centripetal: moving toward the center

impetuous: characterized by sudden or rash action or emotion

petulant: showing sudden irritation, esp. over some annoyance

PHIL: LOVE

philosophy: the rational investigation of the truths and principles of being, knowledge, or conduct

philatelist: one who loves or collects postage stamps

philology: the study of literary texts to establish their authenticity and determine their meaning

bibliophile: one who loves or collects books

PLAC/PLAIS: TO PLEASE

placid: pleasantly calm or peaceful

placebo: a substance with no pharmacological effect which acts to placate a patient who believes it to be a medicine

implacable: unable to be pleased

complacent: self-satisfied, unconcerned

complaisant: inclined or disposed to please

PLE: TO FILL

complete: having all parts or elements

deplete: to decrease seriously or exhaust the supply of

supplement: something added to supply a deficiency

implement: an instrument, tool, or utensil for accomplishing work

replete: abundantly supplied

plethora: excess, overabundance

PLEX/PLIC/PLY: TO FOLD, TWIST, TANGLE, OR BEND

complex: composed of many interconnected parts

replica: any close copy or reproduction

implicit: not expressly stated, implied

implicate: to show to be involved, usually in an incriminating manner

duplicity: deceitfulness in speech or conduct, double-dealing

supplicate: to make humble and earnest entreaty

PON/POS/POUND: TO PUT; TO PLACE

component: a constituent part, elemental ingredient

expose: to lay open to danger, attack, or harm

expound: to set forth in detail

juxtapose: to place close together or side by side, esp. for contrast

repository: a receptacle or place where things are deposited

PORT: TO CARRY

import: to bring in from a foreign country

export: to transmit abroad

portable: easily carried

deportment: conduct, behavior

disport: to divert or amuse oneself

importune: to urge or press with excessive persistence

POST: AFTER

posthumous: after death

posterior: situated at the rear

posterity: succeeding in future generations collectively

post facto: after the fact

PRE: BEFORE

precarious: dependent on circumstances beyond one's control

precocious: unusually advanced or mature in mental development or talent

premonition: a feeling of anticipation over a future event

presentiment: foreboding

precedent: an act that serves as an example for subsequent situations

precept: a commandment given as a rule of action or conduct

PREHEND/PRISE: TO TAKE; TO GET; TO SEIZE

surprise: to strike with an unexpected feeling of wonder or astonishment

enterprise: a project undertaken

reprehensible: deserving rebuke or censure

comprise: to include or contain

reprisals: retaliation against an enemy

apprehend: to take into custody

PRO: MUCH, FOR, A LOT

prolific: highly fruitful

profuse: spending or giving freely

prodigal: wastefully or recklessly extravagant

prodigious: extraordinary in size, amount, or extent

proselytize: to convert or attempt to recruit

propound: to set forth for consideration

provident: having or showing foresight

PROB: TO PROVE; TO TEST

probe: to search or examine thoroughly

approbation: praise, consideration

opprobrium: the disgrace incurred by shameful conduct

reprobate: a depraved or wicked person

problematic: questionable

probity: honesty, high-mindedness

PUG: TO FIGHT

pugnacious: to quarrel or fight readily

impugn: to challenge as false

repugnant: objectionable or offensive

pugilist: a fighter or boxer

PUNC/PUNG/POIGN: TO POINT; TO PRICK

point: a sharp or tapering end

puncture: the act of piercing

pungent: caustic or sharply expressive

compunction: a feeling of uneasiness for doing wrong

punctilious: strict or exact in the observance of formalities

expunge: to erase, eliminate completely

QUE/QUIS: TO SEEK

acquire: to come into possession of

exquisite: of special beauty or charm

conquest: vanquishment

inquisitive: given to research, eager for knowledge

query: a question, inquiry

querulous: full of complaints

perquisite: a gratuity, tip

QUI: QUIET

quiet: making little or no sound

disquiet: lack of calm or peace

tranquil: free from commotion or tumult

acquiesce: to comply, give in

quiescence: the condition of being at rest, still, inactive

RID/RIS: TO LAUGH

riddle: a conundrum

derision: the act of mockery

risible: causing laughter

ROG: TO ASK

interrogate: to ask questions of, esp. formally

arrogant: making claims to superior importance or rights

abrogate: to abolish by formal means

surrogate: a person appointed to act for another

derogatory: belittling, disparaging

arrogate: to claim unwarrantably or presumptuously

SACR/SANCT/SECR: SACRED

sacred: devoted or dedicated to a deity or religious purpose

sacrifice: the offering of some living or inanimate thing to a deity in homage

sanctify: to make holy

sanction: authoritative permission or approval

execrable: abominable

sacrament: something regarded as possessing sacred character

sacrilege: the violation of anything sacred

SAL/SIL/SAULT/SULT: TO LEAP; TO JUMP

insult: to treat with contemptuous rudeness

assault: a sudden or violent attack

somersault: to roll the body end over end, making a complete revolution

salient: prominent or conspicuous

resilient: able to spring back to an original form after compression

insolent: boldly rude or disrespectful

exult: to show or feel triumphant joy

desultory: at random, unmethodical

SCI: TO KNOW

conscious: aware of one's own existence

conscience: the inner sense of what is right or wrong, impelling one toward right action

unconscionable: unscrupulous

omniscient: knowing everything

prescient: having knowledge of things before they happen

SCRIBE/SCRIP: TO WRITE

scribble: to write hastily or carelessly
describe: to tell or depict in words
script: handwriting
postscript: any addition or supplement
proscribe: to condemn as harmful or odious
ascribe: to credit or assign, as to a cause or course
conscription: draft
transcript: a written or typed copy
circumscribe: to draw a line around

SE: APART

select: to choose in preference to another
separate: to keep apart, divide
seduce: to lead astray
segregate: to separate or set apart from others
secede: to withdraw formally from an association
sequester: to remove or withdraw into solitude or retirement
sedition: incitement of discontent or rebellion against a government

SEC/SEQU: TO FOLLOW

second: next after the first
prosecute: to seek to enforce by legal process
sequence: the following of one thing after another
obsequious: fawning
non sequitur: an inference or a conclusion that does not follow from the premises

SED/SESS/SID: TO SIT; TO BE STILL; TO PLAN; TO PLOT

preside: to exercise management or control
resident: a person who lives in a place
sediment: the matter that settles to the bottom of a liquid
dissident: disagreeing, as in opinion or attitude
residual: remaining, leftover
subsidiary: serving to assist or supplement
insidious: intended to entrap or beguile
assiduous: diligent, persistent, hardworking

SENS/SENT: TO FEEL; TO BE AWARE

sense: any of the faculties by which humans and animals perceive stimuli originating outside the body
sensory: of or pertaining to the senses or sensation
sentiment: an attitude or feeling toward something

presentiment: a feeling that something is about to happen
dissent: to differ in opinion, esp. from the majority
resent: to feel or show displeasure
sentinel: a person or thing that stands watch
insensate: without feeling or sensitivity

SOL: TO LOOSEN; TO FREE

dissolve: to make a solution of, as by mixing in a liquid
soluble: capable of being dissolved or liquefied
resolution: a formal expression of opinion or intention made
dissolution: the act or process of dissolving into parts or elements
dissolute: indifferent to moral restraints
absolution: forgiveness for wrongdoing

SPEC/SPIC/SPIT: TO LOOK; TO SEE

perspective: one's mental view of facts, ideas, and their interrelationships
speculation: the contemplation or consideration of some subject
suspicious: inclined to suspect
spectrum: a broad range of related things that form a continuous series
retrospective: contemplative of past situations
circumspect: watchful and discreet, cautious
perspicacious: having keen mental perception and understanding
conspicuous: easily seen or noticed; readily observable
specious: deceptively attractive

STA/STI: TO STAND; TO BE IN PLACE

static: of bodies or forces at rest or in equilibrium
destitute: without means of subsistence
obstinate: stubbornly adhering to a purpose, opinion, or course of action
constitute: to make up
stasis: the state of equilibrium or inactivity caused by opposing equal forces
apostasy: renunciation of an object of one's previous loyalty

SUA: SMOOTH

suave: smoothly agreeable or polite
persuade: to encourage; to convince

dissuade: to deter
assuage: to make less severe, ease, relieve

SUB/SUP: BELOW

submissive: inclined or ready to submit
subsidiary: serving to assist or supplement
subliminal: existing or operating below the threshold of confidence
subtle: thin, tenuous, or rarefied
subterfuge: an artifice or expedient used to evade a rule
supposition: the act of assuming

SUPER/SUR: ABOVE

surpass: to go beyond in amount, extent, or degree
superlative: the highest kind or order
supersede: to replace in power, as by another person or thing
supercilious: arrogant, haughty, condescending
superfluous: extra, more than necessary
surmount: to get over or across, to prevail
surveillance: a watch kept over someone or something

TAC/TIC: TO BE SILENT

reticent: disposed to be silent or not to speak freely
tacit: unspoken understanding
taciturn: uncommunicative

TAIN/TEN/TENT/TIN: TO HOLD

detain: to keep from proceeding
pertain: to have reference or relation
tenacious: holding fast
abstention: the act of refraining voluntarily
tenure: the holding or possessing of anything
tenable: capable of being held, maintained, or defended
sustenance: nourishment, means of livelihood
pertinacious: persistent, stubborn

TEND/TENS/TENT/TENU: TO STRETCH; TO THIN

tension: the act of stretching or straining
tentative: of the nature of, or done as a trial, attempt
tendentious: having a predisposition toward a point of view
distend: to expand by stretching
attenuate: to weaken or reduce in force
extenuating: making less serious by offering excuses
contentious: quarrelsome, disagreeable, belligerent

THEO: GOD

atheist: one who does not believe in a deity or divine system
theocracy: a form of government in which a deity is recognized as the supreme ruler
theology: the study of divine things and the divine faith
apotheosis: glorification, glorified ideal

TRACT: TO DRAG; TO PULL; TO DRAW

tractor: a powerful vehicle used to pull farm machinery
attract: to draw either by physical force or by an appeal to emotions or senses
contract: a legally binding document
detract: to take away from, esp. a positive thing
abstract: to draw or pull away, remove
tractable: easily managed or controlled
protract: to prolong, draw out, extend

TRANS: ACROSS

transaction: the act of carrying on or conduct to a conclusion or settlement
transparent: easily seen through, recognized, or detected
transition: a change from one way of being to another
transgress: to violate a law, command, or moral code
transcendent: going beyond ordinary limits
intransigent: refusing to agree or compromise

US/UT: TO USE

abuse: to use wrongly or improperly
usage: a customary way of doing something
usurp: to seize and hold
utilitarian: efficient, functional, useful

VEN/VENT: TO COME OR TO MOVE TOWARD

convene: to assemble for some public purpose
venturesome: showing a disposition to undertake risks
intervene: to come between disputing factions, mediate
contravene: to come into conflict with
adventitious: accidental

VER: TRUTH

verdict: any judgment or decision
veracious: habitually truthful

verity: truthfulness

verisimilitude: the appearance or semblance of truth

aver: to affirm, to declare to be true

VERD: GREEN

verdant: green with vegetation; inexperienced

verdure: fresh, rich vegetation

VERS/VERT: TO TURN

controversy: a public dispute involving a matter of opinion

revert: to return to a former habit

diverse: of a different kind, form, character

aversion: dislike

introvert: a person concerned primarily with inner thoughts and feelings

extrovert: an outgoing person

inadvertent: unintentional

covert: hidden, clandestine

avert: to turn away from

VI: LIFE

vivid: strikingly bright or intense

vicarious: performed, exercised, received, or suffered in place of another

viable: capable of living

vivacity: the quality of being lively, animated, spirited

joie de vivre: joy of life (French expression)

convivial: sociable

VID/VIS: TO SEE

evident: plain or clear to the sight or understanding

video: the elements of television pertaining to the transmission or reception of the image

adviser: one who gives counsel

vista: a view or prospect

VIL: BASE, MEAN

vilify: to slander, to defame

revile: to criticize with harsh language

vile: loathsome, unpleasant

VOC/VOK: TO CALL

vocabulary: the stock of words used by or known to a particular person or group

advocate: to support or urge by argument

equivocate: to use ambiguous or unclear expressions

vocation: a particular occupation

avocation: something one does in addition to a principle occupation

vociferous: crying out noisily

convoke: to call together

invoke: to call on a deity

VOL: TO WISH

voluntary: undertaken of one's own accord or by free choice

malevolent: characterized by or expressing bad will

benevolent: characterized by or expressing goodwill

volition: free choice, free will; act of choosing

VOR: TO EAT

voracious: having a great appetite

carnivorous: meat-eating

omnivorous: eating or absorbing everything

GRE Words in Context

The GRE tests the same kinds of words over and over again. Here you will find the most popular GRE words with their definitions in context to help you to remember them. If you see a word that's unfamiliar to you, take a moment to study the definition and, most importantly, reread the sentence with the word's definition in mind.

Remember: Learning vocabulary words in context is one of the best ways for your brain to retain the words' meanings. A broader vocabulary will serve you well on all four GRE Verbal question types and will also be extremely helpful in the Analytical Writing section.

ABATE: TO REDUCE IN AMOUNT, DEGREE, OR SEVERITY

As the hurricane's force ABATED, the winds dropped and the sea became calm.

ABSCOND: TO LEAVE SECRETLY

The patron ABSCONDED from the restaurant without paying his bill by sneaking out the back door.

ABSTAIN: TO CHOOSE NOT TO DO SOMETHING

She ABSTAINED from choosing a mouthwatering dessert from the tray.

ABYSS: AN EXTREMELY DEEP HOLE

The submarine dove into the ABYSS to chart the previously unseen depths.

ADULTERATE: TO MAKE IMPURE

The restaurateur made his ketchup last longer by ADULTERATING it with water.

ADVOCATE: TO SPEAK IN FAVOR OF

The vegetarian ADVOCATED a diet containing no meat.

AESTHETIC: CONCERNING THE APPRECIATION OF BEAUTY

Followers of the AESTHETIC Movement regarded the pursuit of beauty as the only true purpose of art.

AGGRANDIZE: TO INCREASE IN POWER, INFLUENCE, AND REPUTATION

The supervisor sought to AGGRANDIZE himself by claiming that the achievements of his staff were actually his own.

ALLEVIATE: TO MAKE MORE BEARABLE

Taking aspirin helps to ALLEVIATE a headache.

AMALGAMATE: TO COMBINE; TO MIX TOGETHER

Giant Industries AMALGAMATED with Mega Products to form Giant-Mega Products Incorporated.

AMBIGUOUS: DOUBTFUL OR UNCERTAIN; ABLE TO BE INTERPRETED SEVERAL WAYS

The directions she gave were so AMBIGUOUS that we disagreed on which way to turn.

AMELIORATE: TO MAKE BETTER; TO IMPROVE

The doctor was able to AMELIORATE the patient's suffering using painkillers.

ANACHRONISM: SOMETHING OUT OF PLACE IN TIME

The aged hippie used ANACHRONISTIC phrases like *groovy* and *far out* that had not been popular for years.

ANALOGOUS: SIMILAR OR ALIKE IN SOME WAY; EQUIVALENT TO

In a famous argument for the existence of God, the universe is ANALOGOUS to a mechanical timepiece, the creation of a divinely intelligent "clockmaker."

ANOMALY: DEVIATION FROM WHAT IS NORMAL

Albino animals may display too great an ANOMALY in their coloring to attract normally colored mates.

ANTAGONIZE: TO ANNOY OR PROVOKE TO ANGER

The child discovered that he could ANTAGONIZE the cat by pulling its tail.

ANTIPATHY: EXTREME DISLIKE

The ANTIPATHY between the French and the English regularly erupted into open warfare.

APATHY: LACK OF INTEREST OR EMOTION

The APATHY of voters is so great that less than half the people who are eligible to vote actually bother to do so.

ARBITRATE: TO JUDGE A DISPUTE BETWEEN TWO OPPOSING PARTIES

Since the couple could not come to agreement, a judge was forced to ARBITRATE their divorce proceedings.

ARCHAIC: ANCIENT, OLD-FASHIONED

Her ARCHAIC Commodore computer could not run the latest software.

ARDOR: INTENSE AND PASSIONATE FEELING

Bishop's ARDOR for landscape was evident when he passionately described the beauty of the scenic Hudson Valley.

ARTICULATE: ABLE TO SPEAK CLEARLY AND EXPRESSIVELY

She is such an ARTICULATE defender of labor that unions are among her strongest supporters.

ASSUAGE: TO MAKE SOMETHING UNPLEASANT LESS SEVERE

Serena used aspirin to ASSUAGE her pounding headache.

ATTENUATE: TO REDUCE IN FORCE OR DEGREE; TO WEAKEN

The Bill of Rights ATTENUATED the traditional power of government to change laws at will.

AUDACIOUS: FEARLESS AND DARING

Her AUDACIOUS nature allowed her to fulfill her dream of skydiving.

AUSTERE: SEVERE OR STERN IN APPEARANCE; UNDECORATED

The lack of decoration makes Zen temples seem AUSTERE to the untrained eye.

BANAL: PREDICTABLE, CLICHÉD, BORING

He used BANAL phrases like *Have a nice day* or *Another day, another dollar.*

BOLSTER: TO SUPPORT; TO PROP UP

The presence of giant footprints BOLSTERED the argument that Sasquatch was in the area.

BOMBASTIC: POMPOUS IN SPEECH AND MANNER

The dictator's speeches were mostly BOMBASTIC; his boasting and outrageous claims had no basis in fact.

CACOPHONY: HARSH, JARRING NOISE

The junior high orchestra created an almost unbearable CACOPHONY as they tried to tune their instruments.

CANDID: IMPARTIAL AND HONEST IN SPEECH

The observations of a child can be charming since they are CANDID and unpretentious.

CAPRICIOUS: CHANGING ONE'S MIND QUICKLY AND OFTEN

Queen Elizabeth I was quite CAPRICIOUS; her courtiers could never be sure which of their number would catch her fancy.

CASTIGATE: TO PUNISH OR CRITICIZE HARSHLY

Americans are amazed at how harshly the authorities in Singapore CASTIGATE perpetrators of what would be considered minor crimes in the United States.

CATALYST: SOMETHING THAT BRINGS ABOUT A CHANGE IN SOMETHING ELSE

The imposition of harsh taxes was the CATALYST that finally brought on the revolution.

CAUSTIC: BITING IN WIT

Dorothy Parker gained her reputation for CAUSTIC wit from her cutting, yet clever, insults.

CHAOS: GREAT DISORDER OR CONFUSION

In most religious traditions, God created an ordered universe from CHAOS.

CHAUVINIST: SOMEONE PREJUDICED IN FAVOR OF A GROUP TO WHICH HE OR SHE BELONGS

The attitude that men are inherently superior to women and therefore must be obeyed is common among male CHAUVINISTS.

CHICANERY: DECEPTION BY MEANS OF CRAFT OR GUILE

Dishonest used car salesmen often use CHICANERY to sell their beat-up old cars.

COGENT: CONVINCING AND WELL REASONED

Swayed by the COGENT argument of the defense, the jury had no choice but to acquit the defendant.

CONDONE: TO OVERLOOK, PARDON, OR DISREGARD

Some theorists believe that failing to prosecute minor crimes is the same as CONDONING an air of lawlessness.

CONVOLUTED: INTRICATE AND COMPLICATED

Although many people bought *A Brief History of Time*, few could follow its CONVOLUTED ideas and theories.

CORROBORATE: TO PROVIDE SUPPORTING EVIDENCE

Fingerprints CORROBORATED the witness's testimony that he saw the defendant in the victim's apartment.

CREDULOUS: TOO TRUSTING; GULLIBLE

Although some four-year-olds believe in the Easter Bunny, only the most CREDULOUS nine-year-olds also believe in him.

CRESCENDO: STEADILY INCREASING VOLUME OR FORCE

The CRESCENDO of tension became unbearable as Evel Knievel prepared to jump his motorcycle over the school buses.

DECORUM: APPROPRIATENESS OF BEHAVIOR OR CONDUCT; PROPRIETY

The countess complained that the vulgar peasants lacked the DECORUM appropriate for a visit to the palace.

DEFERENCE: RESPECT, COURTESY

The respectful young law clerk treated the Supreme Court justice with the utmost DEFERENCE.

DERIDE: TO SPEAK OF OR TREAT WITH CONTEMPT; TO MOCK

The awkward child was often DERIDED by his "cooler" peers.

DESICCATE: TO DRY OUT THOROUGHLY

After a few weeks of lying on the desert's baking sands, the cow's carcass became completely DESICCATED.

DESULTORY: JUMPING FROM ONE THING TO ANOTHER; DISCONNECTED

Diane had a DESULTORY academic record; she had changed majors 12 times in three years.

DIATRIBE: AN ABUSIVE, CONDEMNATORY SPEECH

The trucker bellowed a DIATRIBE at the driver who had cut him off.

DIFFIDENT: LACKING SELF-CONFIDENCE

Steve's DIFFIDENT manner during the job interview stemmed from his nervous nature and lack of experience in the field.

DILATE: TO MAKE LARGER; TO EXPAND

When you enter a darkened room, the pupils of your eyes DILATE to let in more light.

DILATORY: INTENDED TO DELAY

The congressman used DILATORY measures to delay the passage of the bill.

DILETTANTE: SOMEONE WITH AN AMATEURISH AND SUPERFICIAL INTEREST IN A TOPIC

Jerry's friends were such DILETTANTES that they seemed to have new jobs and hobbies every week.

DIRGE: A FUNERAL HYMN OR MOURNFUL SPEECH

Melville wrote the poem "A DIRGE for James McPherson" for the funeral of a Union general who was killed in 1864.

DISABUSE: TO SET RIGHT; TO FREE FROM ERROR

Galileo's observations DISABUSED scholars of the notion that the sun revolved around the earth.

DISCERN: TO PERCEIVE; TO RECOGNIZE

It is easy to DISCERN the difference between butter and butter-flavored topping.

DISPARATE: FUNDAMENTALLY DIFFERENT; ENTIRELY UNLIKE

Although the twins appear to be identical physically, their personalities are DISPARATE.

DISSEMBLE: TO PRESENT A FALSE APPEARANCE; TO DISGUISE ONE'S REAL INTENTIONS OR CHARACTER

The villain could DISSEMBLE to the police no longer—he admitted the deed and tore up the floor to reveal the body of the old man.

DISSONANCE: A HARSH AND DISAGREEABLE COMBINATION, OFTEN OF SOUNDS

Cognitive DISSONANCE is the inner conflict produced when long-standing beliefs are contradicted by new evidence.

DOGMA: A FIRMLY HELD OPINION, OFTEN A RELIGIOUS BELIEF

Linus's central DOGMA was that children who believed in the Great Pumpkin would be rewarded.

DOGMATIC: DICTATORIAL IN ONE'S OPINIONS

The dictator was DOGMATIC—he, and only he, was right.

DUPE: TO DECEIVE; A PERSON WHO IS EASILY DECEIVED

Bugs Bunny was able to DUPE Elmer Fudd by dressing up as a lady rabbit.

ECLECTIC: SELECTING FROM OR MADE UP FROM A VARIETY OF SOURCES

Budapest's architecture is an ECLECTIC mix of Eastern and Western styles.

EFFICACY: EFFECTIVENESS

The EFFICACY of penicillin was unsurpassed when it was first introduced; the drug completely eliminated almost all bacterial infections for which it was administered.

ELEGY: A SORROWFUL POEM OR SPEECH

Although Thomas Gray's "ELEGY Written in a Country Churchyard" is about death and loss, it urges its readers to endure this life and to trust in spirituality.

ELOQUENT: PERSUASIVE AND MOVING, ESPECIALLY IN SPEECH

The Gettysburg Address is moving not only because of its lofty sentiments but also because of its ELOQUENT words.

EMULATE: TO COPY; TO TRY TO EQUAL OR EXCEL

The graduate student sought to EMULATE his professor in every way, copying not only how she taught, but also how she conducted herself outside of class.

ENERVATE: TO REDUCE IN STRENGTH

The guerrillas hoped that a series of surprise attacks would ENERVATE the regular army.

ENGENDER: TO PRODUCE, CAUSE, OR BRING ABOUT

His fear and hatred of clowns was ENGENDERED when he witnessed the death of his father at the hands of a clown.

ENIGMA: A PUZZLE; A MYSTERY

Speaking in riddles and dressed in old robes, the artist gained a reputation as something of an ENIGMA.

ENUMERATE: TO COUNT, LIST, OR ITEMIZE

Moses returned from the mountain with tablets on which the commandments were ENUMERATED.

EPHEMERAL: LASTING A SHORT TIME

The lives of mayflies seem EPHEMERAL to us, since the flies' average life span is a matter of hours.

EQUIVOCATE: TO USE EXPRESSIONS OF DOUBLE MEANING IN ORDER TO MISLEAD

When faced with criticism of his policies, the politician EQUIVOCATED and left all parties thinking he agreed with them.

ERRATIC: WANDERING AND UNPREDICTABLE

The plot seemed predictable until it suddenly took a series of ERRATIC turns that surprised the audience.

ERUDITE: LEARNED, SCHOLARLY, BOOKISH

The annual meeting of philosophy professors was a gathering of the most ERUDITE, well-published individuals in the field.

ESOTERIC: KNOWN OR UNDERSTOOD BY ONLY A FEW

Only a handful of experts are knowledgeable about the ESOTERIC world of particle physics.

ESTIMABLE: ADMIRABLE

Most people consider it ESTIMABLE that Mother Teresa spent her life helping the poor of India.

EULOGY: SPEECH IN PRAISE OF SOMEONE

His best friend gave the EULOGY, outlining his many achievements and talents.

EUPHEMISM: USE OF AN INOFFENSIVE WORD OR PHRASE IN PLACE OF A MORE DISTASTEFUL ONE

The funeral director preferred to use the EUPHEMISM *sleeping* instead of the word *dead*.

EXACERBATE: TO MAKE WORSE

It is unwise to take aspirin to try to relieve heartburn; instead of providing relief, the drug will only EXACERBATE the problem.

EXCULPATE: TO CLEAR FROM BLAME; PROVE INNOCENT

The adversarial legal system is intended to convict those who are guilty and to EXCULPATE those who are innocent.

EXIGENT: URGENT; REQUIRING IMMEDIATE ACTION

The patient was losing blood so rapidly that it was EXIGENT to stop the source of the bleeding.

EXONERATE: TO CLEAR OF BLAME

The fugitive was EXONERATED when another criminal confessed to committing the crime.

EXPLICIT: CLEARLY STATED OR SHOWN; FORTHRIGHT IN EXPRESSION

The owners of the house left a list of EXPLICIT instructions detailing their house sitters' duties, including a schedule for watering the house plants.

FANATICAL: ACTING EXCESSIVELY ENTHUSIASTIC; FILLED WITH EXTREME, UNQUESTIONED DEVOTION

The stormtroopers were FANATICAL in their devotion to the Emperor, readily sacrificing their lives for him.

FAWN: TO GROVEL

The understudy FAWNED over the director in hopes of being cast in the part on a permanent basis.

FERVID: INTENSELY EMOTIONAL; FEVERISH

The fans of Maria Callas were unusually FERVID, doing anything to catch a glimpse of the great opera singer.

FLORID: EXCESSIVELY DECORATED OR EMBELLISHED

The palace had been decorated in an excessively FLORID style; every surface had been carved and gilded.

FOMENT: TO AROUSE OR INCITE

The protesters tried to FOMENT feeling against the war through their speeches and demonstrations.

FRUGALITY: A TENDENCY TO BE THRIFTY OR CHEAP

Scrooge McDuck's FRUGALITY was so great that he accumulated enough wealth to fill a giant storehouse with money.

GARRULOUS: TENDING TO TALK A LOT

The GARRULOUS parakeet distracted its owner with its continuous talking.

GREGARIOUS: OUTGOING, SOCIABLE

She was so GREGARIOUS that when she found herself alone she felt quite sad.

GUILE: DECEIT OR TRICKERY

Since he was not fast enough to catch the roadrunner on foot, the coyote resorted to GUILE in an effort to trap his enemy.

GULLIBLE: EASILY DECEIVED

The con man pretended to be a bank officer so as to fool GULLIBLE bank customers into giving him their account information.

HOMOGENOUS: OF A SIMILAR KIND

The class was fairly HOMOGENOUS, since almost all of the students were senior journalism majors.

ICONOCLAST: ONE WHO OPPOSES ESTABLISHED BELIEFS, CUSTOMS, AND INSTITUTIONS

His lack of regard for traditional beliefs soon established him as an ICONOCLAST.

IMPERTURBABLE: NOT CAPABLE OF BEING DISTURBED

The counselor had so much experience dealing with distraught children that she seemed IMPERTURBABLE, even when faced with the wildest tantrums.

IMPERVIOUS: IMPOSSIBLE TO PENETRATE; INCAPABLE OF BEING AFFECTED

A good raincoat will be IMPERVIOUS to moisture.

IMPETUOUS: QUICK TO ACT WITHOUT THINKING

It is not good for an investment broker to be IMPETUOUS, since much thought should be given to all the possible options.

IMPLACABLE: UNABLE TO BE CALMED DOWN OR MADE PEACEFUL

His rage at the betrayal was so great that he remained IMPLACABLE for weeks.

INCHOATE: NOT FULLY FORMED; DISORGANIZED

The ideas expressed in Nietzsche's mature work also appear in an INCHOATE form in his earliest writing.

INGENUOUS: SHOWING INNOCENCE OR CHILDLIKE SIMPLICITY

She was so INGENUOUS that her friends feared that her innocence and trustfulness would be exploited when she visited the big city.

INIMICAL: HOSTILE, UNFRIENDLY

Even though the children had grown up together they were INIMICAL to each other at school.

INNOCUOUS: HARMLESS

Some snakes are poisonous, but most species are INNOCUOUS and pose no danger to humans.

INSIPID: LACKING INTEREST OR FLAVOR

The critic claimed that the painting was INSIPID, containing no interesting qualities at all.

INTRANSIGENT: UNCOMPROMISING; REFUSING TO BE RECONCILED

The professor was INTRANSIGENT on the deadline, insisting that everyone turn the assignment in at the same time.

INUNDATE: TO OVERWHELM; TO COVER WITH WATER

The tidal wave INUNDATED Atlantis, which was lost beneath the water.

IRASCIBLE: EASILY MADE ANGRY

Attila the Hun's IRASCIBLE and violent nature made all who dealt with him fear for their lives.

LACONIC: USING FEW WORDS

She was a LACONIC poet who built her reputation on using words as sparingly as possible.

LAMENT: TO EXPRESS SORROW; TO GRIEVE

The children continued to LAMENT the death of the goldfish weeks after its demise.

LAUD: TO GIVE PRAISE; TO GLORIFY

Parades and fireworks were staged to LAUD the success of the rebels.

LAVISH: TO GIVE UNSPARINGLY

She LAVISHED the puppy with so many treats that it soon became overweight and spoiled.

LETHARGIC: ACTING IN AN INDIFFERENT OR SLOW, SLUGGISH MANNER

The clerk was so LETHARGIC that, even when the store was slow, he always had a long line in front of him.

LOQUACIOUS: TALKATIVE

She was naturally LOQUACIOUS, which was a problem in situations in which listening was more important than talking.

LUCID: CLEAR AND EASILY UNDERSTOOD

The explanations were written in a simple and LUCID manner so that students were immediately able to apply what they learned.

LUMINOUS: BRIGHT, BRILLIANT, GLOWING

The park was bathed in LUMINOUS sunshine which warmed the bodies and the souls of the visitors.

MALINGER: TO EVADE RESPONSIBILITY BY PRETENDING TO BE ILL

A common way to avoid the draft was by MALINGERING—pretending to be mentally or physically ill so as to avoid being taken by the Army.

MALLEABLE: CAPABLE OF BEING SHAPED

Gold is the most MALLEABLE of precious metals; it can easily be formed into almost any shape.

METAPHOR: A FIGURE OF SPEECH COMPARING TWO DIFFERENT THINGS; A SYMBOL

The METAPHOR "a sea of troubles" suggests a lot of troubles by comparing their number to the vastness of the sea.

METICULOUS: EXTREMELY CAREFUL ABOUT DETAILS

To find all the clues at the crime scene, the investigators METICULOUSLY examined every inch of the area.

MISANTHROPE: A PERSON WHO DISLIKES OTHERS

The character Scrooge in *A Christmas Carol* is such a MISANTHROPE that even the sight of children singing makes him angry.

MITIGATE: TO SOFTEN; TO LESSEN

A judge may MITIGATE a sentence if she decides that a person committed a crime out of need.

MOLLIFY: TO CALM OR MAKE LESS SEVERE

Their argument was so intense that is was difficult to believe any compromise would MOLLIFY them.

MONOTONY: LACK OF VARIATION

The MONOTONY of the sound of the dripping faucet almost drove the research assistant crazy.

NAIVE: LACKING SOPHISTICATION OR EXPERIENCE

Having never traveled before, the hillbillies were more NAIVE than the people they met in Beverly Hills.

OBDURATE: HARDENED IN FEELING; RESISTANT TO PERSUASION

The president was completely OBDURATE on the issue, and no amount of persuasion would change his mind.

OBSEQUIOUS: OVERLY SUBMISSIVE AND EAGER TO PLEASE

The OBSEQUIOUS new associate made sure to compliment her supervisor's tie and agree with him on every issue.

OBSTINATE: STUBBORN, UNYIELDING

The OBSTINATE child could not be made to eat any food that he disliked.

OBVIATE: TO PREVENT; TO MAKE UNNECESSARY

The river was shallow enough to wade across at many points, which OBVIATED the need for a bridge.

OCCLUDE: TO STOP UP; TO PREVENT THE PASSAGE OF

A shadow is thrown across the earth's surface during a solar eclipse, when the light from the sun is OCCLUDED by the moon.

ONEROUS: TROUBLESOME AND OPPRESSIVE; BURDENSOME

The assignment was so extensive and difficult to manage that it proved ONEROUS to the team in charge of it.

OPAQUE: IMPOSSIBLE TO SEE THROUGH; PREVENTING THE PASSAGE OF LIGHT

The heavy buildup of dirt and grime on the windows almost made them OPAQUE.

OPPROBRIUM: PUBLIC DISGRACE

After the scheme to embezzle the elderly was made public, the treasurer resigned in utter OPPROBRIUM.

OSTENTATION: EXCESSIVE SHOWINESS

The OSTENTATION of the Sun King's court is evident in the lavish decoration and luxuriousness of his palace at Versailles.

PARADOX: A CONTRADICTION OR DILEMMA

It is a PARADOX that those most in need of medical attention are often those least able to obtain it.

PARAGON: MODEL OF EXCELLENCE OR PERFECTION

She is the PARAGON of what a judge should be: honest, intelligent, hardworking, and just.

PEDANT: SOMEONE WHO SHOWS OFF LEARNING

The graduate instructor's tedious and excessive commentary on the subject soon gained her a reputation as a PEDANT.

PERFIDIOUS: WILLING TO BETRAY ONE'S TRUST

The actress's PERFIDIOUS companion revealed all of her intimate secrets to the gossip columnist.

PERFUNCTORY: DONE IN A ROUTINE WAY; INDIFFERENT

The machinelike bank teller processed the transaction and gave the waiting customer a PERFUNCTORY smile.

PERMEATE: TO PENETRATE

This miraculous new cleaning fluid is able to PERMEATE stains and dissolve them in minutes!

PHILANTHROPY: CHARITY; A DESIRE OR EFFORT TO PROMOTE GOODNESS

New York's Metropolitan Museum of Art owes much of its collection to the PHILANTHROPY of private collectors who willed their estates to the museum.

PLACATE: TO SOOTHE OR PACIFY

The burglar tried to PLACATE the snarling dog by saying, "Nice doggy," and offering it a treat.

PLASTIC: ABLE TO BE MOLDED, ALTERED, OR BENT

The new material was very PLASTIC and could be formed into products of vastly different shape.

PLETHORA: EXCESS

Assuming that more was better, the defendant offered the judge a PLETHORA of excuses.

PRAGMATIC: PRACTICAL AS OPPOSED TO IDEALISTIC

While daydreaming gamblers think they can get rich by frequenting casinos, PRAGMATIC gamblers realize that the odds are heavily stacked against them.

PRECIPITATE: TO THROW VIOLENTLY OR BRING ABOUT ABRUPTLY; LACKING DELIBERATION

Upon learning that the couple married after knowing each other only two months, friends and family members expected such a PRECIPITATE marriage to end in divorce.

PREVARICATE: TO LIE OR DEVIATE FROM THE TRUTH

Rather than admit that he had overslept again, the employee PREVARICATED and claimed that heavy traffic had prevented him from arriving at work on time.

PRISTINE: FRESH AND CLEAN; UNCORRUPTED

Since concerted measures had been taken to prevent looting, the archeological site was still PRISTINE when researchers arrived.

PRODIGAL: LAVISH, WASTEFUL

The PRODIGAL son quickly wasted all of his inheritance on a lavish lifestyle devoted to pleasure.

PROLIFERATE: TO INCREASE IN NUMBER QUICKLY

Although he only kept two guinea pigs initially, they PROLIFERATED to such an extent that he soon had dozens.

PROPITIATE: TO CONCILIATE; TO APPEASE

The management PROPITIATED the irate union by agreeing to raise wages for its members.

PROPRIETY: CORRECT BEHAVIOR; OBEDIENCE TO RULES AND CUSTOMS

The aristocracy maintained a high level of PROPRIETY, adhering to even the most minor social rules.

PRUDENCE: WISDOM, CAUTION, OR RESTRAINT

The college student exhibited PRUDENCE by obtaining practical experience along with her studies, which greatly strengthened her résumé.

PUNGENT: SHARP AND IRRITATING TO THE SENSES

The smoke from the burning tires was extremely PUNGENT.

QUIESCENT: MOTIONLESS

Many animals are QUIESCENT over the winter months, minimizing activity in order to conserve energy.

RAREFY: TO MAKE THINNER OR SPARSER

Since the atmosphere RAREFIES as altitudes increase, the air at the top of very tall mountains is too thin to breathe.

REPUDIATE: TO REJECT THE VALIDITY OF

The old woman's claim that she was Russian royalty was REPUDIATED when DNA tests showed she was of no relation to them.

RETICENT: SILENT, RESERVED

Physically small and RETICENT in her speech, Joan Didion often went unnoticed by those upon whom she was reporting.

RHETORIC: EFFECTIVE WRITING OR SPEAKING

Lincoln's talent for RHETORIC was evident in his beautifully expressed Gettysburg Address.

SATIATE: TO SATISFY FULLY OR OVERINDULGE

His desire for power was so great that nothing less than complete control of the country could SATIATE it.

SOPORIFIC: CAUSING SLEEP OR LETHARGY

The movie proved to be so SOPORIFIC that soon loud snores were heard throughout the theater.

SPECIOUS: DECEPTIVELY ATTRACTIVE; SEEMINGLY PLAUSIBLE BUT FALLACIOUS

The student's SPECIOUS excuse for being late sounded legitimate, but was proved otherwise when her teacher called her home.

STIGMA: A MARK OF SHAME OR DISCREDIT

In *The Scarlet Letter*, Hester Prynne was required to wear the letter "A" on her clothes as a public STIGMA for her adultery.

STOLID: UNEMOTIONAL; LACKING SENSITIVITY

The prisoner appeared STOLID and unaffected by the judge's harsh sentence.

SUBLIME: LOFTY OR GRAND

The music was so SUBLIME that it transformed the crude surroundings into a special place.

TACIT: DONE WITHOUT USING WORDS

Although not a word had been said, everyone in the room knew that a TACIT agreement had been made about which course of action to take.

TACITURN: SILENT, NOT TALKATIVE

The clerk's TACITURN nature earned him the nickname "Silent Bob."

TIRADE: LONG, HARSH SPEECH OR VERBAL ATTACK

Observers were shocked at the manager's TIRADE over such a minor mistake.

TORPOR: EXTREME MENTAL AND PHYSICAL SLUGGISHNESS

After surgery, the patient experienced TORPOR until the anesthesia wore off.

TRANSITORY: TEMPORARY, LASTING A BRIEF TIME

The reporter lived a TRANSITORY life, staying in one place only long enough to cover the current story.

VACILLATE: TO SWAY PHYSICALLY; TO BE INDECISIVE

The customer held up the line as he VACILLATED between ordering chocolate chip or rocky road ice cream.

VENERATE: TO RESPECT DEEPLY

In a traditional Confucian society, the young VENERATE their elders, deferring to the elders' wisdom and experience.

VERACITY: FILLED WITH TRUTH AND ACCURACY

She had a reputation for VERACITY, so everyone trusted her description of events.

VERBOSE: WORDY

The professor's answer was so VERBOSE that his student forgot what the original question had been.

VEX: TO ANNOY

The old man who loved his peace and quiet was VEXED by his neighbor's loud music.

VOLATILE: EASILY AROUSED OR CHANGEABLE; LIVELY OR EXPLOSIVE

His VOLATILE personality made it difficult to predict his reaction to anything.

WAVER: TO FLUCTUATE BETWEEN CHOICES

If you WAVER too long before making a decision about which testing site to register for, you may not get your first choice.

WHIMSICAL: ACTING IN A FANCIFUL OR CAPRICIOUS MANNER; UNPREDICTABLE

The ballet was WHIMSICAL, delighting the children with its imaginative characters and unpredictable sets.

ZEAL: PASSION, EXCITEMENT

She brought her typical ZEAL to the project, sparking enthusiasm in the other team members.

COMMONLY CONFUSED WORDS

Already—by this or that time, previously
He already completed his work.

All ready—completely prepared
The students were all ready to take their exam.

Altogether—entirely, completely
I am altogether certain that I turned in my homework.

All together—in the same place
She kept the figurines all together on her mantle.

Capital—a city containing the seat of government; the wealth or funds owned by a business or individual, resources
Atlanta is the capital of Georgia.
The company's capital gains have diminished in recent years.

Capitol—the building in which a legislative body meets
Our trip included a visit to the Capitol building in Washington, D.C.

Coarse—rough, not smooth; lacking refinement
The truck's large wheels enabled it to navigate the coarse, rough terrain.
His coarse language prevented him from getting hired for the job.

Course—path; series of classes or studies
James's favorite course is biology.
The doctor suggested that Amy rest and let the disease run its course.

Here—in this location
George Washington used to live here.

Hear—to listen to or to perceive by the ear
Did you hear the question?

Its—a personal pronoun that shows possession
Please put the book back in its place.

It's—the contraction of *it is*
It's snowing outside.

Lead—to act as a leader, to go first, or to take a superior position
The guide will lead us through the forest.

Led—past tense of lead
The guide led us through the forest.

Lead—a metal
It is dangerous to inhale fumes from paint containing lead.

Loose—free, to set free; not tight
She always wears loose clothing when she does yoga.

Lose—to become without
Use a bookmark so you don't lose your place in your book.

Passed—the past tense of pass
We passed by her house on Sunday.

Past—that which has gone by or elapsed in time; by
In the past, Abby never used to study.
We drove past her house.

Principal—the head of a school; main or important
The quarterback's injury is the principal reason the team lost.
The principal of the school meets with parents regularly.

Stationary—fixed, not moving
Thomas rode a stationary bicycle at the gym.

Stationery—paper used for letter writing
The principal's stationery has the school's logo on the top.

Their—possessive of *they*
Pau and Ben studied for their test together.

There—a place; in that matter or respect
There are several question types on the GRE.
Please hang up your jacket over there.

They're—contraction of *they are*
Be careful of the bushes as they're filled with thorns.

GRE Opposite Drills

Each of the word lists below relates to two concepts that are opposite in meaning. The words in each list relate to one of the concepts or its opposite. Try to sort out which category each word belongs in. For each word, check the oval under the appropriate concept. If you don't know the meaning of a word, make your best guess using roots, charge (whether the word sounds "good" or "bad"), prefixes, or context to help you.

No definitions are provided. Look up words that you are unsure of in GRE Minidictionary.

HAPPY		SAD
◯	BLITHE	◯
◯	DISCONSOLATE	◯
◯	DISPIRITED	◯
◯	DOLDRUMS	◯
◯	DOLOROUS	◯
◯	EBULLIENT	◯
◯	EUPHORIC	◯
◯	FELICITY	◯
◯	PROVIDENT	◯
◯	RUE	◯
◯	WOE	◯

Answer key on page 145.

TRUE		FALSE	TRUE		FALSE
○	APOCRYPHAL	○	○	FRANKNESS	○
○	CALUMNY	○	○	GUILE	○
○	CANARD	○	○	INDISPUTABLE	○
○	CANDOR	○	○	INDUBITABLE	○
○	CHICANERY	○	○	LEGITIMATE	○
○	DISSEMBLE	○	○	MALINGER	○
○	DISSIMULATE	○	○	MENDACIOUS	○
○	DUPE	○	○	MENDACITY	○
○	DUPLICITY	○	○	PERFIDY	○
○	EQUIVOCATE	○	○	PREVARICATE	○
○	ERRONEOUS	○	○	PROBITY	○
○	ERSATZ	○	○	SINCERE	○
○	FALLACIOUS	○	○	SPECIOUS	○
○	FEALTY	○	○	SPURIOUS	○
○	FEIGNED	○	○	VERACIOUS	○
○	FOIST	○	○	VERITY	○

Answer key on page 145.

AGREEMENT		DISAGREEMENT	AGREEMENT		DISAGREEMENT
○	ACCORD	○	○	DETRACTOR	○
○	ALTERCATE	○	○	DIFFER	○
○	ALTERCATION	○	○	DISPARAGE	○
○	ANTITHETIC	○	○	DISPUTE	○
○	ASKANCE	○	○	DISSENT	○
○	ASSENT	○	○	EXCORIATE	○
○	AVERSE	○	○	FEUD	○
○	BICKER	○	○	HARMONY	○
○	CAVIL	○	○	INIMICAL	○
○	CONCORD	○	○	MOOT	○
○	CONCUR	○	○	POLEMIC	○
○	CONSENSUS	○	○	QUIBBLE	○
○	CONSONANCE	○	○	RAPPORT	○
○	CONTENTION	○	○	SQUABBLE	○
○	CONTENTIOUS	○	○	UNANIMITY	○
○	CONTRADICT	○	○	WRANGLE	○

Answer key on page 146.

ATTRACTION OR LIKE		REPULSION OR DISLIKE	ATTRACTION OR LIKE		REPULSION OR DISLIKE
◯	ABHOR	◯	◯	ENCHANT	◯
◯	ABOMINATE	◯	◯	ENTICE	◯
◯	AFFINITY	◯	◯	ESCHEW	◯
◯	ALLURE	◯	◯	INVEIGLE	◯
◯	ANATHEMA	◯	◯	LOATH	◯
◯	ANTIPATHY	◯	◯	PARRY	◯
◯	BANE	◯	◯	PENCHANT	◯
◯	BEGUILE	◯	◯	PREDILECTION	◯
◯	BENT	◯	◯	PROCLIVITY	◯
◯	CHARM	◯	◯	PROPENSITY	◯
◯	DISSUADE	◯	◯	RANCOR	◯
◯	DRAW	◯	◯	REVILE	◯
◯	ELICIT	◯	◯	SPURN	◯

Answer key on page 146.

BRAVERY OR CONFIDENCE		FEAR OR CAUTION
◯	APLOMB	◯
◯	APPREHENSION	◯
◯	AUDACIOUS	◯
◯	AUDACITY	◯
◯	CHARY	◯
◯	CIRCUMSPECTION	◯
◯	CRAVEN	◯
◯	DAUNTLESS	◯
◯	DOUGHTY	◯
◯	GALLANTRY	◯
◯	GAME	◯
◯	INTREPID	◯
◯	METTLESOME	◯
◯	MISGIVING	◯
◯	PLUCKY	◯
◯	PUSILLANIMOUS	◯
◯	TEMERITY	◯
◯	TREPIDATION	◯
◯	UNDAUNTED	◯
◯	VALIANT	◯
◯	VALOROUS	◯

Answer key on page 147.

CALMNESS		AGITATION	CALMNESS		AGITATION
○	BECALM	○	○	NONCHALANT	○
○	BLUSTER	○	○	PERTURB	○
○	COLLECTED	○	○	PLACID	○
○	COMPOSED	○	○	QUIESCENT	○
○	COMPOSURE	○	○	RAGING	○
○	DETACHED	○	○	RAIL	○
○	DISCOMPOSED	○	○	REPOSE	○
○	DISPASSIONATE	○	○	ROIL	○
○	DISQUIETED	○	○	RUFFLED	○
○	DISTRAUGHT	○	○	SEDENTARY	○
○	FLURRIED	○	○	SERENE	○
○	FLUSTER	○	○	STAID	○
○	FRENETIC	○	○	STEADY	○
○	FULMINATE	○	○	TRANQUIL	○
○	FUROR	○	○	TUMULTUOUS	○
○	IMPERTURBABLE	○	○	TURBID	○
○	INDOLENT	○	○	TURBULENT	○
○	INSURGENT	○	○	UNRUFFLED	○
○	KINETIC	○	○	VEHEMENCE	○
○	LANGUOR	○	○	VERVE	○
○	LULL	○			

Answer key on page 147–148.

CHANGE		LACK OF CHANGE
○	CATALYST	○
○	COMMUTATION	○
○	CONSISTENT	○
○	CONSTANT	○
○	DETERMINATE	○
○	ENTRENCHED	○
○	FIXITY	○
○	IMMUTABLE	○
○	IMPERVIOUS	○
○	INERT	○
○	INGRAINED	○
○	INNOVATIVE	○

(continued on next page)

CHANGE		LACK OF CHANGE
◯	INVARIABLE	◯
◯	INVIOLATE	◯
◯	LODGED	◯
◯	METAMORPHOSIS	◯
◯	MUTABLE	◯
◯	ROOTED	◯
◯	STEADFAST	◯
◯	TRANSFIGURATION	◯
◯	TRANSFORMATION	◯
◯	TRANSLATION	◯
◯	TRANSMOGRIFY	◯
◯	TRANSMUTATION	◯
◯	UNFAILING	◯

Answer key on page 148.

GOODNESS OR MORALITY		EVIL OR IMMORALITY	GOODNESS OR MORALITY		EVIL OR IMMORALITY
◯	ALTRUISM	◯	◯	INVIDIOUS	◯
◯	BACCHANALIAN	◯	◯	LASCIVIOUS	◯
◯	BEATIFIC	◯	◯	LICENTIOUS	◯
◯	BENEFICENT	◯	◯	LURID	◯
◯	BENIGN	◯	◯	MISCREANT	◯
◯	BENISON	◯	◯	NEFARIOUS	◯
◯	CLEMENT	◯	◯	NOBLE	◯
◯	CONTINENCE	◯	◯	PERFIDIOUS	◯
◯	DEBAUCH	◯	◯	PROBITY	◯
◯	DECADENCE	◯	◯	PROFLIGATE	◯
◯	ELEVATED	◯	◯	PRURIENT	◯
◯	ETHICAL	◯	◯	RAPACITY	◯
◯	EXEMPLARY	◯	◯	RECTITUDE	◯
◯	FIENDISH	◯	◯	REPROBATE	◯
◯	ILLICIT	◯	◯	RIGHTEOUS	◯
◯	INFERNAL	◯	◯	TEMPERANCE	◯
◯	INIQUITOUS	◯	◯	TURPITUDE	◯
◯	INTEGRITY	◯	◯	VIRTUE	◯

Answer key on page 149.

LARGE AMOUNT OR EXCESS		SMALL AMOUNT OR SHORTAGE	LARGE AMOUNT OR EXCESS		SMALL AMOUNT OR SHORTAGE
◯	CAPACIOUS	◯	◯	MYRIAD	◯
◯	CAVALCADE	◯	◯	OPULENCE	◯
◯	CLOYING	◯	◯	OVERABUNDANCE	◯
◯	CORNUCOPIA	◯	◯	PAUCITY	◯
◯	DEARTH	◯	◯	PLETHORA	◯
◯	DEFECT	◯	◯	POVERTY	◯
◯	DEFICIENT	◯	◯	PREPONDERANCE	◯
◯	DILATE	◯	◯	PRIVATION	◯
◯	DISTEND	◯	◯	PRODIGIOUS	◯
◯	EFFUSIVE	◯	◯	PROFUSION	◯
◯	FAMINE	◯	◯	REPLETE	◯
◯	FRAUGHT	◯	◯	SCANTINESS	◯
◯	GLUT	◯	◯	SCARCITY	◯
◯	INSUFFICIENCY	◯	◯	STINTING	◯
◯	MANIFOLD	◯	◯	SUPERABUNDANCE	◯
◯	MEAGER	◯	◯	SUPEREROGATORY	◯
◯	MULTIFARIOUS	◯	◯	SUPERFLUITY	◯
			◯	SURFEIT	◯

Answer key on page 149.

GROW		SHRINK
◯	ABATE	◯
◯	ACCRETE	◯
◯	AGGRANDIZE	◯
◯	AMPLIFY	◯
◯	APPEND	◯
◯	AUGMENT	◯
◯	BURGEON	◯
◯	CONSTRICT	◯
◯	CORRODE	◯
◯	DWINDLE	◯
◯	EBB	◯
◯	ERODE	◯
◯	ESCALATE	◯
◯	UPSURGE	◯
◯	WANE	◯
◯	WAX	◯

Answer key on page 150.

GRAND AND IMPORTANT		PETTY OR UNIMPORTANT	GRAND AND IMPORTANT		PETTY OR UNIMPORTANT
◯	ABJECT	◯	◯	MOMENTOUS	◯
◯	APOTHEOSIS	◯	◯	NEGLIGIBLE	◯
◯	ASTRAL	◯	◯	NIGGLING	◯
◯	AUGUST	◯	◯	NONENTITY	◯
◯	CONSEQUENTIAL	◯	◯	OVERWEENING	◯
◯	CONSIDERABLE	◯	◯	PALTRY	◯
◯	DEBASED	◯	◯	PICAYUNE	◯
◯	ELEVATED	◯	◯	PIDDLING	◯
◯	ELOQUENT	◯	◯	PRETENTIOUS	◯
◯	EXALTED	◯	◯	REGAL	◯
◯	FRIVOLOUS	◯	◯	SALIENT	◯
◯	GRANDIOSE	◯	◯	SERVILE	◯
◯	IGNOBLE	◯	◯	SPLENDID	◯
◯	INCONSEQUENTIAL	◯	◯	STATELY	◯
◯	INGLORIOUS	◯	◯	SUBLIME	◯
◯	LOFTY	◯	◯	SUBSTANTIAL	◯
◯	MEANINGFUL	◯	◯	WEIGHTY	◯

Answer key on page 150.

UNLIMITED OR FREE		LIMITED OR CLOSED
◯	CIRCUMSCRIBED	◯
◯	DURESS	◯
◯	EMANCIPATED	◯
◯	ENCUMBRED	◯
◯	FETTERED	◯
◯	HERMETIC	◯
◯	IMMURE	◯
◯	INCOMMUNICADO	◯
◯	INDENTURE	◯
◯	INSULAR	◯
◯	LATITUDE	◯
◯	LAXITY	◯
◯	LICENSE	◯
◯	MANUMISSION	◯
◯	MAVERICK	◯
◯	OCCLUSION	◯
◯	STRICTURE	◯

(continued on next page)

(continued)

UNLIMITED OR FREE		LIMITED OR CLOSED
⭕	STYMIE	⭕
⭕	THRALL	⭕
⭕	TRAMMELED	⭕
⭕	UNBRIDLED	⭕
⭕	UNFETTERED	⭕
⭕	UNTRAMMELED	⭕
⭕	YOKE	⭕

Answer key on page 151.

YOUTH OR IMMATURITY		OLD AGE OR MATURITY
⭕	ABIDING	⭕
⭕	ANTEDELUVIAN	⭕
⭕	CALLOW	⭕
⭕	DOTAGE	⭕
⭕	GERIATRIC	⭕
⭕	GREEN	⭕
⭕	HOARY	⭕
⭕	INVETERATE	⭕
⭕	JUVENILE	⭕
⭕	NEOPHYTE	⭕
⭕	PUERILE	⭕
⭕	SENESCENT	⭕
⭕	SOPHOMORIC	⭕
⭕	STRIPLING	⭕
⭕	SUPERANNUATED	⭕
⭕	TYRO	⭕

Answer key on page 152.

PRAISE		CRITICISM	PRAISE		CRITICISM
○	ACCLAIM	○	○	EULOGIZE	○
○	ACCOLADE	○	○	EXALT	○
○	ADULATORY	○	○	EXTOL	○
○	APPLAUSE	○	○	HAIL	○
○	APPROBATION	○	○	HOMAGE	○
○	BOUQUET	○	○	HONOR	○
○	CELEBRATE	○	○	IMPUGN	○
○	CENSURE	○	○	KUDOS	○
○	COMMEND	○	○	LAUD	○
○	DEFAME	○	○	PAEAN	○
○	DEMEAN	○	○	PANEGYRIC	○
○	DENIGRATE	○	○	PEJORATIVE	○
○	DENOUNCE	○	○	PLAUDIT	○
○	DENUNCIATE	○	○	TRIBUTE	○
○	DEPRECATE	○	○	VENERATE	○
○	ENCOMIUM	○			

Answer key on page 152.

SWIFTNESS OR BRIEFNESS		DELAY OR SLOWNESS
○	ALACRITY	○
○	CELERITY	○
○	CURSORY	○
○	DALLY	○
○	DILATORY	○
○	EPHEMERAL	○
○	EVANESCENT	○
○	EXTEMPORANEOUS	○
○	IMPROMPTU	○
○	LAGGARD	○
○	MERCURIAL	○
○	PERFUNCTORY	○
○	PERPETUITY	○
○	PRECIPITOUS	○
○	PROCRASTINATION	○
○	PROTRACTED	○
○	RETARD	○
○	SLUGGISH	○
○	TORPID	○
○	TRANSIENT	○

Answer key on page 153.

SUBTLE OR SLIGHT   OBVIOUS

◯	BLATANT	◯
◯	EGREGIOUS	◯
◯	FLAGRANT	◯
◯	GOSSAMER	◯
◯	MANIFEST	◯
◯	MODICUM	◯
◯	NUANCE	◯
◯	OSTENTATIOUS	◯
◯	OVERT	◯
◯	PATENT	◯
◯	RAREFY	◯
◯	REFINED	◯
◯	SCINTILLA	◯

Answer key on page 153.

RUDENESS   POLITENESS

◯	ASOCIAL	◯
◯	BOORISH	◯
◯	CHEEKY	◯
◯	CHURLISH	◯
◯	CIVIL	◯
◯	CRASS	◯
◯	DEFERENTIAL	◯
◯	DEMURE	◯
◯	EARTHY	◯
◯	EFFRONTERY	◯
◯	GALLANT	◯
◯	GENTEEL	◯
◯	OBEISANCE	◯
◯	OBLIGING	◯
◯	OBSTREPEROUS	◯
◯	PHILISTINE	◯
◯	PUNCTILIOUS	◯
◯	RAW	◯
◯	SCABROUS	◯
◯	SOLICITOUS	◯
◯	TACTFUL	◯
◯	UNGRACIOUS	◯
◯	UNPOLISHED	◯
◯	VULGAR	◯

Answer key on page 154.

INTELLIGENCE AND ABILITY		STUPIDITY AND CLUMSINESS	INTELLIGENCE AND ABILITY		STUPIDITY AND CLUMSINESS
○	ACUMEN	○	○	INGENIOUS	○
○	ASININE	○	○	KEN	○
○	ASTUTE	○	○	MALADROIT	○
○	DERANGED	○	○	OMNISCIENT	○
○	DOLTISH	○	○	PERCIPIENT	○
○	FATUOUS	○	○	PERSPICACIOUS	○
○	FINESSE	○	○	PRECOCIOUS	○
○	FLAIR	○	○	PUNDIT	○
○	GAUCHE	○	○	SAGACIOUS	○
○	GULLIBLE	○	○	SAPIENT	○
○	IGNORAMUS	○	○	SIMPLE	○
○	IMPOLITIC	○	○	UNWITTING	○
○	INANE	○	○	VACUOUS	○
○	INCISIVE	○	○	VAPID	○

Answer key on page 154–155.

LOUD, LONG, OR A LOT OF SPEECH		QUIET, SHORT, OR ABSENCE OF SPEECH
○	BOMBAST	○
○	CURT	○
○	DUMB	○
○	ELOQUENT	○
○	GARRULOUS	○
○	GRANDILOQUENT	○
○	LACONIC	○
○	LOQUACIOUS	○
○	MUTE	○
○	OROTUND	○
○	PLANGENT	○
○	PROLIX	○
○	RETICENT	○
○	STENTORIAN	○
○	SUCCINCT	○
○	TACIT	○
○	TACITURN	○
○	TERSE	○
○	TURGID	○
○	VERBOSE	○

Answer key on page 155.

CLEAN		DIRTY
◯	ABLUTION	◯
◯	BESMEAR	◯
◯	BESPATTER	◯
◯	DEFILE	◯
◯	GRIMY	◯
◯	GRUBBY	◯
◯	IMMACULATE	◯
◯	PRISTINE	◯
◯	SLOVENLY	◯
◯	SMUTTY	◯
◯	SULLY	◯
◯	UNSOILED	◯
◯	UNSULLIED	◯
◯	VIRGINAL	◯

Answer key on page 156.

TOGETHER OR CONTINUOUS		SEPARATE OR DISCONTINUOUS	TOGETHER OR CONTINUOUS		SEPARATE OR DISCONTINUOUS
◯	ABUT	◯	◯	DISCRETE	◯
◯	AGGREGATION	◯	◯	DISJOINTED	◯
◯	ASUNDER	◯	◯	DISPERSE	◯
◯	BIFURCATE	◯	◯	DISSIPATE	◯
◯	CABAL	◯	◯	DIVERGE	◯
◯	COLLATE	◯	◯	ESTRANGE	◯
◯	COLLOQUY	◯	◯	HIATUS	◯
◯	COLLUSION	◯	◯	INCONGRUOUS	◯
◯	CONCATENATE	◯	◯	INTERREGNUM	◯
◯	CONCOMITANT	◯	◯	INTERSTICE	◯
◯	CONFLUENCE	◯	◯	RIFT	◯
◯	CONJOIN	◯	◯	SCHISM	◯
◯	CONSENSUS	◯	◯	SEQUESTERED	◯
◯	CONSONANCE	◯	◯	SYNCHRONOUS	◯
◯	COTERIE	◯	◯	SYNTHESIS	◯
◯	DIFFUSE	◯	◯	TANDEM	◯

Answer key on page 156.

STUBBORN		AGREEABLE
◯	ACCEDE	◯
◯	ACCOMMODATING	◯
◯	ACQUIESCE	◯
◯	AMENABLE	◯
◯	CAPITULATE	◯
◯	COMPLY	◯
◯	CONCEDE	◯
◯	CONTUMACIOUS	◯
◯	DOGMATIC	◯
◯	HIDEBOUND	◯
◯	INTRANSIGENT	◯
◯	OBDURACY	◯
◯	OBLIGING	◯
◯	OBSTINATE	◯
◯	OSSIFIED	◯
◯	PERTINACIOUS	◯
◯	RECALCITRANT	◯
◯	REFRACTORY	◯
◯	UNBENDING	◯
◯	UNSWAYABLE	◯

Answer key on page 157.

OPPOSITE DRILL ANSWER KEYS

HAPPY		SAD
●	BLITHE	○
○	DISCONSOLATE	●
○	DISPIRITED	●
○	DOLDRUMS	●
○	DOLOROUS	●
●	EBULLIENT	○
●	EUPHORIC	○
●	FELICITY	○
●	PROVIDENT	○
○	RUE	●
○	WOE	●

DIS means "not," so here the two *DIS* words mean "not consolate" and "not spirited," that is, "sad." Also, *DOL* means "pain," so *dolorous* and *doldrums* also mean "sad."

TRUE		FALSE	TRUE		FALSE
○	APOCRYPHAL	●	●	FRANKNESS	○
○	CALUMNY	●	○	GUILE	●
○	CANARD	●	●	INDISPUTABLE	○
●	CANDOR	○	●	INDUBITABLE	○
○	CHICANERY	●	●	LEGITIMATE	○
○	DISSEMBLE	●	○	MALINGER	●
○	DISSIMULATE	●	○	MENDACIOUS	●
○	DUPE	●	○	MENDACITY	●
○	DUPLICITY	●	○	PERFIDY	●
○	EQUIVOCATE	●	○	PREVARICATE	●
○	ERRONEOUS	●	●	PROBITY	○
○	ERSATZ	●	●	SINCERE	○
○	FALLACIOUS	●	○	SPECIOUS	●
●	FEALTY	○	○	SPURIOUS	●
○	FEIGNED	●	●	VERACIOUS	○
○	FOIST	●	●	VERITY	○

Notice that *veracious* and *verity* both have to do with truthfulness. (The root VER is from the Latin word for truth.) Perhaps you know that Yale's motto is "Lux et veritas," or "light and truth."

AGREEMENT		DISAGREEMENT	AGREEMENT		DISAGREEMENT
●	ACCORD	○	○	DETRACTOR	●
○	ALTERCATE	●	○	DIFFER	●
○	ALTERCATION	●	○	DISPARAGE	●
○	ANTITHETIC	●	○	DISPUTE	●
○	ASKANCE	●	○	DISSENT	●
●	ASSENT	○	○	EXCORIATE	●
○	AVERSE	●	○	FEUD	●
○	BICKER	●	●	HARMONY	○
○	CAVIL	●	○	INIMICAL	●
●	CONCORD	○	○	MOOT	●
●	CONCUR	○	○	POLEMIC	●
●	CONSENSUS	○	○	QUIBBLE	●
●	CONSONANCE	○	●	RAPPORT	○
○	CONTENTION	●	○	SQUABBLE	●
○	CONTENTIOUS	●	●	UNANIMITY	○
○	CONTRADICT	●	○	WRANGLE	●

Notice that all the words that began with *DIS* had to do with disagreement.

ATTRACTION OR LIKE		REPULSION OR DISLIKE	ATTRACTION OR LIKE		REPULSION OR DISLIKE
○	ABHOR	●	●	ENCHANT	○
○	ABOMINATE	●	●	ENTICE	○
●	AFFINITY	○	○	ESCHEW	●
●	ALLURE	○	●	INVEIGLE	○
○	ANATHEMA	●	○	LOATHe	●
○	ANTIPATHY	●	○	PARRY	●
○	BANE	●	●	PENCHANT	○
●	BEGUILE	○	●	PREDILECTION	○
●	BENT	○	●	PROCLIVITY	○
●	CHARM	○	●	PROPENSITY	○
○	DISSUADE	●	○	RANCOR	●
●	DRAW	○	○	REVILE	●
●	ELICIT	○	○	SPURN	●

When you talk about the pros and cons of a situation, you're talking about the positives and negatives. Notice that the words with *PRO* mean "attraction" or "like."

BRAVERY OR CONFIDENCE / FEAR OR CAUTION

BRAVERY OR CONFIDENCE	WORD	FEAR OR CAUTION
●	APLOMB	○
○	APPREHENSION	●
●	AUDACIOUS	○
●	AUDACITY	○
○	CHARY	●
○	CIRCUMSPECTION	●
○	CRAVEN	●
●	DAUNTLESS	○
●	DOUGHTY	○
●	GALLANTRY	○
●	GAME	○
●	INTREPID	○
●	METTLESOME	○
○	MISGIVING	●
●	PLUCKY	○
○	PUSILLANIMOUS	●
●	TEMERITY	○
○	TREPIDATION	●
●	UNDAUNTED	○
●	VALIANT	○
●	VALOROUS	○

Notice that there are several words in this list with the same roots. For instance, *valiant* and *valorous* both use the root *VAL*. If *intrepid* means "fearless," then *trepidation* must be "fear." And *dauntless* and *undaunted* both mean the same thing.

CALMNESS	WORD	AGITATION	CALMNESS	WORD	AGITATION
●	BECALM	○	●	NONCHALANT	○
○	BLUSTER	●	○	PERTURB	●
●	COLLECTED	○	●	PLACID	○
●	COMPOSED	○	●	QUIESCENT	○
●	COMPOSURE	○	○	RAGING	●
●	DETACHED	○	○	RAIL	●
○	DISCOMPOSED	●	●	REPOSE	○
●	DISPASSIONATE	○	○	ROIL	●
○	DISQUIETED	●	○	RUFFLED	●
○	FLURRIED	●	●	SEDENTARY	○
○	FLUSTER	●	●	SERENE	○
○	FRENETIC	●	●	STAID	○

(continued on next page)

(continued)

CALMNESS		AGITATION	CALMNESS		AGITATION
○	FULMINATE	●	●	STEADY	○
○	FUROR	●	●	TRANQUIL	○
●	IMPERTURBABLE	○	○	TUMULTUOUS	●
●	INDOLENT	○	○	TURBID	●
○	INSURGENT	●	○	TURBULENT	●
○	KINETIC	●	●	UNRUFFLED	○
●	LANGUOR	○	○	VEHEMENCE	●
●	LULL	○	○	VERVE	●

On this list, you can use "charge" to answer many of these words. Words like *fluster, frenetic, furor, kinetic, perturb,* and *tumultuous* sound agitating, while *becalm, serene,* and *tranquil* all sound calm.

CHANGE		LACK OF CHANGE
●	CATALYST	○
●	COMMUTATION	○
○	CONSISTENT	●
○	CONSTANT	●
○	DETERMINATE	●
○	ENTRENCHED	●
○	FIXITY	●
○	IMMUTABLE	●
○	IMPERVIOUS	●
○	INERT	●
○	INGRAINED	●
●	INNOVATIVE	○
○	INVARIABLE	●
○	INVIOLATE	●
○	LODGED	●
●	METAMORPHOSIS	○
●	MUTABLE	○
○	ROOTED	●
○	STEADFAST	●
●	TRANSFIGURATION	○
●	TRANSFORMATION	○
●	TRANSLATION	○
●	TRANSMOGRIFY	○
●	TRANSMUTATION	○
○	UNFAILING	●

TRANS means "across," so the five words in this list that begin with this root are all words that have to do with change.

GOODNESS OR MORALITY		EVIL OR IMMORALITY		GOODNESS OR MORALITY		EVIL OR IMMORALITY
●	ALTRUISM	○		○	INVIDIOUS	●
○	BACCHANALIAN	●		○	LASCIVIOUS	●
●	BEATIFIC	○		○	LICENTIOUS	●
●	BENEFICENT	○		○	LURID	●
●	BENIGN	○		○	MISCREANT	●
●	BENISON	○		○	NEFARIOUS	●
●	CLEMENT	○		●	NOBLE	○
●	CONTINENCE	○		○	PERFIDIOUS	●
○	DEBAUCH	●		●	PROBITY	○
○	DECADENCE	●		○	PROFLIGATE	●
●	ELEVATED	○		○	PRURIENT	●
●	ETHICAL	○		○	RAPACITY	●
●	EXEMPLARY	○		●	RECTITUDE	○
○	FIENDISH	●		○	REPROBATE	●
○	ILLICIT	●		●	RIGHTEOUS	○
○	INFERNAL	●		●	TEMPERANCE	○
○	INIQUITOUS	●		○	TURPITUDE	●
●	INTEGRITY	○		●	VIRTUE	○

The root *BEN* means "good." Notice that the three words in this list that include this root all mean something having to do with goodness or morality.

LARGE AMOUNT OR EXCESS		SMALL AMOUNT OR SHORTAGE		LARGE AMOUNT OR EXCESS		SMALL AMOUNT OR SHORTAGE
●	CAPACIOUS	○		●	MYRIAD	○
●	CAVALCADE	○		●	OPULENCE	○
●	CLOYING	○		●	OVERABUNDANCE	○
●	CORNUCOPIA	○		○	PAUCITY	●
○	DEARTH	●		●	PLETHORA	○
○	DEFECT	●		○	POVERTY	●
○	DEFICIENT	●		●	PREPONDERANCE	○
●	DILATE	○		○	PRIVATION	●
●	DISTEND	○		●	PRODIGIOUS	○
●	EFFUSIVE	○		●	PROFUSION	○
○	FAMINE	●		●	REPLETE	○
●	FRAUGHT	○		○	SCANTINESS	●
●	GLUT	○		○	SCARCITY	●
○	INSUFFICIENCY	●		○	STINTING	●
●	MANIFOLD	○		●	SUPERABUNDANCE	○
○	MEAGER	●		●	SUPEREROGATORY	○
●	MULTIFARIOUS	○		●	SUPERFLUITY	○
				●	SURFEIT	○

Notice that all the words that start with *SUPER* have to do with excess.

GROW		SHRINK
○	ABATE	●
●	ACCRETE	○
●	AGGRANDIZE	○
●	AMPLIFY	○
●	APPEND	○
●	AUGMENT	○
●	BURGEON	○
○	CONSTRICT	●
○	CORRODE	●
○	DWINDLE	●
○	EBB	●
○	ERODE	●
●	ESCALATE	○
●	UPSURGE	○
●	WANE	○
○	WAX	●

Here you might want to think of clichéd phrases. For instance, an *ebb tide* is a tide that's going out. A *burgeoning debt* is a debt that's increasing at a healthy rate. And the moon has *waxing* (growing) and *waning* (shrinking) phases.

GRAND AND IMPORTANT		PETTY OR UNIMPORTANT
○	ABJECT	●
●	APOTHEOSIS	○
●	ASTRAL	○
●	AUGUST	○
●	CONSEQUENTIAL	○
●	CONSIDERABLE	○
○	DEBASED	●
●	ELEVATED	○
●	ELOQUENT	○
●	EXALTED	○
○	FRIVOLOUS	●
●	GRANDIOSE	○
○	IGNOBLE	●
○	INCONSEQUENTIAL	●
○	INGLORIOUS	●
●	LOFTY	○
●	MEANINGFUL	○

GRAND AND IMPORTANT		PETTY OR UNIMPORTANT
●	MOMENTOUS	○
○	NEGLIGIBLE	●
○	NIGGLING	●
○	NONENTITY	●
●	OVERWEENING	○
○	PALTRY	●
○	PICAYUNE	●
○	PIDDLING	●
●	PRETENTIOUS	○
●	REGAL	○
●	SALIENT	○
○	SERVILE	●
●	SPLENDID	○
●	STATELY	○
●	SUBLIME	○
●	SUBSTANTIAL	○
●	WEIGHTY	○

This is another list in which common phrases can help you figure out the meaning of words. For instance, if someone makes a *salient point*, it's central to an argument. In physics, certain forces, such as air resistance, are often considered *negligible*, or ignored.

UNLIMITED OR FREE		LIMITED OR CLOSED
○	CIRCUMSCRIBED	●
○	DURESS	●
●	EMANCIPATED	○
○	ENCUMBRED	●
○	FETTERED	●
○	HERMETIC	●
○	IMMURE	●
○	INCOMMUNICADO	●
○	INDENTURE	●
○	INSULAR	●
●	LATITUDE	○
●	LAXITY	○
●	LICENSE	○
●	MANUMISSION	○
●	MAVERICK	○
○	OCCLUSION	●
○	STRICTURE	●
○	STYMIE	●
○	THRALL	●
○	TRAMMELED	●
●	UNBRIDLED	○
●	UNFETTERED	○
●	UNTRAMMELED	○
○	YOKE	●

Notice that *trammeled* and *fettered* are joined on this list by untrammeled and unfettered. Also, notice that all the words with *UN* are free.

YOUTH OR IMMATURITY		OLD AGE OR MATURITY
○	ABIDING	●
○	ANTEDELUVIAN	●
●	CALLOW	○
○	DOTAGE	●
○	GERIATRIC	●
●	GREEN	○
○	HOARY	●
○	INVETERATE	●
●	JUVENILE	○
●	NEOPHYTE	○
●	PUERILE	○
○	SENESCENT	●
●	SOPHOMORIC	○
●	STRIPLING	○
○	SUPERANNUATED	●
●	TYRO	○

This list is full of roots to help you figure things out: *NEO* means "new." *GERI* means "old." *Senescent* comes from the Latin *senex*, which means "old man." *Superannuated* has to do with lots of years.

PRAISE		CRITICISM	PRAISE		CRITICISM
●	ACCLAIM	○	●	EULOGIZE	○
●	ACCOLADE	○	●	EXALT	○
●	ADULATORY	○	●	EXTOL	○
●	APPLAUSE	○	●	HAIL	○
●	APPROBATION	○	●	HOMAGE	○
●	BOUQUET	○	●	HONOR	○
●	CELEBRATE	○	○	IMPUGN	●
○	CENSURE	●	●	KUDOS	○
●	COMMEND	○	●	LAUD	○
○	DEFAME	●	●	PAEAN	○
○	DEMEAN	●	●	PANEGYRIC	○
○	DENIGRATE	●	○	PEJORATIVE	●
○	DENOUNCE	●	●	PLAUDIT	○
○	DENUNCIATE	●	●	TRIBUTE	○
○	DEPRECATE	●	●	VENERATE	○
●	ENCOMIUM	○			

In this exercise, every word that uses *DE*, which can mean "down," as a prefix is negative. For instance, *denounce* means "to speak down" or "to criticize."

SWIFTNESS OR BRIEFNESS		DELAY OR SLOWNESS
●	ALACRITY	○
●	CELERITY	○
●	CURSORY	○
○	DALLY	●
○	DILATORY	●
●	EPHEMERAL	○
●	EVANESCENT	○
●	EXTEMPORANEOUS	○
●	IMPROMPTU	○
○	LAGGARD	●
●	MERCURIAL	○
●	PERFUNCTORY	○
○	PERPETUITY	●
●	PRECIPITOUS	○
○	PROCRASTINATION	●
○	PROTRACTED	●
○	RETARD	●
○	SLUGGISH	●
○	TORPID	●
●	TRANSIENT	○

Mercurial is a word based on a mythological figure. Mercury was the messenger of the gods who traveled with winged sandals. Thus, *mercurial* is fast.

SUBTLE OR SLIGHT		OBVIOUS
○	BLATANT	●
○	EGREGIOUS	●
○	FLAGRANT	●
●	GOSSAMER	○
○	MANIFEST	●
●	MODICUM	○
●	NUANCE	○
○	OSTENTATIOUS	●
○	OVERT	●
○	PATENT	●
●	RAREFY	○
●	REFINED	○
●	SCINTILLA	○

This list has several words that you can probably recognize from when they are used in context. For instance, people often refer to an "*egregious* error" or a "*modicum* of respect."

RUDENESS		POLITENESS
●	ASOCIAL	○
●	BOORISH	○
●	CHEEKY	○
●	CHURLISH	○
○	CIVIL	●
●	CRASS	○
○	DEFERENTIAL	●
○	DEMURE	●
●	EARTHY	○
●	EFFRONTERY	○
○	GALLANT	●
○	GENTEEL	●
○	OBEISANCE	●
○	OBLIGING	●
●	OBSTREPEROUS	○
●	PHILISTINE	○
○	PUNCTILIOUS	●
●	RAW	○
●	SCABROUS	○
○	SOLICITOUS	●
○	TACTFUL	●
●	UNGRACIOUS	○
●	UNPOLISHED	○
●	VULGAR	○

The word *Philistine* comes from a reference to the ancient people of Philistia. These people had a reputation for being smug and ignorant, particularly in the area of art and culture.

INTELLIGENCE AND ABILITY		STUPIDITY AND CLUMSINESS	INTELLIGENCE AND ABILITY		STUPIDITY AND CLUMSINESS
●	ACUMEN	○	●	INGENIOUS	○
○	ASININE	●	●	KEN	○
●	ASTUTE	○	○	MALADROIT	●
○	DERANGED	●	●	OMNISCIENT	○
○	DOLTISH	●	●	PERCIPIENT	○
○	FATUOUS	●	●	PERSPICACIOUS	○
●	FINESSE	○	●	PRECOCIOUS	○
●	FLAIR	○	●	PUNDIT	○

(continued on next page)

INTELLIGENCE AND ABILITY		STUPIDITY AND CLUMSINESS
○	GAUCHE	●
○	GULLIBLE	●
○	IGNORAMUS	●
○	IMPOLITIC	●
○	INANE	●
●	INCISIVE	○

INTELLIGENCE AND ABILITY		STUPIDITY AND CLUMSINESS
●	SAGACIOUS	○
●	SAPIENT	○
○	SIMPLE	●
○	UNWITTING	●
○	VACUOUS	●
○	VAPID	●

Many of these words have roots that can lead you to the answer. *MAL* means "bad," so *maladroit* deals with clumsiness. *OMNI* means "all," and *SCI* means "knowing," so *omniscient* means "all-knowing."

LOUD, LONG, OR A LOT OF SPEECH		QUIET, SHORT, OR ABSENCE OF SPEECH
●	BOMBAST	○
○	CURT	●
○	DUMB	●
●	ELOQUENT	○
●	GARRULOUS	○
●	GRANDILOQUENT	○
○	LACONIC	●
●	LOQUACIOUS	○
○	MUTE	●
●	OROTUND	○
●	PLANGENT	○
●	PROLIX	○
○	RETICENT	●
●	STENTORIAN	○
○	SUCCINCT	●
○	TACIT	●
○	TACITURN	●
○	TERSE	●
●	TURGID	○
●	VERBOSE	○

Notice that there are three different words with the root *LOQU* in this list. *LOQU* means "word, speech," so these three words all have to do with a lot of speech.

CLEAN		DIRTY
●	ABLUTION	○
○	BESMEAR	●
○	BESPATTER	●
○	DEFILE	●
○	GRIMY	●
○	GRUBBY	●
●	IMMACULATE	○
●	PRISTINE	○
○	SLOVENLY	●
○	SMUTTY	●
○	SULLY	●
●	UNSOILED	○
●	UNSULLIED	○
●	VIRGINAL	○

In this case, the sound of the words tell you a lot about the words themselves. If the word sounds dirty, as the words *besmear, bespatter, defile,* or *slovenly* do, you can bet that's what it means.

TOGETHER OR CONTINUOUS		SEPARATE OR DISCONTINUOUS	TOGETHER OR CONTINUOUS		SEPARATE OR DISCONTINUOUS
●	ABUT	○	○	DISCRETE	●
●	AGGREGATION	○	○	DISJOINTED	●
○	ASUNDER	●	○	DISPERSE	●
○	BIFURCATE	●	○	DISSIPATE	●
●	CABAL	○	○	DIVERGE	●
●	COLLATE	○	○	ESTRANGE	●
●	COLLOQUY	○	○	HIATUS	●
●	COLLUSION	○	○	INCONGRUOUS	●
●	CONCATENATE	○	○	INTERREGNUM	●
●	CONCOMITANT	○	○	INTERSTICE	●
●	CONFLUENCE	○	○	RIFT	●
●	CONJOIN	○	○	SCHISM	●
●	CONSENSUS	○	○	SEQUESTERED	●
●	CONSONANCE	○	●	SYNCHRONOUS	○
●	COTERIE	○	●	SYNTHESIS	○
○	DIFFUSE	●	●	TANDEM	○

This list is full of roots. *SYN* means "same"; *CON, COM,* and *COLL* mean "with"; and *DIS* means "away from" or "apart." Use your knowledge of these roots to make your decisions.

STUBBORN		AGREEABLE
⬭	ACCEDE	⬬
⬭	ACCOMMODATING	⬬
⬭	ACQUIESCE	⬬
⬭	AMENABLE	⬬
⬭	CAPITULATE	⬬
⬭	COMPLY	⬬
⬭	CONCEDE	⬬
⬬	CONTUMACIOUS	⬭
⬬	DOGMATIC	⬭
⬬	HIDEBOUND	⬭
⬬	INTRANSIGENT	⬭
⬬	OBDURACY	⬭
⬭	OBLIGING	⬬
⬬	OBSTINATE	⬭
⬬	OSSIFIED	⬭
⬬	PERTINACIOUS	⬭
⬬	RECALCITRANT	⬭
⬬	REFRACTORY	⬭
⬬	UNBENDING	⬭
⬬	UNSWAYABLE	⬭

UN means "not," so *unswayable* and *unbending* both mean "stubborn."

GRE Minidictionary

This Minidictionary provides you with the definitions of many common GRE words. Use this list not only when you work with the vocabulary exercises but whenever you encounter an unfamiliar word anywhere—such as in released tests or everyday reading.

A

ABANDON (n)   total lack of inhibition

ABASE   to humble, disgrace

ABASH   to embarrass

ABATEMENT   decrease, reduction

ABDICATE   to give up a position, right, or power

ABERRANT   atypical, not normal

ABERRATION   something different from the usual or normal

ABET   to aid, act as accomplice

ABEYANCE   temporary suppression or suspension

ABHOR   to loathe, detest

ABIDING   enduring, continuing

ABJECT   miserable, pitiful

ABJURE   to reject, abandon formally

ABLUTION   act of cleansing

ABNEGATE   to deny, renounce

ABOLITIONIST   one who opposes the practice of slavery

ABOMINATE   to hate

ABORTIVE   interrupted while incomplete

ABRIDGE   to condense, shorten

ABROGATE   to abolish or invalidate by authority

ABRUPT   sudden, unexpected

ABSCOND   to depart secretly

ABSOLVE   to forgive, free from blame

ABSTAIN   to refrain deliberately from something

ABSTEMIOUS   moderate in appetite

ABSTRACT (adj)   theoretical; complex, difficult

ABSTRUSE   difficult to comprehend

ABUT   to touch, to be in contact with

ABYSS   an extremely great depth

ACCEDE   to express approval; agree to

ACCESSIBLE   attainable, available; approachable

ACCESSORY   attachment, ornament; accomplice, partner

ACCLAIM   praise

ACCOLADE   praise, distinction

ACCOMMODATING   helpful

ACCORD   to reconcile, come to an agreement

ACCOST   to approach and speak to someone

ACCRETION   growth in size or increase in amount

ACCRUE   to accumulate, grow by additions

ACERBIC   bitter, sharp in taste or temper

ACIDULOUS   sour in taste or manner

ACME   highest point, summit

ACQUIESCE   to agree, comply quietly

ACQUITTAL   release from blame

ACRID   harsh, bitter

ACRIMONY   bitterness, animosity

ACUITY   sharpness

ACUMEN   sharpness of insight

ACUTE   sharp, pointed

ADAGE   old saying or proverb

ADAMANT   uncompromising, unyielding

ADAPT   to accommodate, adjust

ADHERE   to cling or to follow without deviation

ADJACENT   next to

ADJUNCT   something added, attached, or joined

ADMONISH   to caution or reprimand

ADROIT   skillful, accomplished, highly competent

ADULATION   high praise

ADULTERATE   to corrupt or make impure

ADUMBRATE   to sketch, outline in a shadowy way

ADVANTAGEOUS   favorable, useful

ADVENTITIOUS   accidental

ADVERSARIAL   antagonistic, competitive

ADVERSE   unfavorable, unlucky, harmful

ADVOCATE   to speak in favor of

AERIAL   having to do with the air

AERIE   nook or nest built high in the air

AERODYNAMIC   relating to objects moving through the air

AESTHETIC   pertaining to beauty or art

AFFABLE   friendly, easy to approach

AFFECTED (adj)   pretentious, phony

AFFINITY   fondness, liking; similarity

AFFLUENT   rich, abundant

AFFRONT (n)   personal offense, insult

AGENDA   plan, schedule

AGGRANDIZE   to make larger or greater in power

AGGREGATE (n)   collective mass or sum; total

AGGRIEVE   to afflict, distress

AGILE   well coordinated, nimble

AGITATION   commotion, excitement; uneasiness

AGNOSTIC   one doubting that people can know God

AGRARIAN   relating to farming or rural matters

ALACRITY   cheerful willingness, eagerness; speed

ALCHEMY   medieval chemical philosophy based on quest to change metal into gold

ALGORITHM   mechanical problem-solving procedure

ALIAS   assumed name

ALIENATED   distanced, estranged

ALIGNED   precisely adjusted; committed to one side or party

ALLAY   to lessen, ease, or soothe

ALLEGORY   symbolic representation

ALLEVIATE   to relieve, improve partially

ALLITERATION   repetition of the beginning sounds of words

ALLOCATION   allowance, portion, share

ALLURE (v)   to entice by charm; attract

ALLUSION   indirect reference

ALLUSIVENESS   quality of making many indirect references

ALOOF   detached, indifferent

ALTERCATION   noisy dispute

ALTRUISM   unselfish concern for others' welfare

AMALGAM   mixture, combination, alloy

AMBIDEXTROUS   able to use both hands equally well

AMBIGUOUS   uncertain; subject to multiple interpretations

AMBIVALENCE   attitude of uncertainty; conflicting emotions

AMBULATORY   itinerant; related to walking around

AMELIORATE   to make better, improve

AMENABLE   agreeable, cooperative

AMEND   to improve or correct flaws in

AMENITY   pleasantness; something increasing comfort

AMIABLE   friendly, pleasant, likable

AMICABLE   friendly, agreeable

AMITY   friendship

AMORAL   unprincipled, unethical

AMOROUS   strongly attracted to love; showing love

AMORPHOUS   having no definite form

AMORTIZE   to diminish by installment payments

AMPHIBIAN (n)   creature equally at home on land or in water

AMPHITHEATER   arena theater with rising tiers around a central open space

AMPLE   abundant, plentiful

AMPLIFY   to increase, intensify

AMULET   ornament worn as a charm against evil spirits

ANACHRONISM   something chronologically inappropriate

ANACHRONISTIC   outdated

ANALGESIA   a lessening of pain

ANALOGOUS   comparable, parallel

ANARCHY   absence of government or law; chaos

ANATHEMA   ban, curse; something shunned or disliked

ANCILLARY   accessory, subordinate, helping

ANECDOTE   short, usually funny account of an event

ANGULAR   characterized by sharp angles; lean and gaunt

ANIMATION   enthusiasm, excitement

ANIMOSITY   hatred, hostility

ANNUL   to cancel, nullify, declare void, or make legally invalid

ANODYNE   something that calms or soothes pain

ANOINT   to apply oil to, esp. as a sacred rite

ANOMALY   irregularity or deviation from the norm

ANONYMITY   condition of having no name or an unknown name

ANTAGONIST   foe, opponent, adversary

ANTECEDENT (adj)   coming before in place or time

ANTEDATE   dated prior to the actual occurrence

ANTEDILUVIAN   prehistoric, ancient beyond measure

ANTEPENULTIMATE   third from last

ANTERIOR   preceding, previous, before, prior (to)

ANTHOLOGY   collection of literary works

ANTHROPOMORPHIC   attributing human qualities to nonhumans

ANTIPATHY   dislike, hostility; extreme opposition or aversion

ANTIQUATED   outdated, obsolete

ANTIQUITY   ancient times; the quality of being old or ancient

ANTITHESIS   exact opposite or direct contrast

APACE   done quickly

APATHETIC   indifferent, unconcerned

APATHY   lack of feeling or emotion

APERTURE   an opening or hole

APHASIA   inability to speak or use words

APHELION   point in a planet's orbit that is farthest from the sun

APHORISM   old saying or short pithy statement

APLOMB   poise, confidence

APOCRYPHAL   not genuine; fictional

APOSTATE (n)   one who renounces a religious faith

APOSTROPHE   speech to the reader or someone not present; a superscript sign (')

APOTHEGM   a short, instructive saying

APOTHEOSIS   glorification; glorified ideal

APPEASE   to satisfy, placate, calm, pacify

APPEND   to attach

APPLAUSE   praise

APPRAISE   to evaluate the value of something

APPREHENSION   the act of comprehending; fear, foreboding

APPRISE   to give notice of; inform

APPROBATION   praise; official approval

APPROPRIATE (v)   to take possession of

AQUATIC   belonging or living in water

ARABLE   suitable for cultivation

ARBITRARY   depending solely on individual will; inconsistent

ARBITRATOR   mediator, negotiator

ARBOREAL   relating to trees; living in trees

ARBORETUM   place where trees are displayed and studied

ARCANE   secret, obscure, known only to a few

ARCHAIC   antiquated, from an earlier time; outdated

ARCHIPELAGO   large group of islands

ARDENT   passionate, enthusiastic, fervent

ARDOR   great emotion or passion

ARDUOUS   extremely difficult, laborious

ARID   extremely dry or deathly boring

ARRAIGN   to call to court to answer a charge

ARROGATE   to demand, claim arrogantly

ARSENAL   ammunition storehouse

ARTICULATE (adj)   well-spoken, expressing oneself clearly

ARTIFACT   historical relic, item made by human craft

ARTISAN   craftsperson; expert

ARTLESS   open and honest

ASCEND   to rise or climb

ASCENDANCY   state of rising, ascending; power or control

ASCERTAIN   to determine, discover, make certain of

ASCETIC (adj)   self-denying, abstinent, austere

ASCRIBE   to attribute to, assign

ASHEN   resembling ashes; deathly pale

ASININE   lacking intelligence or sound judgment

ASKANCE   scornfully

ASKEW   crooked, tilted

ASOCIAL   unable or unwilling to interact socially

ASPERITY   harshness, roughness

ASPERSION   false rumor, damaging report, slander

ASPIRE   to have great hopes; to aim at a goal

ASSAIL   to attack, assault

ASSAY   to analyze or estimate

ASSENT (v)   to express agreement

ASSERT   to affirm, attest

ASSIDUOUS   diligent, persistent, hardworking

ASSIGNATION   appointment for lovers' meeting; assignment

ASSIMILATION   act of blending in, becoming similar

ASSONANCE   resemblance in sound, especially in vowel sounds; partial rhyme

ASSUAGE   to make less severe, ease, relieve

ASTRAL   exalted, elevated in position; relating to the stars

ASTRINGENT   harsh, severe, stern

ASTUTE   having good judgment

ASUNDER (adv)   into different parts

ASYMMETRICAL   not corresponding in size, shape, position, etc.

ATONE   to make amends for a wrong

ATROCIOUS   monstrous, shockingly bad, wicked

ATROPHY (v)   to waste away, wither from disuse

ATTAIN   to accomplish, gain

ATTENUATE   to make thin or slender; weaken

ATTEST   to testify, stand as proof of, bear witness

AUDACIOUS   bold, daring, fearless

AUDIBLE   capable of being heard

AUDIT (n)   formal examination of financial records

AUDITORY   having to do with hearing

AUGMENT   to expand, extend

AUGURY (adj)   prophecy, prediction of events

AUGUST   dignified, awe-inspiring, venerable

AUSPICIOUS   having favorable prospects, promising

AUSTERE   stern, strict, unadorned

AUTHORITARIAN   extremely strict, bossy

AUTOCRAT   dictator

AUTONOMOUS   separate, independent

AUXILIARY   supplementary, reserve

AVARICE   greed

AVENGE   to retaliate, take revenge for an injury or crime

AVER   to declare to be true, affirm

AVERSE   being disinclined towards something

AVERSION   intense dislike

AVERT   to turn (something) away; prevent

AVIARY   large enclosure housing birds

AVOW   to state openly or declare

AWRY   crooked, askew, amiss

AXIOM   premise, postulate, self-evident truth

B

BACCHANALIAN   drunkenly festive

BALEFUL   harmful, with evil intentions

BALK (v)   to refuse, shirk; prevent

BALLAD   folk song, narrative poem

BALM   soothing, healing influence

BAN (v)   to forbid, outlaw

BANAL   trite and overly common

BANE   something causing ruin, death, or destruction

BANTER   playful conversation

BASE   being of low value or position

BASTION   fortification, stronghold

BAY (v)   to bark, especially in a deep, prolonged way

BEATIFIC   appearing to be saintly, angelic

BECALM   to make calm or still; keep motionless by lack of wind

BECLOUD   to confuse; darken with clouds

BEGUILE   to deceive, mislead; charm

BEHEMOTH   huge creature

BELABOR   to insist repeatedly or harp on

BELATED   late

BELEAGUER   to harass, plague

BELFRY   bell tower, room in which a bell is hung

BELIE   to misrepresent; expose as false

BELITTLE   to represent as unimportant, make light of

BELLICOSE   warlike, aggressive

BELLIGERENT   hostile, tending to fight

BELLOW   to roar, shout

BEMUSE   to confuse, stupefy; plunge deep into thought

BENCHMARK   standard of measure

BENEFACTOR   someone giving aid or money

BENEFICENT   kindly, charitable; doing good deeds; producing good effects

BENEFICIAL   advantageous

BENIGHTED   unenlightened

BENIGN   kindly, gentle or harmless

BENISON   blessing

BENT   a natural inclination towards something

BEQUEATH   to give or leave through a will; to hand down

BERATE   to scold harshly

BEREAVED   suffering the death of a loved one

BESEECH   to beg, plead, implore

BESMEAR   to smear

BESPATTER   to spatter

BESTIAL   beastly, animal-like

BESTOW   to give as a gift

BETOKEN   to indicate, signify, give evidence of

BEVY   group

BIAS   prejudice, slant

BIBLIOGRAPHY   list of books

BIBLIOPHILE   book lover

BICKER   to have a petty argument

BIFURCATE   divide into two parts

BILATERAL   two sided

BILIOUS   bad-natured

BILK   to cheat, defraud

BILLET   board and lodging for troops

BIPED   two-footed animal

BISECT   to cut into two (usually equal) parts

BLANCH   to pale; take the color out of

BLANDISH   to coax with flattery

BLASPHEMOUS   cursing, profane, irreverent

BLATANT   glaring, obvious, showy

BLIGHT (v)   to afflict, destroy

BLITHE   joyful, cheerful, or without appropriate thought

BLUDGEON   to hit as with a short, heavy club

BLUSTER   to boast or make threats loudly

BOISTEROUS   rowdy, loud, unrestrained

BOLSTER   to support; reinforce

BOMBASTIC   using high-sounding but meaningless language

BONANZA   extremely large amount; something profitable

BONHOMIE   good-natured geniality; atmosphere of good cheer

BOON   blessing, something to be thankful for

BOOR   crude person, one lacking manners or taste

BOTANIST   scientist who studies plants

BOUNTIFUL   plentiful

BOUQUET   a bunch of cut flowers

BOURGEOIS   middle class

BOVINE   relating to cows

BRAZEN   bold, shameless, impudent; of or like brass

BREACH   act of breaking, violation

BREVITY   the quality of being brief in time

BRIGAND   bandit, outlaw

BROACH   to mention or suggest for the first time

BROMIDE   a dull, commonplace person or idea

BRUSQUE   rough and abrupt in manner

BUFFET (v)   to strike, hit

BUFFOON   clown or fool

BULWARK   defense wall; anything serving as defense

BURGEON   to sprout or flourish

BURLY   brawny, husky

BURNISH   to polish, make smooth and bright

BURSAR   treasurer

BUSTLE   commotion, energetic activity

BUTT   person or thing that is object of ridicule

BUTTRESS (v)   to reinforce or support

BYWAY   back road

C

CABAL   a secret group seeking to overturn something

CACOPHONOUS   jarring, unpleasantly noisy

CADAVER   dead body

CADENCE   rhythmic flow of poetry; marching beat

CAJOLE   to flatter, coax, persuade

CALAMITOUS   disastrous, catastrophic

CALLOUS   thick-skinned, insensitive

CALLOW   immature, lacking sophistication

CALUMNY   false and malicious accusation, misrepresentation, slander

CANARD   a lie

CANDID   frank or fair

CANDOR   honesty of expression

CANNY   smart; founded on common sense

CANONIZE   to declare a person a saint; raise to highest honors

CANVASS   to examine thoroughly; conduct a poll

CAPACIOUS   large, roomy; extensive

CAPITULATE   to submit completely, surrender

CAPRICIOUS   impulsive, whimsical, without much thought

CARDIOLOGIST   physician specializing in diseases of the heart

CAREEN   to lean to one side

CARICATURE   exaggerated portrait, cartoon

CARNAL   of the flesh

CARNIVOROUS   meat-eating

CAROM   to strike and rebound

CARP (v)   to find fault, complain constantly

CARTOGRAPHY   science or art of making maps

CAST (n)   copy, replica

CAST (v)   to fling, to throw

CASTIGATE   to punish, chastise, criticize severely

CATACLYSMIC   disastrous

CATALYST   something causing change without being changed

CATEGORICAL   absolute, without exception

CATHARSIS   purification, cleansing

CATHOLIC   universal; broad and comprehensive

CAUCUS   smaller group within an organization; a meeting of such a group

CAULK   to make watertight

CAUSALITY   cause-and-effect relationship

CAUSTIC   biting, sarcastic; able to burn

CAVALCADE   a procession

CAVALIER (adj)   carefree, happy; with lordly disdain

CAVIL   to raise trivial objections

CAVORT   to frolic, frisk

CEDE   to surrender possession of something

CELEBRITY   fame, widespread acclaim

CELERITY   quick moving or acting

CENSORIOUS   severely critical

CENSURE   to criticize or find fault with

CENTRIPETAL   directed or moving towards the center

CERTITUDE   assurance, certainty

CESSATION   temporary or complete halt

CESSION   act of surrendering something

CHAGRIN   shame, embarrassment, humiliation

CHALICE   goblet, cup

CHAMP (v)   chew noisily

CHAMPION (v)   to defend or support

CHAOS   confusion

CHAOTIC   extremely disorderly

CHARLATAN   quack, fake

CHARM   compelling attractiveness

CHARY   watchful, cautious, extremely shy

CHASTISE   to punish, discipline, scold

CHATTEL   piece of personal property

CHAUVINIST   someone prejudiced in the belief of their kind's superiority

CHEEKY   lacking prudence or discretion

CHERUBIC   sweet, innocent, resembling a cherub angel

CHICANERY   trickery, fraud, deception

CHIDE   to scold, express disapproval

CHIMERICAL   fanciful, imaginary, visionary; impossible

CHOICE (adj)   specially selected, preferred

CHOLERIC   easily angered, short-tempered

CHORTLE   to chuckle

CHROMATIC   relating to color

CHRONICLER   one who keeps records of historical events

CHURLISH   rude

CIRCUITOUS   roundabout

CIRCUMFERENCE   boundary or distance around a circle or sphere

CIRCUMLOCUTION   roundabout, lengthy way of saying something

CIRCUMNAVIGATE   to sail completely around

CIRCUMSCRIBE   to encircle; set limits on, confine

CIRCUMSPECT   cautious, wary

CIRCUMVENT   to go around; avoid

CISTERN   tank for rainwater

CITADEL   fortress or stronghold

CIVIL   polite; relating to citizens

CIVILITY   courtesy, politeness

CLAIRVOYANT (adj)   having ESP, psychic

CLAMOR (n)   noisy outcry

CLAMOR (v)   to make a noisy outcry

CLANDESTINE   secretive, concealed for a darker purpose

CLARITY   clearness; clear understanding

CLAUSTROPHOBIA   fear of small, confined places

CLEAVE   to split or separate; to stick, cling, adhere

CLEMENCY   merciful leniency

CLEMENT   mild

CLOISTER (v)   to confine, seclude

CLOYING   indulging to excess

COAGULATE   to clot or change from a liquid to a solid

COALESCE   to grow together or cause to unite as one

CODDLE   to baby, treat indulgently

COERCE   to compel by force or intimidation

COFFER   strongbox, large chest for money

COGENT   logically forceful, compelling, convincing

COGNATE   related, similar, akin

COGNITION   mental process by which knowledge is acquired

COGNOMEN   family name; any name, especially a nickname

COHABIT   to live together

COHERENT   intelligible, lucid, understandable

COLLATE   to arrange in an order

COLLATERAL   accompanying

COLLECTED   acting calm and composed

COLLOQUIAL   characteristic of informal speech

COLLOQUY   dialog or conversation, conference

COLLUSION   collaboration, complicity, conspiracy

COMELINESS   physical grace and beauty

COMMEND   to compliment, praise

COMMENSURATE   proportional

COMMISSION   fee payable to an agent; authorization

COMMODIOUS   roomy, spacious

COMMONPLACE   ordinary, found every day

COMMUNICABLE   transmittable

COMMUTE   to change a penalty to a less severe one

COMPATRIOT   fellow countryman

COMPELLING (adj)   having a powerful and irresistible effect

COMPENDIOUS   summarizing completely and briefly

COMPENSATE   to repay or reimburse

COMPLACENT   self-satisfied, smug, affable

COMPLAISANT   agreeable, friendly

COMPLEMENT   to complete, perfect

COMPLIANT   submissive and yielding

COMPLICITY   knowing partnership in wrongdoing

COMPOSED   acting calm

COMPOSURE   a calm manner or appearance

COMPOUND (adj)   complex; composed of several parts

COMPOUND (v)   to combine, add to

COMPRESS (v)   to reduce, squeeze

COMPULSIVE   obsessive, fanatic

COMPUNCTION   feeling of uneasiness caused by guilt or regret

COMPUNCTIOUS   feeling guilty or having misgivings

CONCATENATE   linked together

CONCAVE   curving inward

CONCEDE   to yield, admit

CONCEPTUALIZE   to envision, imagine

CONCERN   a matter of importance or worthy of consideration

CONCERTO   musical composition for orchestra and soloist(s)

CONCILIATORY   overcoming distrust or hostility

CONCOMITANT   accompanying something

CONCORD   agreement

CONCUR   to agree

CONDONE   to pardon or forgive; overlook, justify, or excuse a fault

CONDUIT   tube, pipe, or similar passage

CONFECTION   something sweet to eat

CONFISCATE   to appropriate, seize

CONFLAGRATION   big, destructive fire

CONFLUENCE   meeting place; meeting of two streams

CONFOUND   to baffle, perplex

CONGEAL   to become thick or solid, as a liquid freezing

CONGENIAL   similar in tastes and habits

CONGENITAL   existing since birth

CONGLOMERATE   collected group of varied things

CONGRESS   formal meeting or assembly

CONGRUITY   correspondence, harmony, agreement

CONJECTURE   speculation, prediction

CONJOIN   to join together

CONJUGAL   pertaining to marriage

CONJURE   to evoke a spirit, cast a spell

CONNIVE   to conspire, scheme

CONNOISSEUR   a person with refined taste

CONSANGUINEOUS   of the same origin; related by blood

CONSCIENTIOUS   governed by conscience; careful and thorough

CONSECRATE   to declare sacred; dedicate to a goal

CONSENSUS   unanimity, agreement of opinion or attitude

CONSEQUENTIAL   important

CONSIDERABLE   significant, worth considering

CONSIGN   to commit, entrust

CONSISTENT   containing no contradictions, being harmonious

CONSOLATION   something providing comfort or solace for a loss or hardship

CONSOLIDATE   to combine, incorporate

CONSONANT (adj)   consistent with, in agreement with

CONSTANT   completely uniform and unchanging

CONSTITUENT   component, part; citizen, voter

CONSTRAINED   forced, compelled; confined, restrained

CONSTRAINT   something that forces or compels; something that restrains or confines

CONSTRICT   to inhibit

CONSTRUE   to explain or interpret

CONSUMMATE (adj)   accomplished, complete, perfect

CONSUMMATE (v)   to complete, fulfill

CONTEND   to battle, clash; compete

CONTENTIOUS   quarrelsome, disagreeable, belligerent

CONTINENCE   self-control, self-restraint

CONTRADICT   to deny or oppose

CONTRAVENE   to contradict, deny, act contrary to

CONTRITE   deeply sorrowful and repentant for a wrong

CONTUMACIOUS   rebellious

CONTUSION   bruise

CONUNDRUM   riddle, puzzle, or problem with no solution

CONVALESCENCE   gradual recovery after an illness

CONVENE   to meet, come together, assemble

CONVENTIONAL   typical, customary, commonplace

CONVEX   curved outward

CONVIVIAL   sociable; fond of eating, drinking, and people

CONVOKE   to call together, summon

CONVOLUTED   twisted, complicated, involved

COPIOUS   abundant, plentiful

COQUETTE   woman who flirts

CORNUCOPIA   abundance

CORPOREAL   having to do with the body; tangible, material

CORPULENCE   obesity, fatness, bulkiness

CORRELATION   association, mutual relation of two or more things

CORROBORATE   to confirm, verify

CORRODE   to weaken or destroy

CORRUGATE   to mold in a shape with parallel grooves and ridges

COSMETIC (adj)   relating to beauty; affecting the surface of something

COSMOGRAPHY   science that deals with the nature of the universe

COSMOPOLITAN   sophisticated, free from local prejudices

COSSET   to pamper, treat with great care

COTERIE   small group of persons with a common interest or a similar purpose

COUNTENANCE (n)   facial expression; look of approval or support

COUNTENANCE (v)   to favor, support

COUNTERMAND   to annul, cancel, make a contrary order

COUNTERVAIL   to counteract, exert force against

COVEN   group of witches

COVERT   hidden; secret

COVET   to strongly desire something possessed by another

COWER   to cringe in fear

CRASS   crude, unrefined

CRAVEN   cowardly

CREDENCE   acceptance of something as true or real

CREDIBLE   plausible, believable

CREDULOUS   gullible, trusting

CREED   statement of belief or principle

CRESCENDO   gradual increase in volume of sound

CRINGE   to shrink in fear

CRITERION   standard for judging, rule for testing

CRYPTIC   puzzling

CUISINE   characteristic style of cooking

CULMINATION   climax, final stage

CULPABLE   guilty, responsible for wrong

CULPRIT   guilty person

CUMULATIVE   resulting from gradual increase

CUPIDITY   greed

CURATOR   caretaker and overseer of an exhibition, esp. in a museum

CURMUDGEON   cranky person

CURSORY   hastily done, superficial

CURT   abrupt, blunt

CURTAIL   to shorten

CUTLERY   cutting instruments; tableware

CYGNET   young swan

CYNIC   person who distrusts the motives of others

D

DALLY   to act playfully or waste time

DAUNT   to discourage, intimidate

DEARTH   lack, scarcity, insufficiency

DEBASE   to degrade or lower in quality or stature

DEBAUCH   to corrupt, seduce from virtue or duty; indulge

DEBILITATE   to weaken, enfeeble

DEBUNK   to discredit, disprove

DEBUTANTE   young woman making debut in high society

DECADENCE   decline or decay, deterioration

DECAMP   to leave suddenly

DECAPITATE   to behead

DECATHLON   athletic contest with ten events

DECIDUOUS   losing leaves in the fall; short-lived, temporary

DECLIVITY   downward slope

DECOROUS   proper, tasteful, socially correct

DECORUM   proper behavior, etiquette

DECRY   to belittle, openly condemn

DEFACE   to mar the appearance of, vandalize

DEFAMATORY   slanderous, injurious to the reputation

DEFAME   to disgrace or slander

DEFECT   an imperfection or shortcoming

DEFENDANT   person required to answer a legal action or suit

DEFER   to submit or yield

DEFERENCE   respect, honor

DEFERENTIAL   respectful and polite in a submissive way

DEFICIENT   defective, not meeting a normal standard

DEFILE   to make unclean or dishonor

DEFINITIVE   clear-cut, explicit or decisive

DEFLATION   decrease, depreciation

DEFORM   to disfigure, distort

DEFT   skillful, dexterous

DEFUNCT   no longer existing, dead, extinct

DELECTABLE   appetizing, delicious

DELEGATE (v)   to give powers to another

DELETERIOUS   harmful, destructive, detrimental

DELINEATION   depiction, representation

DELTA   tidal deposit at the mouth of a river

DELUGE (n)   flood

DELUGE (v)   to submerge, overwhelm

DEMAGOGUE   leader or rabble-rouser who usually uses appeals to emotion or prejudice

DEMARCATION   borderline; act of defining or marking a boundary or distinction

DEMEAN   to degrade, humiliate, humble

DEMISE   death

DEMOGRAPHICS   data relating to study of human population

DEMOTE   to reduce to a lower grade or rank

DEMOTION   lowering in rank or grade

DEMUR   to express doubts or objections

DEMYSTIFY   to remove mystery from, clarify

DENIGRATE   to slur or blacken someone's reputation

DENOUNCE   to accuse, blame

DENUDE   to make bare, uncover, undress

DENUNCIATION   public condemnation

DEPICT   to describe, represent

DEPLETE   to use up, exhaust

DEPLORE   to express or feel disapproval of; regret strongly

DEPLOY   to spread out strategically over an area

DEPOSE   to remove from a high position, as from a throne

DEPRAVITY   sinfulness, moral corruption

DEPRECATE   to belittle, disparage

DEPRECIATE   to lose value gradually

DERANGED   to be disturbed or insane

DERIDE   to mock, ridicule, make fun of

DERISIVE   expressing ridicule or scorn

DERIVATIVE   copied or adapted; not original

DERIVE   to originate; take from a certain source

DEROGATE   to belittle, disparage

DESCRY   to discover or reveal

DESECRATE   to abuse something sacred

DESICCATE   to dry completely, dehydrate

DESIST   to stop doing something

DESPONDENT   feeling discouraged and dejected

DESPOT   tyrannical ruler

DESTITUTE   very poor, poverty-stricken

DESULTORY   at random, rambling, unmethodical

DETACHED   separate, unconnected

DETER   to discourage; prevent from happening

DETERMINATE   having defined limits; conclusive

DETESTATION   extreme hatred

DETRACTOR   one who takes something away

DETRIMENTAL   causing harm or injury

DEVIATE   to stray, wander

DEVIATION   departure, exception, anomaly

DEVOID   totally lacking

DEVOUT   deeply religious

DEXTEROUS   skilled physically or mentally

DIABOLICAL   fiendish; wicked

DIALECT   regional style of speaking

DIAPHANOUS   allowing light to show through; delicate

DIATRIBE   bitter verbal attack

DICHOTOMY   division into two parts

DICTUM   authoritative statement; popular saying

DIDACTIC   excessively instructive

DIFFER   disagree

DIFFERENTIATE   to distinguish between two items

DIFFIDENCE   shyness, lack of confidence

DIFFRACT   to cause to separate into parts, esp. light

DIFFUSE   widely spread out

DIGRESS   to turn aside; to stray from the main point

DILAPIDATED   in disrepair, run-down, neglected

DILATE   to enlarge, swell, extend

DILATORY   slow, tending to delay

DILETTANTE   an amateur

DILUVIAL   relating to a flood

DIMINUTIVE   small

DIPLOMACY   discretion, tact

DIRGE   funeral hymn

DISABUSE   to free from a misconception

DISAFFECTED   discontented and disloyal

DISARRAY   clutter, disorder

DISBAND   to break up

DISBAR   to expel from legal profession

DISBURSE   to pay out

DISCERN   to perceive something obscure

DISCLAIM   to deny, disavow

DISCLOSE   to confess, divulge

DISCOMFIT   to cause perplexity and embarrassment

DISCOMPOSE   to disturb the composure or serenity

DISCONCERTING   bewildering, perplexing, slightly disturbing

DISCONSOLATE   unable to be consoled; extremely sad

DISCORDANT   harsh-sounding, badly out of tune

DISCREDIT   to dishonor or disgrace

DISCREDITED   disbelieved, discounted; disgraced, dishonored

DISCREPANCY   difference between

DISCRETE   distinct, separate

DISCRETIONARY   subject to one's own judgment

DISCURSIVE   wandering from topic to topic

DISDAIN   to regard with scorn and contempt

DISDAINFUL   contemptuous, scornful

DISENGAGED   disconnected, disassociated

DISGORGE   to vomit, discharge violently

DISHEVELED   untidy, disarranged, unkempt

DISINCLINED   averse, unwilling, lacking desire

DISINGENUOUS   sly and crafty

DISINTEREST   lack of interest or a disadvantage

DISJOINTED   lacking coherence or order, being separated

DISPARAGE   to belittle, speak disrespectfully about

DISPARATE   dissimilar, different in kind

DISPARITY   contrast, dissimilarity

DISPASSIONATE   free from emotion; impartial, unbiased

DISPEL   to drive out or scatter

DISPENSE   to distribute, administer

DISPENSE WITH   to suspend the operation of, do without

DISPERSE   to break up, scatter

DISPIRIT   to dishearten, make dejected

DISPUTE   to debate, to quarrel

DISQUIETED   feeling anxiety, being disturbed, lacking peace

DISREGARD   to neglect, pay no attention to

DISREPUTE   disgrace, dishonor

DISSEMBLE   to pretend, disguise one's motives

DISSEMINATE   to spread far and wide

DISSENSION   difference of opinion

DISSIMULATE   to disguise or put on a false appearance

DISSIPATE   to scatter; to pursue pleasure to excess

DISSOCIATE   to separate; remove from an association

DISSONANT   harsh and unpleasant sounding

DISSUADE   to persuade someone to alter original intentions

DISTAFF   the female branch of a family

DISTEND   to swell, inflate, bloat

DISTRAUGHT   very worried and distressed

DISTRUST (n)   disbelief and suspicion

DITHER (v)   to move or act confusedly or without clear purpose

DIURNAL   daily

DIVERGE   to move in different directions, to deviate from a source

DIVERSE   differing

DIVERT   to turn from one course to another

DIVEST   to get rid of

DIVINE (v)   to foretell or know by inspiration

DIVISIVE   creating disunity or conflict

DOCILE   tame, willing to be taught

DOCTRINAIRE   rigidly devoted to theories

DOGGED (adj)   persistent, stubborn

DOGMATIC   rigidly fixed in opinion, opinionated

DOLDRUMS   a period of despondency

DOLEFUL   sad, mournful

DOLOR   sadness

DOLT   idiot, dimwit, foolish person

DOMINEER   to rule over something in a tyrannical way

DONOR   benefactor, contributor

DORMANT   at rest, inactive, in suspended animation

DOTAGE   senile condition, mental decline

DOTARD   senile old person

DOTING   excessively fond, loving to excess

DOUGHTY   courageous

DOUR   sullen and gloomy; stern and severe

DOWRY   money or property given by a bride to her husband

DRAFT (v)   to plan, outline; to recruit, conscript

DRAW   to attract, to pull toward

DRIVEL   stupid talk; slobber

DROLL   amusing in a wry, subtle way

DROSS   waste produced during metal smelting; garbage

DUDGEON   angry indignation

DULCET   pleasant sounding, soothing to the ear

DUMB   unable to speak

DUPE (n)   fool, pawn

DUPE (v)   to deceive, trick

DUPLICITY   deception, dishonesty, double-dealing

DURABILITY   strength, sturdiness

DURATION   period of time that something lasts

DURESS   threat of force or intimidation; imprisonment

DWINDLE   to shrink or decrease

DYSPEPTIC   suffering from indigestion; gloomy and irritable

E

EARTHY   crude

EBB (v)   to fade away, recede

EBULLIENT   exhilarated, full of enthusiasm and high spirits

ECLECTIC   selecting from various sources

ECSTATIC   joyful

EDDY   air or wind current

EDICT   law, command, official public order

EDIFICE   building

EDIFY   to instruct morally and spiritually

EDITORIALIZE   to express an opinion on an issue

EFFACE   to erase or make illegible

EFFERVESCENT   bubbly, lively

EFFICACIOUS   effective, efficient

EFFIGY   stuffed doll; likeness of a person

EFFLUVIA   outpouring of gases or vapors

EFFRONTERY   impudent boldness; audacity

EFFULGENT   brilliantly shining

EFFUSIVE   expressing emotion without restraint

EGOCENTRIC   acting as if things are centered around oneself

EGREGIOUS   conspicuously bad

EGRESS   exit

ELATION   exhilaration, joy

ELEGY   mournful poem, usually about the dead

ELEVATED   high in status, exalted

ELICIT   to draw out, provoke

ELOQUENCE   fluent and effective speech

ELUCIDATE   to explain, clarify

EMACIATED   skinny, scrawny, gaunt, esp. from hunger

EMANCIPATE   to set free, liberate

EMBELLISH   to ornament, make attractive with decoration or details; add details to a statement

EMBEZZLE   to steal money in violation of a trust

EMBROIL   to involve in; cause to fall into disorder

EMEND   to correct a text

EMINENT   celebrated, distinguished; outstanding, towering

EMOLLIENT   having soothing qualities, esp. for skin

EMOTIVE   appealing to or expressing emotion

EMPATHY   identification with another's feelings

EMULATE   to copy, imitate

ENCHANT   to charm or attract

ENCIPHER   to translate a message into code

ENCOMIUM   warm praise

ENCORE   additional performance, often demanded by audience

ENCUMBER   to hinder, burden, restrict motion

ENDEMIC   belonging to a particular area, inherent

ENDOGAMOUS   marrying within a specific group due to law or custom

ENDURANCE   ability to withstand hardships

ENERVATE   to weaken, sap strength from

ENGENDER   to produce, cause, bring about

ENIGMATIC   puzzling, inexplicable

ENJOIN   to urge, order, command; forbid or prohibit, as by judicial order

ENMITY   hostility, antagonism, ill-will

ENNUI   boredom, lack of interest and energy

ENORMITY   state of being gigantic or terrible

ENSCONCE   to settle comfortably into a place

ENSHROUD   to cover, enclose with a dark cover

ENTAIL   to involve as a necessary result, necessitate

ENTHRALL   to captivate, enchant, enslave

ENTICE   to lure or tempt

ENTITY   something with its own existence or form

ENTOMOLOGIST   scientist who studies insects

ENTREAT   to plead, beg

ENTRENCHED   established solidly

ENUMERATE   to count, list, itemize

ENUNCIATE   to pronounce clearly

EON   indefinitely long period of time

EPHEMERAL   momentary, transient, fleeting

EPICURE   person with refined taste in food and wine

EPIGRAM   short, witty saying or poem

EPIGRAPH   quotation at the beginning of a literary work

EPILOGUE   concluding section of a literary work

EPITHET   an abusive word or phrase

EPITOME   representative of an entire group; summary

EPOCHAL   very significant or influential; defining an epoch or time period

EQUANIMITY   calmness, composure

EQUESTRIAN (n)   one who rides on horseback

EQUINE   relating to horses

EQUITABLE   fair

EQUITY   justice, fairness

EQUIVOCAL   ambiguous, open to two interpretations

EQUIVOCATE   to use vague or ambiguous language intentionally

ERADICATE   to erase or wipe out

ERODE   to diminish or destroy over a period of time

ERRANT   straying, mistaken, roving

ERRATIC   wandering and unpredictable

ERRONEOUS   in error; mistaken

ERSATZ   fake

ERUDITE   learned, scholarly

ESCALATE   to increase the intensity or scope of

ESCHEW   to abstain from, avoid

ESOTERIC   understood only by a learned few

ESPOUSE   to support or advocate; to marry

ESTIMABLE   admirable

ESTRANGE   to alienate, keep at a distance

ESURIENT   hungry, greedy

ETHEREAL   not earthly, spiritual, delicate

ETHICAL   moral, abiding by an accepted code of conduct

ETHOS   beliefs or character of a group

ETYMOLOGY   origin and history of a word; study of words

EULOGY   high praise, often in a public speech

EUPHEMISM   use of an inoffensive word or phrase in place of a more distasteful one

EUPHONY   pleasant, harmonious sound

EUPHORIA   feeling of well-being or happiness

EURYTHMICS   art of harmonious bodily movement

EUTHANASIA   mercy killing; intentional, easy and painless death

EVADE   to avoid, dodge

EVANESCENT   momentary, transitory, short-lived

EVICT   to put out or force out

EVIDENT   clear, able to be understood

EVINCE   to show clearly, display, signify

EVOKE   to inspire memories; to produce a reaction

EXACERBATE   to aggravate, intensify the bad qualities of

EXALT   to glorify, to elevate

EXASPERATION   irritation

EXCERPT (n)   selection from a book or play

EXCOMMUNICATE   to bar from membership in the church

EXCORIATE   to denounce

EXCRUCIATING   agonizing, intensely painful

EXCULPATE   to clear of blame or fault

EXECRABLE   utterly detestable

EXEMPLARY   serving as an example, commendable

EXHILARATION   state of being energetic or filled with happiness

EXHORT   to urge or incite by strong appeals

EXHUME   to remove from a grave; uncover a secret

EXIGENT   urgent; excessively demanding

EXONERATE   to clear of blame

EXORBITANT   extravagant, greater than reasonable

EXORCISE   to expel evil spirits

EXOTIC   foreign; romantic, excitingly strange

EXPANSIVE   sweeping, comprehensive; tending to expand

EXPATIATE   to wander; to discuss or describe at length

EXPATRIATE (n)   one who lives outside one's native land

EXPATRIATE (v)   to drive someone from his or her native land

EXPEDIENT (adj)   convenient, efficient, practical

EXPIATE   to atone for, make amends for

EXPIRE   to come to an end; die; breathe out

EXPLICABLE   capable of being explained

EXPLICIT   clearly defined, specific; forthright in expression

EXPLODE   to debunk, disprove; blow up, burst

EXPONENT   one who champions or advocates

EXPOUND   to elaborate; to expand or increase

EXPUNGE   to erase, eliminate completely

EXPURGATE   to censor

EXTEMPORANEOUS   unrehearsed, on the spur of the moment

EXTENUATE   to lessen the seriousness, strength, or effect of

EXTINCTION   end of a living thing or species

EXTOL   to praise

EXTORT   to obtain something by threats

EXTRANEOUS   irrelevant, unrelated, unnecessary

EXTRAPOLATE   to estimate

EXTREMITY   outermost or farthest point

EXTRICATE   to free from, disentangle, free

EXTRINSIC   not inherent or essential, coming from without

EXTROVERT   an outgoing person

EXUBERANT   lively, happy, and full of good spirits

EXUDE   to give off, ooze

EXULT   to rejoice

F

FABRICATE   to make or devise; construct

FABRICATED   constructed, invented; faked, falsified

FACADE   face, front; mask, superficial appearance

FACETIOUS   witty in an inappropriate way

FACILE   very easy

FACILITATE   to aid, assist

FACILITY   aptitude, ease in doing something

FACSIMILE   an exact copy

FALLACIOUS   wrong, unsound, illogical

FALLIBLE   capable of failing

FALLOW   uncultivated, unused

FAMINE   extreme scarcity of food

FANATICISM   extreme devotion to a cause

FARCICAL   absurd, ludicrous

FASTIDIOUS   careful with details

FATHOM (v)   to measure the depth of, gauge; to understand

FATUOUS   stupid; foolishly self-satisfied

FAULT   break in a rock formation; mistake or error

FAWN (v)   to flatter excessively, seek the favor of

FAZE   to bother, upset, or disconcert

FEALTY   intense loyalty

FEASIBLE   possible, capable of being done

FECKLESS   ineffective, careless, irresponsible

FECUND   fertile, fruitful, productive

FEDERATION   union of organizations; union of several states, each of which retains local power

FEIGN   to pretend, give a false impression; to invent falsely

FEISTY   excitable, easily drawn into quarrels

FELICITOUS   suitable, appropriate; well-spoken

FELICITY   feeling great happiness

FELL (v)   to chop, cut down

FELL (adj)   cruel

FERVID   passionate, intense zealous

FETID   foul-smelling, putrid

FETTER   to bind, chain, confine

FEUD   a prolonged quarrel between families

FEY   otherworldly; doomed

FIASCO   disaster, utter failure

FICKLE   unreliable

FICTIVE   fictional, imaginary

FIDELITY   loyalty

FIENDISH   excessively bad or cruel

FILCH   to steal

FILIAL   appropriate for a child

FILIBUSTER   use of obstructive tactics in a legislative assembly to prevent adoption of a measure

FINESSE   refinement or skill at a task or in a situation

FINICKY   fussy, difficult to please

FISSION   process of splitting into two parts

FISSURE   a crack or break

FITFUL   intermittent, irregular

FIXITY   being fixed or stable

FLACCID   limp, flabby, weak

FLAG   to loose energy and strength

FLAGRANT   outrageous, shameless

FLAIR   a natural inclination towards something

FLAMBOYANT   flashy, garish; exciting, dazzling

FLAMMABLE   combustible, being easily burned

FLAUNT   to show off

FLEDGLING   young bird just learning to fly; beginner, novice

FLIPPANT   disrespectful, casual

FLORA   plants

FLORID   gaudy, extremely ornate; ruddy, flushed

FLOUNDER   to falter, waver; to muddle, struggle

FLOUT   to treat contemptuously, scorn

FLUCTUATE   to alternate, waver

FLURRIED   to become agitated and confused

FLUSTER   to agitate or confuse

FODDER   raw material; feed for animals

FOIBLE   minor weakness or character flaw

FOIL (v)   to defeat, frustrate

FOIST   to pass off as genuine

FOLIATE   to grow, sprout leaves

FOMENT   to arouse or incite

FORAGE   to wander in search of food

FORBEARANCE   patience, restraint, leniency

FORD (v)   to cross a body of water at a shallow place

FOREBODING   dark sense of evil to come

FORECLOSE   to rule out; to seize debtor's property for lack of payments

FORENSIC   relating to legal proceedings; relating to debates

FORENSICS   study of argumentation and debate

FORESTALL   to prevent, delay; anticipate

FORETHOUGHT   anticipation, foresight

FORFEND   to prevent

FORGO   to go without, refrain from

FORLORN   dreary, deserted; unhappy; hopeless, despairing; pitiful in appearance

FORMULATE   to conceive, devise; to draft, plan; to express, state

FORSAKE   to abandon, withdraw from

FORSWEAR   to repudiate, renounce, disclaim, reject

FORTE (n)   strong point, something a person does well

FORTNIGHT   two weeks

FORTUITOUS   happening by luck, fortunate

FOSTER (v)   to nourish, cultivate, promote

FOUNDATION   groundwork, support; institution established by donation to aid a certain cause

FOUNDER (v)   to fall helplessly; sink

FRACAS   noisy dispute

FRACTIOUS   unruly, rebellious

FRAGMENTATION   division, separation into parts, disorganization

FRANK   honest and straightforward

FRATRICIDE   the killing of a brother or sister

FRAUD   deception, hoax

FRAUDULENT   deceitful, dishonest, unethical

FRAUGHT   full of, accompanied by

FRENETIC   wildly frantic, frenzied, hectic

FRENZIED   feverishly fast, hectic, and confused

FRIVOLOUS   petty, trivial; flippant, silly

FROND   leaf

FRUGAL   thrifty; cheap

FULMINATE   to explode with anger

FULSOME   excessive, overdone, sickeningly abundant

FUNEREAL   mournful, appropriate to a funeral

FUROR   rage, fury

FURTIVE   secret, stealthy

FUSION   process of merging things into one

G

GAINSAY   to deny

GALL (n)   bitterness; careless nerve

GALL (v)   to exasperate and irritate

GALLANT   a very fashionable young man

GAMBOL   to dance or skip around playfully

GAME (adj)   courageous

GARGANTUAN   giant, tremendous

GARNER   to gather and store

GARRULOUS   very talkative

GAUCHE   crude, socially awkward

GAUCHERIE   a tactless or awkward act

GAUNT   thin and bony

GAVEL   mallet used for commanding attention

GENRE   type, class, category

GENTEEL   stylish, elegant in manner or appearance

GERIATRIC   relating to old age or the process of aging

GERMINATE   to begin to grow (as in a seed or idea)

GESTATION   growth process from conception to birth

GIBE (v)   to make heckling, taunting remarks

GIRTH   distance around something

GLIB   fluent in an insincere manner; offhand, casual

GLOBAL   involving the entire world; relating to a whole

GLOWER   to glare, stare angrily and intensely

GLUTTONY   eating and drinking to excess

GNARL   to make knotted, deform

GNOSTIC   having to do with knowledge

GOAD   to prod or urge

GOSSAMER   something light, delicate, or tenuous

GOUGE   scoop out; extort

GRADATION   process occurring by regular degrees or stages; variation in color

GRANDILOQUENCE   pompous talk, fancy but meaningless language

GRANDIOSE   magnificent and imposing; exaggerated and pretentious

GRANULAR   having a grainy texture

GRASP (v)   to perceive and understand; to hold securely

GRATIS   free, costing nothing

GRATUITOUS   free, voluntary; unnecessary and unjustified

GRATUITY   something given voluntarily, tip

GREGARIOUS   outgoing, sociable

GRIEVOUS   causing grief or sorrow; serious and distressing

GRIMACE   facial expression showing pain or disgust

GRIMY   dirty, filthy

GROSS (adj)   obscene; blatant, flagrant

GROSS (n)   total before deductions

GROVEL   to humble oneself in a demeaning way

GRUBBY   dirty, sloppy

GUILE   trickery, deception

GULLIBLE   easily deceived

GUSTATORY   relating to sense of taste

GYRATE   to move in a circular motion

H

HABITAT   dwelling place

HACKNEYED   worn out by overuse

HAIL   to greet with praise

HALLOW   to make holy; treat as sacred

HAMLET   small village

HAPLESS   unfortunate, having bad luck

HARANGUE   a pompous speech

HARBINGER   precursor, sign of something to come

HARDY   robust, vigorous

HARMONY   accord, tranquillity, agreement

HARROWING   extremely distressing, terrifying

HASTEN   to hurry, to speed up

HAUGHTY   arrogant and condescending

HEADLONG   recklessly

HEADSTRONG   reckless; insisting on one's own way

HEATHEN   pagan; uncivilized and irreligious

HECTIC   hasty, hurried, confused

HECTOR   a bully, braggart

HEDONISM   pursuit of pleasure as a goal

HEGEMONY   leadership, domination, usually by a country

HEIGHTEN   to raise

HEINOUS   shocking, wicked, terrible

HEMICYCLE   semicircular form or structure

HEMORRHAGE (n)   heavy bleeding

HEMORRHAGE (v)   to bleed heavily

HERETICAL   opposed to an established religious orthodoxy

HERMETIC   tightly sealed

HETERODOX   unorthodox, not widely accepted

HETEROGENEOUS   composed of unlike parts, different, diverse

HEW   to cut with an ax

HIATUS   a gap or a break

HIDEBOUND   excessively rigid; dry and stiff

HINDER   to hamper

HINDSIGHT   perception of events after they happen

HINTERLAND   wilderness

HOARY   very old; whitish or gray from age

HOLISTIC   emphasizing importance of the whole and interdependence of its parts

HOLOCAUST   widespread destruction, usually by fire

HOMAGE   public honor and respect

HOMOGENEOUS   composed of identical parts

HOMONYM   word identical in pronunciation but different in meaning

HONE   to sharpen

HONOR (v)   to praise, glorify, pay tribute to

HUMANE   merciful, kindly

HUSBAND (v)   to farm; manage carefully and thriftily

HUTCH   pen or coop for animals; shack, shanty

HYDRATE   to add water to

HYGIENIC   clean, sanitary

HYMN   religious song, usually of praise or thanks

HYPERBOLE   purposeful exaggeration for effect

HYPERVENTILATE   to breathe abnormally fast

HYPOCHONDRIA   unfounded belief that one is often ill

HYPOCRITE   person claiming beliefs or virtues he or she doesn't really possess

HYPOTHERMIA   abnormally low body temperature

HYPOTHESIS   assumption subject to proof

HYPOTHETICAL   theoretical, speculative

I

ICONOCLAST   one who attacks traditional beliefs

IDEALISM   pursuit of noble goals

IDIOSYNCRASY   peculiarity of temperament, eccentricity

IGNOBLE   dishonorable, not noble in character

IGNOMINIOUS   disgraceful and dishonorable

IGNORAMUS   an ignorant person

ILK   type or kind

ILLICIT   illegal, improper

ILLIMITABLE   limitless

ILLUSORY   unreal, deceptive

ILLUSTRIOUS   famous, renowned

IMBUE   to infuse; dye, wet, moisten

IMMACULATE   spotless; free from error

IMMATERIAL   extraneous, inconsequential, nonessential; not consisting of matter

IMMENSE   enormous, huge

IMMERSE   to bathe, dip; to engross, preoccupy

IMMOBILE   not moveable; still

IMMUNE   exempt; protected from harm or disease; unresponsive to

IMMUNOLOGICAL   relating to immune system

IMMURE   to imprison

IMMUTABLE   unchangeable, invariable

IMPAIR   to damage, injure

IMPASSE   blocked path, dilemma with no solution

IMPASSIONED   with passion

IMPASSIVE   showing no emotion

IMPEACH   to charge with misdeeds in public office; accuse

IMPECCABLE   flawless, without fault

IMPECUNIOUS   poor, having no money

IMPEDIMENT   barrier, obstacle; speech disorder

IMPERATIVE   essential; mandatory

IMPERIOUS   arrogantly self-assured, domineering, overbearing

IMPERTINENT   rude

IMPERTURBABLE   not capable of being disturbed

IMPERVIOUS   impossible to penetrate; incapable of being affected

IMPETUOUS   quick to act without thinking

IMPIOUS   not devout in religion

IMPLACABLE   inflexible, incapable of being pleased

IMPLANT   to set securely or deeply; to instill

IMPLAUSIBLE   improbable, inconceivable

IMPLICATE   to involve in a crime, incriminate

IMPLICIT   implied, not directly expressed

IMPOLITIC   unwise

IMPORTUNE   to ask repeatedly, beg

IMPOSE   to inflict, force upon

IMPOSING   dignified, grand

IMPOTENT   powerless, ineffective, lacking strength

IMPOUND   to seize and confine

IMPOVERISH   to make poor or bankrupt

IMPRECATION   curse

IMPREGNABLE   totally safe from attack, able to resist defeat

IMPRESSIONABLE   easily influenced or affected

IMPROMPTU   spontaneous, without rehearsal

IMPROVIDENT   without planning or foresight, negligent

IMPRUDENT   unwise

IMPUDENT   arrogant and rude

IMPUGN   to call into question, attack verbally

IMPULSE   sudden tendency, inclination

IMPULSIVE   spontaneous, unpredictable

INADVERTENTLY   unintentionally

INANE   foolish, silly, lacking significance

INAUGURATE   to begin or start officially; to induct into office

INCANDESCENT   shining brightly

INCARCERATE   to put in jail; to confine

INCARCERATION   imprisonment

INCARNADINE   blood-red in color

INCARNATE   having bodily form

INCENDIARY   combustible, flammable, burning easily

INCENSE (v)   to infuriate, enrage

INCEPTION   beginning

INCESSANT   continuous, never ceasing

INCHOATE   just begun; disorganized

INCIPIENT   beginning to exist or appear; in an initial stage

INCISIVE   perceptive, penetrating

INCLINATION   tendency towards

INCLUSIVE   comprehensive, all-encompassing

INCOGNITO   in disguise, concealing one's identity

INCOMMUNICADO   lacking a means to communicate

INCONCEIVABLE   impossible, unthinkable

INCONGRUOUS   incompatible, not harmonious

INCONSEQUENTIAL   unimportant, trivial

INCONTROVERTIBLE   unquestionable, beyond dispute

INCORRIGIBLE   incapable of being corrected

INCREDULOUS   skeptical, doubtful

INCULCATE   to teach, impress in the mind

INCULPATE   to blame, charge with a crime

INCUMBENT (adj)   holding a specified office, often political; required, obligatory

INCURSION   sudden invasion

INDEFATIGABLE   never tired

INDEFENSIBLE   inexcusable, unforgivable

INDELIBLE   permanent, not erasable

INDENTURE   bound to another by contract

INDICATIVE   showing or pointing out, suggestive of

INDICT   to accuse formally, charge with a crime

INDIGENOUS   native, occurring naturally in an area

INDIGENT   very poor

INDIGNANT   angry, incensed, offended

INDISPUTABLE   not disputed, unquestioned

INDOLENT   habitually lazy, idle

INDOMITABLE   fearless, unconquerable

INDUBITABLE   unquestionable

INDUCE   to persuade; bring about

INDUCT   to place ceremoniously in office

INDULGE   to give in to a craving or desire

INDUSTRY   business or trade; diligence, energy

INEBRIATED   drunk, intoxicated

INEPT   clumsy, awkward

INERT   unable to move, tending to inactivity

INESTIMABLE   too great to be estimated

INEVITABLE   certain, unavoidable

INEXORABLE   inflexible, unyielding

INEXTRICABLE   incapable of being disentangled

INFALLIBLE   incapable of making a mistake

INFAMY   reputation for bad deeds

INFANTILE   childish, immature

INFATUATED   strongly or foolishly attached to, inspired with foolish passion, overly in love

INFER   to conclude, deduce

INFERNAL   hellish, diabolical

INFILTRATE   to pass secretly into enemy territory

INFINITESIMAL   extremely tiny

INFIRMITY   disease, ailment

INFRINGE   to encroach, trespass; to transgress, violate

INFURIATE   to anger, provoke, outrage

INFURIATING   provoking anger or outrage

INGENIOUS   original, clever, inventive

INGENUOUS   straightforward, open; naive and unsophisticated

INGLORIOUS   lacking fame or honor, shameful

INGRAINED   an innate quality, deep-seated

INGRATE   ungrateful person

INGRATIATE   to bring oneself purposely into another's good graces

INGRESS   entrance

INHIBIT   to hold back, prevent, restrain

INIMICAL   hostile, unfriendly

INIQUITY   sin, evil act

INITIATE   to begin, introduce; to enlist, induct

INJECT   to force into; to introduce into conversation

INJUNCTION   command, order

INJURIOUS   causing injury

INKLING   hint; vague idea

INNATE   natural, inborn

INNATENESS   state of being natural or inborn

INNOCUOUS   harmless; inoffensive

INNOVATE   to invent, modernize, revolutionize

INNUENDO   indirect and subtle criticism, insinuation

INNUMERABLE   too many to be counted

INOFFENSIVE   harmless, innocent

INOPERABLE   not operable; incurable by surgery

INQUEST   investigation; court or legal proceeding

INQUISITIVE   curious

INSATIABLE   never satisfied

INSCRUTABLE   impossible to understand fully

INSENTIENT   unfeeling, unconscious

INSIDIOUS   sly, treacherous, devious

INSINUATE   to suggest, say indirectly, imply

INSIPID   bland, lacking flavor; lacking excitement

INSOLENT   insulting and arrogant

INSOLUBLE   not able to be solved or explained

INSOLVENT   bankrupt, unable to pay one's debts

INSTIGATE   to incite, urge, agitate

INSUBSTANTIAL   modest, insignificant

INSUFFICIENCY   lacking in something

INSULAR   isolated, detached

INSUPERABLE   insurmountable, unconquerable

INSURGENT (adj)   rebellious, insubordinate

INSURRECTION   rebellion

INTEGRAL   central, indispensable

INTEGRATED   unified

INTEGRITY   decency, honest; wholeness

INTEMPERATE   not moderate

INTER   to bury

INTERDICT   to forbid, prohibit

INTERJECT   to interpose, insert

INTERLOCUTOR   someone taking part in a dialog

INTERLOPER   trespasser; meddler in others' affairs

INTERMINABLE   endless

INTERMITTENT   starting and stopping

INTERNECINE   deadly to both sides

INTERPOLATE   to insert; change by adding new words or material

INTERPOSE   to insert; to intervene

INTERREGNUM   interval between reigns

INTERROGATE   to question formally

INTERSECT   to divide by passing through or across

INTERSPERSE   to distribute among, mix with

INTERSTICE   a space between things

INTIMATION   clue, suggestion

INTRACTABLE   not easily managed

INTRAMURAL   within an institution like a school

INTRANSIGENT   uncompromising, refusing to be reconciled

INTREPID   fearless

INTRIGUED   interested, curious

INTRINSIC   inherent, internal

INTROSPECTIVE   contemplating one's own thoughts
  and feelings

INTROVERT   someone given to self-analysis

INTRUSION   trespass, invasion of another's privacy

INTUITIVE   instinctive, untaught

INUNDATE   to cover with water; overwhelm

INURE   to harden; accustom; become used to

INVALIDATE   to negate or nullify

INVARIABLE   constant, not changing

INVECTIVE   verbal abuse

INVEIGH   protest strongly

INVESTITURE   ceremony conferring authority

INVETERATE   confirmed, long-standing, deeply rooted

INVIDIOUS   likely to provoke ill will, offensive

INVINCIBLE   invulnerable, unbeatable

INVIOLABLE   safe from violation or assault

INVOKE   to call upon, request help

IOTA   very tiny amount

IRASCIBLE   easily angered

IRIDESCENT   showing many colors

IRRESOLVABLE   unable to be resolved; not analyzable

IRREVERENT   disrespectful

IRREVOCABLE   conclusive, irreversible

ITINERANT   wandering from place to place, unsettled

ITINERARY   route of a traveler's journey

J

JADED   tired by excess or overuse; slightly cynical

JANGLING   clashing, jarring; harshly unpleasant (in sound)

JARGON   nonsensical talk; specialized language

JAUNDICE   yellowish discoloration of skin

JAUNDICED   affected by jaundice; prejudiced or embittered

JETTISON   to cast off, throw cargo overboard

JIBE   to shift suddenly from one side to the other

JINGOISM   belligerent support of one's country

JOCULAR   jovial, playful, humorous

JUBILEE   special anniversary

JUDICIOUS   sensible, showing good judgment

JUGGERNAUT   huge force destroying everything in its path

JUNCTURE   point where two things are joined

JURISPRUDENCE   philosophy of law

JUVENILE   young or childish acting

JUXTAPOSITION   side-by-side placement

K

KEEN   having a sharp edge; intellectually sharp, perceptive

KERNEL   innermost, essential part; seed grain, often in a shell

KEYNOTE   note or tone on which a musical key is founded;
  main idea of a speech, program, etc.

KINDLE   to set fire to or ignite; excite or inspire

KINETIC   relating to motion; characterized by movement

KISMET   fate

KNELL   sound of a funeral bell; omen of death or failure

KUDOS   fame, glory, honor

L

LABYRINTH   maze

LACERATION   cut or wound

LACHRYMOSE   tearful

LACKADAISICAL   idle, lazy; apathetic, indifferent

LACKLUSTER   dull

LACONIC   using few words

LAGGARD   dawdler, loafer, lazy person

LAMBASTE   disapprove angrily

LAMENT (v)   to deplore, grieve

LAMPOON (v)   to attack with satire, mock harshly

LANGUID   lacking energy, indifferent, slow

LANGUOR   listlessness

LAP (v)   to drink using the tongue; to wash against

LAPIDARY   relating to precious stones

LARCENY   theft of property

LARDER   place where food is stored

LARGESS   generosity; gift

LARYNX   organ containing vocal cords

LASCIVIOUS   lewd, lustful

LASSITUDE   lethargy, sluggishness

LATENT   present but hidden; potential

LATITUDE   freedom of action or choice

LAUDABLE   deserving of praise

LAVISH   to give plentiful amounts of

LAXITY   carelessness

LEERY   suspicious

LEGERDEMAIN   trickery

LEGIBLE   readable

LEGISLATE   to decree, mandate, make laws

LEGITIMATE   adhering to the law, rightful

LENIENT   easygoing, permissive

LETHARGY   indifferent inactivity

LEVITATE   to rise in the air or cause to rise

LEVITY   humor, frivolity, gaiety

LEXICON   dictionary, list of words

LIBERAL (adj)   tolerant, broad-minded; generous, lavish

LIBERATION   freedom, emancipation

LIBERTARIAN   one who believes in unrestricted freedom

LIBERTINE   one without moral restraint

LIBIDINOUS   lustful

LICENSE   freedom to act

LICENTIOUS   immoral; unrestrained by society

LIEN   right to possess and sell the property of a debtor

LIMPID   clear and simple; serene; transparent

LINEAGE   ancestry

LINGUISTICS   study of language

LINIMENT   medicinal liquid used externally to ease pain

LIONIZE   to treat as a celebrity

LISSOME   easily flexed, limber, agile

LISTLESS   lacking energy and enthusiasm

LITERAL   word for word; upholding the exact meaning of a word

LITERATE   able to read and write; well-read and educated

LITHE   moving and bending with ease; graceful

LITIGATION   lawsuit

LIVID   discolored from a bruise; reddened with anger

LOATHE   to abhor, despise, hate

LOCOMOTION   movement from place to place

LODGED   fixed in one position

LOFTY   noble, elevated in position

LOGO   corporate symbol

LOITER   to stand around idly

LOQUACIOUS   talkative

LOW (v)   to make a sound like a cow, moo

LUCID   clear and easily understood

LUDICROUS   laughable, ridiculous

LUGUBRIOUS   sorrowful, mournful

LULL   to soothe

LUMBER (v)   to move slowly and awkwardly

LUMINARY   bright object; celebrity; source of inspiration

LUMINOUS   bright, brilliant, glowing

LUNAR   relating to the moon

LURID   harshly shocking, sensational; glowing

LURK   to prowl, sneak

LUSCIOUS   very good-tasting

LUXURIANCE   elegance, lavishness

LYRICAL   suitable for poetry and song; expressing feeling

M

MACABRE   gruesome, producing horror

MACHINATION   plot or scheme

MACROBIOTICS   art of prolonging life by special diet of organic, nonmeat substances

MACROCOSM   system regarded as an entity with subsystems

MAELSTROM   whirlpool; turmoil; agitated state of mind

MAGNANIMOUS   generous, noble in spirit

MAGNATE   powerful or influential person

MAGNITUDE   extent, greatness of size

MAINSTAY   chief support

MALADROIT   clumsy, tactless

MALADY   illness

MALAPROPISM   humorous misuse of a word

MALCONTENT   discontented person, one who holds a grudge

MALEDICTION   curse

MALEFACTOR   evil-doer; culprit

MALEVOLENT   ill-willed; causing evil or harm to others

MALFUNCTION (n)   breakdown, failure

MALFUNCTION (v)   to fail to work

MALICE   animosity, spite, hatred

MALINGER   to evade responsibility by pretending to be ill

MALLEABLE   capable of being shaped

MALNUTRITION   undernourishment

MALODOROUS   foul-smelling

MANDATORY   necessary, required

MANIFEST (adj)   obvious

MANIFOLD   diverse, varied, comprised of many parts

MANNERED   artificial or stilted in character

MANUAL (adj)   hand-operated; physical

MANUMISSION   release from slavery

MAR   to damage, deface; spoil

MARGINAL   barely sufficient

MARITIME   relating to the sea or sailing

MARTIAL   warlike, pertaining to the military

MARTINET   strict disciplinarian, one who rigidly follows rules

MARTYR   person dying for his or her beliefs

MASOCHIST   one who enjoys pain or humiliation

MASQUERADE   disguise; action that conceals the truth

MATERIALISM   preoccupation with material things

MATRICULATE   to enroll as a member of a college or university

MATRILINEAL   tracing ancestry through mother's line rather than father's

MAUDLIN   overly sentimental

MAVERICK   a person who resists adherence to a group

MAWKISH   sickeningly sentimental

MEAGER   scanty, sparse

MEANDER   to wander aimlessly without direction

MEANINGFUL   significant

MEDDLER   person interfering in others' affairs

MEDIEVAL   relating to the Middle Ages

MEGALITH   huge stone used in prehistoric structures

MEGALOMANIA   mental state with delusions of wealth and power

MELANCHOLY   sadness, depression

MELODIOUS   having a pleasing melody

MELODY   pleasing musical sounds; tune

MENAGERIE   various animals kept together for exhibition

MENDACIOUS   dishonest

MENDACITY   a lie, falsehood

MENDICANT   beggar

MENTOR   experienced teacher and wise adviser

MERCENARY (adj)   motivated only by greed

MERCENARY (n)   soldier for hire in foreign countries

MERCURIAL   quick, shrewd, and unpredictable

MERETRICIOUS   gaudy, falsely attractive

MERIDIAN   circle passing through the two poles of the earth

MERITORIOUS   deserving reward or praise

METAMORPHOSIS   change, transformation

METAPHOR   figure of speech comparing two different things

METICULOUS   extremely careful, fastidious, painstaking

METRONOME   time-keeping device used in music

METTLE   courageousness; endurance

MICROBE   microorganism

MICROCOSM   tiny system used as analogy for larger system

MIGRATORY   wandering from place to place with the seasons

MILITATE   to operate against, work against

MILLENNIUM   one thousand years

MINATORY   menacing, threatening

MINIMAL   smallest in amount, least possible

MINUSCULE   very small

MIRTH   frivolity, gaiety, laughter

MISANTHROPE   person who hates human beings

MISAPPREHEND   to misunderstand, fail to know

MISCONSTRUE   to misunderstand, fail to discover

MISCREANT   one who behaves criminally

MISERLINESS   extreme stinginess

MISGIVING   apprehension, doubt, sense of foreboding

MISHAP   accident; misfortune

MISNOMER   an incorrect name or designation

MISSIVE   note or letter

MITIGATE   to soften, or make milder

MNEMONIC   relating to memory; designed to assist memory

MOBILITY   ease of movement

MOCK (v)   to deride, ridicule

MODERATE (adj)   reasonable, not extreme

MODERATE (v)   to make less excessive, restrain; regulate

MODICUM   a small amount

MOLLIFY   to calm or make less severe

MOLLUSK   sea animal with a soft body

MOLT (v)   to shed hair, skin, or an outer layer periodically

MOMENTOUS   important

MONASTIC   extremely plain or secluded, as in a monastery

MONOCHROMATIC   having one color

MONOGAMY   custom of marriage to one person at a time

MONOLITH   large block of stone

MONOLOGUE   dramatic speech performed by one actor

MONOTONY   lack of variation; wearisome sameness

MONTAGE   composite picture

MOOT   debatable; previously decided

MORBID   gruesome; relating to disease; abnormally gloomy

MORDACIOUS   caustic, biting

MORDANT   sarcastic

MORES   customs or manners

MORIBUND   dying, decaying

MOROSE   gloomy, sullen, or surly

MORSEL   small bit of food

MOTE   small particle, speck

MOTLEY   many-colored; composed of diverse parts

MOTTLE   to mark with spots

MULTIFACETED   having many parts, many-sided

MULTIFARIOUS   diverse

MUNDANE   worldly; commonplace

MUNIFICENT   generous

MUNITIONS   ammunition

MUTABILITY   changeability

MUTE   unable to speak

MYOPIC   near-sighted

MYRIAD   immense number, multitude

N

NADIR   lowest point

NAIVE   lacking sophistication

NAIVETÉ   a lack of worldly wisdom

NARRATIVE   account, story

NASCENT   starting to develop, coming into existence

NATAL   relating to birth

NEBULOUS   vague, cloudy

NECROMANCY   black magic

NEFARIOUS   vicious, evil

NEGLIGENT   careless, inattentive

NEGLIGIBLE   not worth considering

NEMESIS   a formidable, often victorious opponent

NEOLOGISM   new word or expression

NEONATE   newborn child

NEOPHYTE   novice, beginner

NETHER   located under or below

NETTLE (v)   to irritate

NEUTRALITY   disinterest, impartiality

NEUTRALIZE   to balance, offset

NICETY   elegant or delicate feature; minute distinction

NICHE   recess in a wall; best position for something

NIGGARDLY   stingy

NIGGLING   trifle, petty

NIHILISM   belief that existence and all traditional values are meaningless

NOBLE   illustrious, moral

NOCTURNAL   pertaining to night; active at night

NOISOME   stinking, putrid

NOMADIC   moving from place to place

NOMENCLATURE   terms used in a particular science or discipline

NOMINAL   existing in name only; negligible

NON SEQUITUR   conclusion not following from apparent evidence

NONCHALANT   unconcerned, indifferent

NONDESCRIPT   lacking interesting or distinctive qualities; dull

NONENTITY   an insignificant person

NOTORIETY   fame; unfavorable fame

NOVICE   apprentice, beginner

NOVITIATE   period of being a beginner or novice

NOXIOUS   harmful, unwholesome

NUANCE   shade of meaning

NULLIFY   to make legally invalid; to counteract the effect of

NUMISMATICS   coin collecting

NUPTIAL   relating to marriage

NUTRITIVE   relating to nutrition or health

O

OBDURATE   stubborn

OBEISANCE   a show of respect or submission

OBFUSCATE   to confuse, obscure

OBJURGATE   scold

OBLIGING   accommodating, agreeable

OBLIQUE   indirect, evasive; misleading, devious

OBLITERATE   demolish completely, wipe out

OBLIVIOUS   unaware, inattentive

OBLOQUY   abusive language; ill repute

OBSCURE (adj)   dim, unclear; not well known

OBSCURITY   place or thing that's hard to perceive

OBSEQUIOUS   overly submissive, brownnosing

OBSEQUY   funeral ceremony

OBSESSIVE   preoccupying, all-consuming

OBSOLETE   no longer in use

OBSTINATE   stubborn

OBSTREPEROUS   troublesome, boisterous, unruly

OBTRUSIVE   pushy, too conspicuous

OBTUSE   insensitive, stupid, dull

OBVIATE   to make unnecessary; to anticipate and prevent

OCCLUDE   to shut, block

ODIOUS   hateful, contemptible

OFFICIOUS   too helpful, meddlesome

OFFSHOOT   branch

OMINOUS   menacing, threatening, indicating misfortune

OMNIPOTENT   having unlimited power

OMNISCIENT   having infinite knowledge

OMNIVOROUS   eating everything; absorbing everything

ONEROUS   burdensome

ONTOLOGY   theory about the nature of existence

OPALESCENT   iridescent, displaying colors

OPAQUE   impervious to light; difficult to understand

OPERATIVE   functioning, working

OPINE   to express an opinion

OPPORTUNE   appropriate, fitting

OPPORTUNIST   one who takes advantage of circumstances

OPPROBRIOUS   disgraceful, contemptuous

OPTIMUM   the most favorable degree

OPULENCE   wealth

ORACLE   person who foresees the future and gives advice

ORATION   lecture, formal speech

ORATOR   lecturer, speaker

ORB   spherical body; eye

ORCHESTRATE   to arrange music for performance; to coordinate, organize

ORDAIN   to make someone a priest or minister; to order

ORIFICE   an opening

ORNITHOLOGIST   scientist who studies birds

OROTUND   pompous

OSCILLATE   to move back and forth

OSSIFY   to turn to bone; to become rigid

OSTENSIBLE   apparent

OSTENTATIOUS   showy

OSTRACISM   exclusion, temporary banishment

OUSTER   expulsion, ejection

OVERABUNDANCE   excess, surfeit

OVERSTATE   to embellish, exaggerate

OVERT   in the open, obvious

OVERTURE   musical introduction; proposal, offer

OVERWEENING   arrogant

OVERWROUGHT   agitated, overdone

P

PACIFIC   calm, peaceful

PACIFIST   one opposed to war

PACIFY   to restore calm, bring peace

PAEAN   a song of praise or thanksgiving

PALATIAL   like a palace, magnificent

PALAVER   idle talk

PALEONTOLOGY   study of past geological eras through fossil remains

PALETTE   board for mixing paints; range of colors

PALISADE   fence made up of stakes

PALL (n)   covering that darkens or obscures; coffin

PALL (v)   to lose strength or interest

PALLIATE   to make less serious, ease

PALLID   lacking color or liveliness

PALPABLE   obvious, real, tangible

PALPITATION   trembling, shaking, irregular beating

PALTRY   pitifully small or worthless

PANACEA   cure-all

PANACHE   flamboyance, verve

PANDEMIC   spread over a whole area or country

PANEGYRIC   elaborate praise; formal hymn of praise

PANOPLY   impressive array

PANORAMA   broad view; comprehensive picture

PARADIGM   ideal example, model

PARADOX   contradiction, incongruity; dilemma, puzzle

PARADOXICAL   self-contradictory but true

PARAGON   model of excellence or perfection

PARAMOUNT   supreme, dominant, primary

PARAPHRASE   to reword, usually in simpler terms

PARASITE   person or animal that lives at another's expense

PARCH   to dry or shrivel

PARE   to trim

PARIAH   outcast

PARITY   equality

PARLEY   discussion, usually between enemies

PAROCHIAL   of limited scope or outlook, provincial

PARODY   humorous imitation

PAROLE   conditional release of a prisoner

PARRY   to ward off or deflect

PARSIMONY   stinginess

PARTISAN (adj)   biased in favor of

PARTISAN (n)   strong supporter

PASTICHE   piece of literature or music imitating other works

PATENT (adj)   obvious, unconcealed

PATENT (n)   official document giving exclusive right to sell an invention

PATERNITY   fatherhood; descent from father's ancestors

PATHOGENIC   causing disease

PATHOS   pity, compassion

PATRICIAN   aristocrat

PATRICIDE   murder of one's father

PATRIMONY   inheritance or heritage derived from one's father

PATRONIZE   to condescend to, disparage; to buy from

PAUCITY   scarcity, lack

PAUPER   very poor person

PAVILION   tent or light building used for shelter or exhibitions

PECCADILLO   minor sin or offense

PECULATION   theft of money or goods

PEDAGOGUE   teacher

PEDANT   one who pays undue attention to book learning and rules; one who displays learning ostentatiously

PEDESTRIAN (adj)   commonplace

PEDIATRICIAN   doctor specializing in children and their ailments

PEDIMENT   triangular gable on a roof or facade

PEER (n)   contemporary, equal, match

PEERLESS   unequaled

PEJORATIVE   having bad connotations; disparaging

PELLUCID   transparent; translucent; easily understood

PENANCE   voluntary suffering to repent for a wrong

PENCHANT   inclination

PENDING (prep)   during, while awaiting

PENITENT   expressing sorrow for sins or offenses, repentant

PENSIVE   thoughtful

PENULTIMATE   next to last

PENUMBRA   partial shadow

PENURY   extreme poverty

PERAMBULATE   walk about

PERCIPIENT   discerning, able to perceive

PERDITION   complete and utter loss; damnation

PEREGRINATE   to wander from place to place

PEREMPTORY   imperative; dictatorial

PERENNIAL   present throughout the years; persistent

PERFIDIOUS   faithless, disloyal, untrustworthy

PERFUNCTORY   done in a routine way; indifferent

PERIHELION   point in orbit nearest to the sun

PERIPATETIC   moving from place to place

PERIPHRASTIC   containing too many words

PERJURE   to tell a lie under oath

PERMEABLE   penetrable

PERNICIOUS   very harmful

PERPETUAL   endless, lasting

PERPETUITY   continuing forever

PERPLEXING   puzzling, bewildering

PERSONIFICATION   act of attributing human qualities to objects or abstract qualities

PERSPICACIOUS   shrewd, astute, keen-witted

PERT   lively and bold

PERTINACIOUS   persistent, stubborn

PERTINENT   applicable, appropriate

PERTURBATION   disturbance

PERUSAL   close examination

PERVASIVE   present throughout

PERVERT (v)   to cause to change in immoral way; to misuse

PESTILENCE   epidemic, plague

PETTISH   fretful

PETULANCE   rudeness, peevishness

PHALANX   massed group of soldiers, people, or things

PHILANDERER   pursuer of casual love affairs

PHILANTHROPY   love of humanity; generosity to worthy causes

PHILISTINE   narrow-minded person, someone lacking appreciation for art or culture

PHILOLOGY   study of words

PHLEGM   coldness or indifference

PHLEGMATIC   calm in temperament; sluggish

PHOBIA   anxiety, horror

PHOENIX   mythical, immortal bird that lives for 500 years, burns itself to death, and rises from its ashes

PHONETICS   study of speech sounds

PHONIC   relating to sound

PICAYUNE   petty, of little value

PIDDLING   trivial

PIETY   devoutness

PILFER   to steal

PILLAGE   to loot, especially during a war

PILLORY   ridicule and abuse

PINNACLE   peak, highest point of development

PIOUS   dedicated, devout, extremely religious

PIQUE   fleeting feeling of hurt pride

PITHY   profound, substantial; concise, succinct, to the point

PITTANCE   meager amount or wage

PLACATE   to soothe or pacify

PLACID   calm

PLAGIARIST   one who steals words or ideas

PLAINTIFF   injured person in a lawsuit

PLAINTIVE   expressing sorrow

PLAIT   to braid

PLANGENT   loud sound; wailing sound

PLASTIC   flexible; pliable

PLATITUDE   stale, overused expression

PLAUDIT   applause

PLEBEIAN   crude, vulgar; low-class

PLENITUDE   abundance, plenty

PLETHORA   excess, overabundance

PLIANT   pliable, yielding

PLUCK   to pull strings on musical instrument

PLUCKY   courageous, spunky

PLUMMET   to fall, plunge

PLURALISTIC   including a variety of groups

PLY (v)   to use diligently; to engage; to join together

PNEUMATIC   relating to air; worked by compressed air

POACH   to steal game or fish; cook in boiling liquid

PODIUM   platform or lectern for orchestra conductors or speakers

POIGNANT   emotionally moving

POLAR   relating to a geographic pole; exhibiting contrast

POLARIZE   to tend towards opposite extremes

POLEMIC   controversy, argument; verbal attack

POLITIC   shrewd and practical; diplomatic

POLYGLOT   speaker of many languages

POMPOUS   self-important

PONDEROUS   weighty, heavy, large

PONTIFICATE   to speak in a pretentious manner

PORE (v)   to study closely or meditatively

POROUS   full of holes, permeable to liquids

PORTENT   omen

PORTLY   stout, dignified

POSIT   to put in position; to suggest an idea

POSTERIOR   bottom, rear

POSTERITY   future generations; all of a person's descendants

POTABLE   drinkable

POTENTATE   monarch or ruler with great power

POVERTY   lacking money or possessions

PRAGMATIC   practical; moved by facts rather than abstract ideals

PRATTLE   meaningless, foolish talk

PRECARIOUS   uncertain

PRECEPT   principle; law

PRECIPICE   edge, steep overhang

PRECIPITATE (adj)   sudden and unexpected

PRECIPITATE (v)   to throw down from a height; to cause to happen

PRECIPITOUS   hasty, quickly, with too little caution

PRÉCIS   short summary of facts

PRECISION   state of being precise; exactness

PRECLUDE   to rule out

PRECOCIOUS   unusually advanced at an early age

PRECURSOR   forerunner, predecessor

PREDATOR   one that preys on others, destroyer, plunderer

PREDESTINE   to decide in advance

PREDICAMENT   difficult situation

PREDICATE (v)   to found or base on

PREDICTIVE   relating to prediction, indicative of the future

PREDILECTION   preference, liking

PREDISPOSITION   tendency, inclination

PREEMINENT   celebrated, distinguished

PREFACE   introduction to a book; introductory remarks to a speech

PREMEDITATE   to consider, plan beforehand

PREMONITION   forewarning; presentiment

PREPONDERANCE   majority in number; dominance

PREPOSSESSING   attractive, engaging, appealing

PREPOSTEROUS   absurd, illogical

PRESAGE   to foretell, indicate in advance

PRESCIENT   having foresight

PRESCRIBE   to set down a rule; to recommend a treatment

PRESENTIMENT   premonition, sense of foreboding

PRESTIDIGITATION   sleight of hand

PRESUMPTUOUS   rude, improperly bold

PRETENTIOUS   showy, self-important

PRETEXT   excuse, pretended reason

PREVALENT   widespread

PREVARICATE   to lie, evade the truth

PRIMEVAL   ancient, primitive

PRIMORDIAL   original, existing from the beginning

PRISTINE   untouched, uncorrupted

PRIVATION   lack of usual necessities or comforts

PROBITY   honesty, high-mindedness

PROCLIVITY   tendency, inclination

PROCRASTINATION   putting off something that must be done

PROCRASTINATOR   one who continually and unjustifiably postpones

PROCURE   to obtain

PRODIGAL   wasteful, extravagant, lavish

PRODIGIOUS   vast, enormous, extraordinary

PROFANE   impure; contrary to religion; sacrilegious

PROFICIENT   expert, skilled in a certain subject

PROFLIGATE   corrupt, degenerate

PROFUNDITY   great depth

PROFUSE   lavish, extravagant

PROGENITOR   originator, forefather, ancestor in a direct line

PROGENY   offspring, children

PROGNOSIS   prediction of disease outcome; any prediction

PROGNOSTICATE   to predict

PROGRESSIVE   favoring progress or change; moving forward

PROLIFERATION   propagation, reproduction; enlargement, expansion

PROLIFIC   productive, fertile

PROLIX   tedious; wordy

PROLOGUE   introductory section of a literary work or play

PROMONTORY   piece of land or rock higher than its surroundings

PROMULGATE   to make known publicly

PROPAGATE   to breed

PROPENSITY   inclination, tendency

PROPINQUITY   nearness

PROPITIATE   to win over, appease

PROPITIOUS   favorable, advantageous

PROPONENT   advocate, defender, supporter

PROPRIETY   appropriateness

PROSAIC   relating to prose; dull, commonplace

PROSCRIBE   to condemn; to forbid, outlaw

PROSE   ordinary language used in everyday speech

PROSECUTOR   person who initiates a legal action or suit

PROSELYTIZE   to convert to a particular belief or religion

PROSTRATE   lying face downward, lying flat on the ground

PROTAGONIST   main character in a play or story, hero

PROTEAN   readily assuming different forms or characters

PROTESTATION   declaration

PROTOCOL   ceremony and manners observed by diplomats

PROTRACT   to prolong, draw out, extend

PROTRUSION   something that sticks out

PROVIDENT   prudent, frugal

PROVIDENTIAL   prudent, lucky

PROVINCIAL   rustic, unsophisticated, limited in scope

PROVOCATION   cause, incitement to act or respond

PROWESS   bravery, skill

PROXIMITY   nearness

PROXY   power to act as substitute for another

PRUDE   one who is excessively proper or modest

PRUDENT   careful, cautious

PRURIENT   lustful, exhibiting lewd desires

PRY   to intrude into; force open

PSEUDONYM   pen name; fictitious or borrowed name

PSYCHIC (adj)   having to do with the mind; perceptive of nonmaterial, spiritual forces

PUDGY   chubby, overweight

PUERILE   childish, immature, silly

PUGILISM   boxing

PUGNACIOUS   quarrelsome, eager and ready to fight

PULCHRITUDE   beauty

PULVERIZE   to pound, crush, or grind into powder; destroy

PUMMEL   to pound, beat

PUNCTILIOUS   careful in observing rules of behavior or ceremony

PUNDIT   an authority or critic

PUNGENT   strong or sharp in smell or taste

PUNITIVE   having to do with punishment

PURGATION   process of cleansing, purification

PURGE (v)   to cleanse or free from impurities

PURITANICAL   adhering to a rigid moral code

PURPORT   to profess, suppose, claim

PUSILLANIMOUS   cowardly

PUTRID   rotten

Q

QUACK (n)   faker; one who falsely claims to have medical skill

QUADRILATERAL   four-sided polygon

QUADRUPED   animal having four feet

QUAFF   to drink heartily

QUAGMIRE   marsh; difficult situation

QUALIFY   to provide with needed skills; modify, limit

QUANDARY   dilemma, difficulty

QUARANTINE   isolation period, originally 40 days, to prevent spread of disease

QUATERNARY   consisting of or relating to four units or members

QUELL   to crush or subdue

QUERULOUS   inclined to complain, irritable

QUERY (n)   question

QUIBBLE   to argue about insignificant and irrelevant details

QUICKEN   to hasten, arouse, excite

QUIESCENCE   inactivity, stillness

QUIESCENT   inactive, at rest

QUINTESSENCE   most typical example; concentrated essence

QUIVER (v)   to shake slightly, tremble, vibrate

QUIXOTIC   overly idealistic, impractical

QUOTIDIAN   occurring daily; commonplace

R

RACONTEUR   witty, skillful storyteller

RADICAL (adj)   fundamental; drastic

RAGING   violent, wild

RAIL (v)   to scold with bitter or abusive language

RAILLERY   lighthearted jesting

RALLY (v)   to assemble; recover, recuperate

RAMBLE (v)   to roam, wander; to babble, digress

RAMIFICATION   implication, outgrowth, or consequence

RAMPANT   unrestrained

RAMSHACKLE   likely to collapse

RANCID   spoiled, rotten

RANCOR   bitter hatred

RANT   to harangue, rave, forcefully scold

RAPACIOUS   greedy; predatory

RAPPORT   relationship of trust and respect

RAPPROCHEMENT   having a cordial relationship

RAPT   deeply absorbed

RAREFY   to make thinner, purer, or more refined

RASH (adj)   careless, hasty, reckless

RATIFY   to approve formally, confirm

RATIOCINATION   methodical, logical reasoning

RATION (n)   portion, share

RATION (v)   to supply; to restrict consumption of

RATIONAL   logical, reasonable

RATIONALE   line of reasoning

RAUCOUS   harsh-sounding; boisterous

RAVAGE   to destroy, devastate

RAVENOUS   extremely hungry

RAVINE   deep, narrow gorge

RAW   vulgar, coarse

RAZE   to tear down, demolish

REACTIONARY (adj)   marked by extreme conservatism, esp. in politics

REBARBATIVE   irritating; repellent

REBUFF (n)   blunt rejection

REBUKE (v)   to reprimand, scold

REBUT   to refute by evidence or argument

RECALCITRANT   resisting authority or control

RECANT   to retract a statement, opinion, etc.

RECAPITULATE   to review with a brief summary

RECEPTIVE   open to others' ideas; congenial

RECIDIVISM   tendency to repeat previous behavior

RECIPROCATE   to show or feel in return

RECLUSIVE   shut off from the world

RECONDITE   relating to obscure learning; known to only a few

RECOUNT (v)   to describe facts or events

RECREANT   disloyal; cowardly

RECRUIT (v)   to draft, enlist; to seek to enroll

RECTIFY   to correct

RECTITUDE   moral uprightness

RECURRENCE   repetition

REDRESS (n)   relief from wrong or injury

REDUNDANCY   unnecessary repetition

REFECTORY   room where meals are served

REFLECTION   image, likeness; opinion, thought, impression

REFORM (v)   to change, correct

REFRACT   to deflect sound or light

REFRACTORY   obstinately resistant

REFUGE   escape, shelter

REFURBISH   to renovate

REFUTE   to contradict, discredit

REGAL   magnificent, splendid, fit for royalty

REGARD   high esteem

REGIMEN   government rule; systematic plan

REGRESS   to move backward; revert to an earlier form or state

REHABILITATE   to restore to good health or condition; reestablish a person's good reputation

REITERATE   to say again, repeat

REJOINDER   response

REJUVENATE   to make young again; renew

RELEGATE   to assign to a class, especially to an inferior one

RELENT   to become gentler in attitude

RELINQUISH   to renounce or surrender something

RELISH (v)   to enjoy greatly

REMEDIABLE   capable of being corrected

REMEDY (v)   to cure, correct

REMINISCENCE   remembrance of past events

REMISSION   lessening, relaxation

REMIT   to send (usually money) as payment

REMONSTRATE   to protest or object

REMOTE   distant, isolated

REMUNERATION   pay or reward for work, trouble, etc.

RENASCENT   reborn, coming into being again

RENEGADE   traitor, person abandoning a cause

RENEGE   to go back on one's word

RENITENT   resisting pressure, obstinate

RENOUNCE   to give up or reject a right, title, person, etc.

RENOWN   fame, widespread acclaim

RENT   (adj) torn apart

REPAST   meal or mealtime

REPEAL   to revoke or formally withdraw (often a law)

REPEL   to rebuff, repulse; disgust, offend

REPENT   to regret a past action

REPENTANT   apologetic, guilty, remorseful

REPLETE   abundantly supplied

REPLICATE   to duplicate, repeat

REPOSE   relaxation, leisure

REPREHEND   to criticize

REPREHENSIBLE   blameworthy, disreputable

REPRESS   to restrain or hold in

REPRESSION   act of restraining or holding in

REPRISE   repetition, esp. of a piece of music

REPROACH (v)   to find fault with; blame

REPROBATE   morally unprincipled person

REPROVE   to criticize or correct

REPUDIATE   to reject as having no authority

REPULSE   to repel, fend off; sicken, disgust

REQUIEM   hymns or religious service for the dead

REQUITE   to return or repay

RESCIND   to repeal, cancel

RESIDUE   remainder, leftover, remnant

RESILIENT   able to recover quickly after illness or bad luck;
able to bounce back into shape

RESOLUTE   determined; with a clear purpose

RESOLVE (n)   determination, firmness of purpose

RESOLVE (v)   to conclude, determine

RESONATE   to echo

RESPIRE   to breathe

RESPITE   interval of relief

RESPLENDENT   splendid, brilliant

RESTITUTION   act of compensating for loss or damage

RESTIVE   impatient, uneasy, restless

RESTORATIVE   having the power to renew or revitalize

RESTRAINED   controlled, repressed, restricted

RESUSCITATE   to revive, bring back to life

RETAIN   to hold, keep possession of

RETARD (v)   to slow, hold back

RETICENT   not speaking freely; reserved

RETINUE   group of attendants with an important person

RETIRING   shy, modest, reserved

RETORT   cutting response

RETRACT   to draw in or take back

RETRENCH   to regroup, reorganize

RETRIEVE   to bring, fetch; reclaim

RETROACTIVE   applying to an earlier time

RETROGRADE   having a backward motion or direction

RETROSPECTIVE   looking back to the past

REVELRY   boisterous festivity

REVERE   to worship, regard with awe

REVERT   to backslide, regress

REVILE   to criticize with harsh language, verbally abuse

REVITALIZE   to renew; give new energy to

REVOKE   to annul, cancel, call back

REVULSION   strong feeling of repugnance or dislike

RHAPSODY   emotional literary or musical work

RHETORIC   persuasive use of language

RHYTHM   regular pattern or variation of sounds and stresses

RIBALD   humorous in a vulgar way

RIDDLE (v)   to make many holes in; permeate

RIFE   widespread, prevalent; abundant

RIFT   an open space; to divide

RIGHTEOUS   morally right

RIPOSTE   a retort

RISQUÉ   bordering on being inappropriate or indecent

ROBUST   strong and healthy; hardy

ROCOCO   very highly ornamented

ROIL   to disturb or cause disorder

ROOT (v)   to dig with a snout (like a pig)

ROOTED   to have an origin or base

ROSTRUM   stage for public speaking

ROTUND   round in shape; fat

RUE   to regret

RUFFLED   irritated

RUMINATE   to contemplate, reflect upon

RUSTIC   rural

S

SACCHARINE   excessively sweet or sentimental

SACROSANCT   extremely sacred; beyond criticism

SAGACIOUS   shrewd, wise

SALACIOUS   lustful

SALIENT   prominent or conspicuous

SALLOW   sickly yellow in color

SALUBRIOUS   healthful

SALUTATION   greeting

SANCTION   permission, support; law; penalty

SANCTUARY   haven, retreat

SANGUINE   ruddy; cheerfully optimistic

SAP (v)   to weaken gradually

SAPIENT   wise

SARDONIC   cynical, scornfully mocking

SATIATE   to satisfy

SAUNTER   to amble; walk in a leisurely manner

SAVANT   learned person

SAVORY   agreeable in taste or smell

SCABBARD   sheath for sword or dagger

SCABROUS   dealing with indecent things; blemished

SCALE (v)   to climb to the top of

SCANTINESS   barely enough, meager

SCARCITY   not enough, insufficient

SCATHING   harshly critical; painfully hot

SCENARIO   plot outline; possible situation

SCHISM   a division or separation; disharmony

SCINTILLA   very small amount

SCINTILLATE   to sparkle, flash

SCION   descendent, child

SCOFF   to deride, ridicule

SCORE (n)   notation for a musical composition

SCORE (v)   to make a notch or scratch

SCRIVENER   professional copyist

SCRUPULOUS   restrained; careful and precise

SCRUTINY   careful observation

SCURRILOUS   vulgar, low, indecent

SECANT   straight line intersecting a curve at two points

SECEDE   to withdraw formally from an organization

SECLUDED   isolated and remote

SECTARIAN   narrow-minded; relating to a group or sect

SECULAR   not specifically pertaining to religion

SEDENTARY   inactive, stationary; sluggish

SEDITION   behavior promoting rebellion

SEISMOLOGY   science of earthquakes

SEMINAL   relating to the beginning or seeds of something

SENESCENT   aging, growing old

SENSUAL   satisfying or gratifying the senses; suggesting sexuality

SENTENTIOUS   having a moralizing tone

SENTIENT   aware, conscious, able to perceive

SEPULCHRAL   typical of a place of burial

SEQUEL   anything that follows

SEQUESTER   to remove or set apart; put into seclusion

SERAPHIC   angelic, pure, sublime

SERENDIPITY   habit of making fortunate discoveries by chance

SERENITY   calm, peacefulness

SERPENTINE   serpent-like; twisting, winding

SERRATED   saw-toothed, notched

SERVILE   submissive, obedient

SHARD   piece of broken glass or pottery

SHEEPISH   timid, meek, or bashful

SHIRK   to avoid a task due to laziness or fear

SIDLE   to cause to turn sideways; to move along one side

SIGNIFY   denote, indicate; symbolize

SIMIAN   apelike; relating to apes

SIMPER   to smirk, smile foolishly

SIMPLE   lacking in knowledge or intelligence

SIMULATED   fake, made to look real

SINCERE   genuine, true

SINECURE   well-paying job or office that requires little or no work

SINGE   to burn slightly, scorch

SINUOUS   winding; intricate, complex

SKEPTICAL   doubtful, questioning

SKULK   to move in a stealthy or cautious manner; sneak

SLAKE   to calm down or moderate

SLIGHT   to treat as unimportant; insult

SLIPSHOD   careless, hasty

SLOTH   sluggishness, laziness

SLOUGH   to discard or shed

SLOVENLY   untidy, messy

SLUGGARD   lazy, inactive person

SMELT (v)   to melt metal in order to refine it

SMUTTY   obscene, indecent

SNIPPET   tiny part, tidbit

SOBRIETY   seriousness

SOBRIQUET   nickname

SODDEN   thoroughly soaked; saturated

SOJOURN   visit, stay

SOLACE   comfort in distress; consolation

SOLARIUM   room or glassed-in area exposed to the sun

SOLECISM   grammatical mistake

SOLICITOUS   concerned, attentive; eager

SOLIDARITY   unity based on common aims or interests

SOLILOQUY   literary or dramatic speech by one character, not
  addressed to others

SOLIPSISM   belief that the self is the only reality

SOLSTICE   shortest or longest day of the year

SOLUBLE   capable of being solved or dissolved

SOMBER   dark and gloomy; melancholy, dismal

SOMNAMBULIST   sleepwalker

SOMNOLENT   drowsy, sleepy; inducing sleep

SONIC   relating to sound

SONOROUS   producing a full, rich sound

SOPHIST   person good at arguing deviously

SOPHISTRY   deceptive reasoning or argumentation

SOPHOMORIC   immature and overconfident

SOPORIFIC   sleepy or tending to cause sleep

SORDID   filthy; contemptible and corrupt

SOVEREIGN   having supreme power

SPARTAN   austere, severe, grave; simple, bare

SPAWN   to generate, produce

SPECIOUS   deceptively attractive

SPECULATION   contemplation; act of taking business risks for
  financial gain

SPECULATIVE   involving assumption; uncertain; theoretical

SPLENDID   grand, illustrious

SPONTANEOUS   on the spur of the moment, impulsive

SPORADIC   infrequent, irregular

SPORTIVE   frolicsome, playful

SPRIGHTLY   lively, animated, energetic

SPUR (v)   to prod

SPURIOUS   lacking authenticity; counterfeit, false

SPURN   to reject or refuse contemptuously; to scorn

SQUABBLE   quarrel

SQUALID   filthy; morally repulsive

SQUANDER   to waste

STACCATO   marked by abrupt, clear-cut sounds

STAGNANT   immobile, stale

STAID   self-restrained to the point of dullness

STALK (v)   to hunt, pursue

STALWART   strong, unwavering

STAND (n)   group of trees

STARK   bare, empty, vacant

STASIS   motionless state; standstill

STATELY   grand, unapproachable

STEADFAST   immovable

STEADY   stable, unfaltering

STENTORIAN   extremely loud

STIFLE   to smother or suffocate; suppress

STIGMA   mark of disgrace or inferiority

STILTED   stiff, unnatural

STINT (n)   period of time spent doing something

STINT (v)   to be sparing or frugal

STIPEND   allowance; fixed amount of money paid regularly

STOCKADE   enclosed area forming defensive wall

STOIC   indifferent to or unaffected by emotions

STOLID   having or showing little emotion

STRATAGEM   trick designed to deceive an enemy

STRATIFY   to arrange into layers

STRIATE   striped, grooved

STRICTURE   something that restrains; negative criticism

STRIDENT   loud, harsh, unpleasantly noisy

STRINGENT   imposing severe, rigorous standards

STRIPLING   an adolescent boy

STULTIFY   to impair or reduce to uselessness

STUNTED   having arrested growth or development

STUPEFY   to dull the senses of; stun, astonish

STYLIZE   to fashion, formalize

STYMIE   to block or thwart

SUAVE   smoothly gracious or polite; blandly ingratiating

SUBDUED   suppressed, stifled

SUBJECTION   dependence, obedience, submission

SUBJUGATE   to conquer, subdue; enslave

SUBLIMATE   to repress impulses

SUBLIME   awe-inspiring; of high spiritual or moral value

SUBLIMINAL   subconscious; imperceptible

SUBMISSIVE   tending to be meek and submit

SUBPOENA   notice ordering someone to appear in court

SUBSEQUENT   following in time or order

SUBSTANTIAL   important, real

SUBTERFUGE   trick or tactic used to avoid something

SUBTERRANEAN   hidden, secret; underground

SUBTLE   hard to detect or describe; perceptive

SUBVERT   to undermine or corrupt

SUCCINCT   terse, brief, concise

SUCCULENT   juicy; full of vitality or freshness

SUFFERABLE   bearable

SUFFRAGIST   one who advocates extended voting rights

SULLEN   brooding, gloomy

SULLY   to soil, stain, tarnish; taint

SUMPTUOUS   lavish, splendid

SUPERABUNDANCE   excessive

SUPERANNUATED   too old, obsolete, outdated

SUPERCILIOUS   arrogant, haughty, overbearing, condescending

SUPEREROGATORY   nonessential

SUPERFICIAL   hasty; shallow and phony

SUPERFLUOUS   extra, more than necessary

SUPERSEDE   to take the place of; replace

SUPERVISE   to direct or oversee the work of others

SUPPLANT   to replace, substitute

SUPPLE   flexible, pliant

SUPPLICANT   one who asks humbly and earnestly

SUPPOSITION   assumption

SURFEIT   excessive amount

SURLY   rude and bad-tempered

SURMISE   to make an educated guess

SURMOUNT   to conquer, overcome

SURPASS   to do better than, be superior to

SURPLUS   excess

SURREPTITIOUS   characterized by secrecy

SURVEY (v)   to examine in a comprehensive way

SUSCEPTIBLE   vulnerable, unprotected

SUSPEND   to defer, interrupt; dangle, hang

SUSTAIN   support, uphold; endure, undergo

SUSTENANCE   supplying the necessities of life

SWARTHY   having a dark complexion

SYBARITE   person devoted to pleasure and luxury

SYCOPHANT   self-serving flatterer, yes-man

SYLLABUS   outline of a course

SYMBIOSIS   cooperation, mutual helpfulness

SYMPOSIUM   meeting with short presentations on related topics

SYNCHRONOUS   happening at the same time

SYNCOPATION   temporary irregularity in musical rhythm

SYNOPSIS   plot summary

SYNTHESIS   blend, combination

SYNTHETIC   artificial, imitation

T

TABLEAU   vivid description, striking incident or scene

TACIT   silently understood or implied

TACITURN   uncommunicative, not inclined to speak much

TACTFUL   skillful in dealing with others

TACTILE   relating to the sense of touch

TAINT   to spoil or infect; to stain honor

TAINTED   stained, tarnished; corrupted, poisoned

TALISMAN   something producing a magical effect

TALON   claw of an animal, esp. a bird of prey

TANDEM   acting as a group or in partnership

TANG   sharp flavor or odor

TANGENTIAL   digressing, diverting

TANGIBLE   able to be sensed; perceptible, measurable

TANTAMOUNT   equivalent in value or significance; amounting to

TARNISHED   corroded, discolored; discredited, disgraced

TAWDRY   gaudy, cheap, showy

TAXONOMY   science of classification

TECHNOCRAT   strong believer in technology; technical expert

TEETER   to waver or move unsteadily

TEMERITY   recklessness

TEMPERANCE   restraint, self-control, moderation

TEMPERED   moderated, restrained

TEMPESTUOUS   stormy, raging, furious

TEMPORAL   relating to time; chronological

TENABLE   defensible, reasonable

TENACIOUS   stubborn, holding firm

TENDENTIOUS   biased

TENET   belief, doctrine

TENSILE   capable of withstanding physical stress

TENUOUS   weak, insubstantial

TEPID   lukewarm; showing little enthusiasm

TERMINAL (adj)   concluding, final; fatal

TERMINAL (n)   depot, station

TERRESTRIAL   earthly; down-to-earth, commonplace

TERSE   concise, brief, free of extra words

TESTAMENT   statement of belief; will

TESTIMONIAL   statement testifying to a truth; something given in tribute to a person's achievement

TETHER (v)   to bind, tie

THEOCRACY   government by priests representing a god

THEOLOGY   study of God and religion

THEORETICAL   abstract

THERAPEUTIC   medicinal

THESAURUS   book of synonyms and antonyms

THESIS   theory or hypothesis; dissertation or long written composition

THRALL   a person in servitude, enslaved

THRENODY   a sad poem or song

THWART   to block or prevent from happening; frustrate

TIDINGS   news

TIMOROUS   timid, shy, full of apprehension

TINGE   to color slightly

TIRADE   long violent speech; verbal assault

TITAN   person of colossal stature or achievement

TOADY   flatterer, hanger-on, yes-man

TOLERANCE   capacity to respect different values; capacity to endure or resist something

TOME   book, usually large and academic

TONAL   relating to pitch or sound

TOPOGRAPHY   art of making maps or charts

TORPID   lethargic; unable to move; dormant

TORRID   burning hot; passionate

TORSION   act of twisting and turning

TORTUOUS   having many twists and turns; highly complex

TOTTERING   barely standing

TOXIN   poison

TRACTABLE   obedient, yielding

TRAMMEL   to impede or hamper

TRANQUIL   to calm or steady

TRANSCEND   to rise above, go beyond

TRANSCENDENT   rising above, going beyond

TRANSCRIPTION   copy, reproduction; record

TRANSFIGURATION   a change; an exalting change

TRANSFORMATION   a change in form or appearance

TRANSGRESS   to trespass, violate a law

TRANSIENT (adj)   temporary, short-lived, fleeting

TRANSITORY   short-lived, existing only briefly

TRANSLATION   a change from one state to another; converting one language into another

TRANSLUCENT   partially transparent

TRANSMUTE   to change in appearance or shape

TRANSPIRE   to happen, occur; become known

TRAVESTY   parody, exaggerated imitation, caricature

TREMULOUS   trembling, quivering; fearful, timid

TRENCHANT   acute, sharp, incisive; forceful, effective

TREPIDATION   fear and anxiety

TRIBUTE   a gift or statement showing respect or gratitude

TRIFLING   of slight worth, trivial, insignificant

TRITE   shallow, superficial

TROUNCE   to beat severely, defeat

TROUPE   group of actors

TRUCULENT   savage and cruel; fierce; ready to fight

TRUISM   something that is obviously true

TRUNCATE   to cut off, shorten by cutting

TRYING   difficult to deal with

TRYST   agreement between lovers to meet; rendezvous

TUMULT   state of confusion; agitation

TUNDRA   treeless plain found in Arctic or subarctic regions

TURBID   muddled; unclear

TURBULENCE   commotion, disorder

TURGID   swollen, bloated

TURPITUDE   inherent vileness, foulness, depravity

TYRANNICAL   oppressive; dictatorial

TYRO   beginner, novice

U

UBIQUITOUS   being everywhere simultaneously

UMBRAGE   offense, resentment

UNADULTERATED   absolutely pure

UNANIMITY   state of total agreement or unity

UNAPPEALING   unattractive, unpleasant

UNAVAILING   hopeless, useless

UNBENDING   inflexible, unyielding

UNBRIDLED   unrestrained

UNCONSCIONABLE   unscrupulous; shockingly unfair or
   unjust

UNCTUOUS   greasy, oily; smug and falsely earnest

UNDAUNTED   resolute even in adversity

UNDERMINE   to sabotage, thwart

UNDOCUMENTED   not certified, unsubstantiated

UNDULATING   moving in waves

UNEQUIVOCAL   absolute, certain

UNFAILING   not likely to fail, constant, infallible

UNFETTERED   free, unrestrained

UNFROCK   to strip of priestly duties

UNGRACIOUS   rude, disagreeable

UNHERALDED   unannounced, unexpected

UNIDIMENSIONAL   having one size or dimension

UNIFORM (adj)   consistent and unchanging; identical

UNIMPEACHABLE   beyond question

UNINITIATED   not familiar with an area of study

UNKEMPT   uncombed, messy in appearance

UNOBTRUSIVE   modest, unassuming

UNPOLISHED   lacking sophistication

UNRUFFLED   poised, calm

UNSCRUPULOUS   dishonest

UNSOILED   clean, pure

UNSOLICITED   unrequested

UNSTINTING   generous

UNSULLIED   clean

UNSWAYABLE   unable to change

UNTOWARD   not favorable; unruly

UNTRAMMELED   unhampered

UNWARRANTED   groundless, unjustified

UNWITTING   unconscious; unintentional

UNYIELDING   firm, resolute

UPBRAID   to scold sharply

UPROARIOUS   loud and forceful

UPSURGE   sudden rise

URBANE   courteous, refined, suave

USURP   to seize by force

USURY   practice of lending money at exorbitant rates

UTILITARIAN   efficient, functional, useful

UTOPIA   perfect place

V

VACILLATE   to waver, show indecision

VACUOUS   empty, void; lacking intelligence, purposeless

VAGRANT   poor person with no home

VALIANT   brave, courageous

VALIDATE   to authorize, certify, confirm

VALOROUS   brave, valiant

VANQUISH   to conquer, defeat

VAPID   tasteless, dull

VARIABLE   changeable, inconstant

VARIEGATED   varied; marked with different colors

VAUNTED   boasted about, bragged about

VEHEMENTLY   strongly, urgently

VENAL   willing to do wrong for money

VENDETTA   prolonged feud marked by bitter hostility

VENERABLE   respected because of age

VENERATION   adoration, honor, respect

VENT (v)   to express, say out loud

VERACIOUS   truthful, accurate

VERACITY   accuracy, truth

VERBATIM   word for word

VERBOSE   wordy

VERDANT   green with vegetation; inexperienced

VERDURE   fresh, rich vegetation

VERIFIED   proven true

VERISIMILITUDE   quality of appearing true or real

VERITY   truthfulness; belief viewed as true and enduring

VERMIN   small creatures offensive to humans

VERNACULAR   everyday language used by ordinary people;
   specialized language of a profession

VERNAL   related to spring

VERSATILE   adaptable, all-purpose

VERVE   energy, vitality

VESTIGE   trace, remnant

VETO (v)   to reject formally

VEX   to irritate, annoy; confuse, puzzle

VIABLE   workable, able to succeed or grow

VIADUCT   series of elevated arches used to cross a valley

VICARIOUS   substitute, surrogate; enjoyed through imagined
   participation in another's experience

VICISSITUDE   change or variation; ups and downs

VIE   to compete, contend

VIGILANT   attentive, watchful

VIGNETTE   decorative design; short literary composition

VILIFY   to slander, defame

VIM   energy, enthusiasm

VINDICATE   to clear of blame; to support a claim

VINDICATION   clearance from blame or suspicion

VINDICTIVE   spiteful, vengeful, unforgiving

VIRGINAL   pure, chaste

VIRILE   manly, having qualities of an adult male

VIRTUE   conforming to what is right

VIRTUOSO   someone with masterly skill; expert musician

VIRULENT   extremely poisonous; malignant; hateful

VISCOUS   thick, syrupy and sticky

VITIATE   reduce in value or effectiveness

VITRIOLIC   burning, caustic; sharp, bitter

VITUPERATE   to abuse verbally

VIVACIOUS   lively, spirited

VIVID   bright and intense in color; strongly perceived

VOCIFEROUS   loud, vocal and noisy

VOID (adj)   not legally enforceable; empty

VOID (n)   emptiness, vacuum

VOID (v)   to cancel, invalidate

VOLATILE   explosive

VOLITION   free choice, free will; act of choosing

VOLLEY (n)   flight of missiles, round of gunshots

VOLUBLE   speaking much and easily, talkative; glib

VOLUMINOUS   large; of great quantity; writing or speaking at great length

VORACIOUS   having a great appetite

VORTEX   swirling, resembling a whirlpool

VULGAR   obscene; common, of low class

VULNERABLE   defenseless, unprotected; innocent, naive

W

WAIVE   to refrain from enforcing a rule; to give up a legal right

WALLOW   to indulge oneself excessively, luxuriate

WAN   sickly pale

WANE   to dwindle, to decrease

WANTON   undisciplined, unrestrained, reckless

WARRANTY   guarantee of a product's soundness

WARY   careful, cautious

WASPISH   rude, behaving badly

WAVER   to show indecision

WAX   to increase

WAYWARD   erratic, unrestrained, reckless

WEATHER (v)   to endure, undergo

WEIGHTY   important, momentous

WELTER (n)   a confused mass; a jumble

WHET   to sharpen, stimulate

WHIMSY   playful or fanciful idea

WILY   clever, deceptive

WINDFALL   sudden, unexpected good fortune

WINSOME   charming, happily engaging

WITHDRAWN   unsociable, aloof; shy, timid

WIZENED   withered, shriveled, wrinkled

WOE   deep suffering or grief

WRAITH   a ghost

WRANGLE   loud quarrel

WRIT   written document, usually in law

WRY   amusing, ironic

X

XENOPHOBIA   fear or hatred of foreigners or strangers

Y

YOKE (v)   to join together

Z

ZEALOT   someone passionately devoted to a cause

ZENITH   highest point, summit

ZEPHYR   gentle breeze

ZOOLOGIST   scientist who studies animals